Lecture Notes in Artificial Intelligence 8235

Subseries of Lecture Notes in Computer Science

LNAI Series Editors

Randy Goebel
University of Alberta, Edmonton, Canada
Yuzuru Tanaka
Hokkaido University, Sapporo, Japan
Wolfgang Wahlster
DFKI and Saarland University, Saarbrücken, Germany

LNAI Founding Series Editor

Joerg Siekmann
DFKI and Saarland University, Saarbrücken, Germany

T0226060

For further volumes:
http://www.springer.com/series/1244

Shah Jamal Alam · H. Van Dyke Parunak (Eds.)

Multi-Agent-Based Simulation XIV

International Workshop, MABS 2013
Saint Paul, MN, USA, May 6–7, 2013
Revised Selected Papers

 Springer

Editors
Shah Jamal Alam
School of Geosciences
University of Edinburgh
Edinburgh
UK

H. Van Dyke Parunak
Soar Technology
Ann Arbor, MI
USA

ISSN 0302-9743   ISSN 1611-3349   (electronic)
ISBN 978-3-642-54782-9   ISBN 978-3-642-54783-6   (eBook)
DOI 10.1007/978-3-642-54783-6
Springer Heidelberg New York Dordrecht London

Library of Congress Control Number: 2014935152

CR Subject Classification (1998): 21017, I21025

LNCS Sublibrary: SL7 – Artificial Intelligence

Printed on acid-free paper

Springer is part of Springer Science+Business Media (www.springer.com)

Preface

This volume contains the revised and selected papers from the 14th edition of the International Multi-Agent-Based Simulation (MABS) workshop series (http://www.pcs.usb.br/~mabs). Since its inception in 1998, the MABS workshop has remained one of the leading scientific forums where high-quality research focusing on the nexus between multiagent systems and social sciences has been reported. It has attracted researchers interested in the application of agent-based simulation for social science research and has enabled the application of insights from social theories to the development and design of multiagent systems. The MABS workshop series has thus provided a solid platform in promoting interdisciplinary and crossdisciplinary research in the field and has attracted researchers with a wide range of backgrounds and expertise.

Following previous editions, this year's MABS main themes included simulation methodologies, simulation of social and economic behavior, and application. Additionally, we solicited papers addressing empirical simulations, MABS that link real-world data in real time, provenance and ontology-driven simulation, and the methods of validating multiagent-based simulations. We received 29 submissions, of which 14 were selected for presentation in the 1.5 days allocated to the workshop. Eleven revised papers are included in this volume.

A recurring theme throughout this year's workshop was the relation of models to data, including the challenges of model validation and verification. (Validation is usually defined as "making the right model," that is, one that meets the needs of the customer, while verification is "making the model right," that is, avoiding programming errors.) The round table discussion that closed the first day's session centered on this theme, with participants actively sharing positions and experiences ranging from an insistence on solid testing with real data to the case for abstract models that explore theoretical constructs and are not intended to align in detail with real data. Our keynote speaker Dr. Charles Macal's invited presentation also focused on validation, drawing on his extensive experience with large models of real-world situations whose users demand clear validation.

The workshop clearly raised consciousness among the MABS community of the importance of considering validation in the life cycle of a model, and provided numerous examples and guidelines of how this can be done. One delegate observed that in some cases, a paper about the validation of a model would be a worthwhile separate publication alongside a paper that motivates a model and describes its behavior. Coupled with the increasing popularity of the ODD protocol for detailed specification of models to enable replication, we are moving toward a tri-partite scheme for a fully documented model in applied domains: main paper to motivate and describe lessons learned, ODD protocol to enable others to replicate the work, and detailed validation study.

MABS workshops have always been held in conjunction with the world's leading conference on autonomous and multiagent systems AAMAS (International Joint Conference on Autonomous Agents and Multiagent Systems). This year's MABS was held with the 12th AAMAS conference in the beautiful city of St. Paul, Minnesota, in the United States. We are grateful to the 2013 AAMAS conference chair Maria Gini and the workshop chairs Satoshi Kurihara and Wolfgang Ketter for their role in the successful organization of this year's MABS workshop. We are also thankful to the AAMAS local organizers for providing us with excellent technical and infrastructural support. We are indebted to the MABS Steering Committee and its coordinator Jaime Sichman for giving us the opportunity to organize the 2013 MABS and for their encouragement and positive feedback throughout this time. Last but not least, we are thankful to the members of the Program Committee for providing constructive and useful reviews of the submitted papers in time, which is no doubt one of the hallmarks of the MABS workshop series.

January 2014   H. Van Dyke Parunak
                                                                Shah Jamal Alam

Organization

General and Program Chairs

Shah Jamal Alam   University of Edinburgh, UK
H. Van Dyke Parunak   Soar Technology, USA

MABS Steering Committee

Frederic Amblard   Université Toulouse 1, France
Luis Antunes   University of Lisbon, Portugal
Rosaria Conte   National Research Council, Italy
Paul Davidsson   Blekinge Institute of Technology, Sweden
Nigel Gilbert   University of Surrey, UK
Scott Moss   University of Koblenz-Landau, Germany
Keith Sawyer   Washington University in St. Louis, USA
Jaime Sichman   University of Sao Paulo, Brazil
Keiki Takadama   The University of Electro-Communications, Japan

Program Committee

Shah Jamal Alam   University of Edinburgh, UK
Frederic Amblard   Université Toulouse 1 Capitole, France
Joao Balsa   Universidade de Lisboa, Portugal
Tibor Bosse   Vrije Universiteit Amsterdam, The Netherlands
Sven A. Brueckner   Soar Technology, USA
Sung-Bae Cho   Yonsei University, Korea
Helder Coelho   Universidade de Lisboa, Portugal
Andrew Crooks   George Mason University, USA
Paul Davidsson   Malmö University, Sweden
Gennaro Di Tosto   Utrecht University, The Netherlands
Virginia Dignum   TU Delft, The Netherlands
Frank Dignum   Utrecht University, The Netherlands
Bruce Edmonds   Manchester Metropolitan University, UK
Armando Geller   Scensei LLC, USA
Nick Gotts   Independent Researcher, UK
William Griffin   Arizona State University, USA
Laszlo Gulyas   Aitia International, Hungary
David Hales   The Open University, UK
Rainer Hegselmann   Bayreuth University, Germany
Marco Janssen   Arizona State University, Germany

William Kennedy	George Mason University, USA
Satoshi Kurihara	Osaka University, Japan
Adolfo Lopez	University of Valladolid, Spain
Ulf Lotzmann	University of Koblenz, Germany
Ed MacKerrow	Los Alamos National Laboratory, USA
Ruth Meyer	Manchester Metropolitan University, UK
Jean-Pierre Muller	CIRAD, France
John Murphy	Argonne National Laboratory, USA
Emma Norling	Manchester Metropolitan University, UK
Michael North	Argonne National Laboratory, USA
Paulo Novais	University of Minho, Portugal
Mario Paolucci	ISTC-CNR Rome, Italy
H. Van Dyke Parunak	Soar Technology, USA
Juan Pavón	Universidad Complutense, Spain
Gary Polhill	The James Hutton Institute, UK
William Rand	University of Maryland, USA
Juliette Rouchier	CNRS-GREQAM, France
Keith Sawyer	Washington University, USA
Jeff Schank	University of California Davis, USA
Jaime Sichman	University of Sao Paulo, Brazil
Carles Sierra	IIIA, Spain
Barry Silverman	University of Pennsylvania, USA
Elizabeth Sklar	City University of New York, USA
Klaus G. Troitzsch	University of Koblenz-Landau, Germany
Harko Verhagen	Stockholm University, Sweden
Yu Zhang	Trinity University, USA

Additional Reviewers

Maria del Carmen Delgado-Roman	IIIA, Spain
Tomas Trescak	IIIA, Spain
Lois Vanhee	Université de Montpellier 2, France

Contents

Simulating Social Phenomena

MABS for Real-Time
and Online Data

Dynamically Tracking the Real World
in an Agent-Based Model

H. Van Dyke Parunak[1](✉), S. Hugh Brooks[2], Sven Brueckner[3],
and Ravi Gupta[3]

[1] Soar Technology, Green Court Suite 600, P.O. Box 3600 Ann Arbor,
MI 48105, USA
van.parunak@soartech.com
[2] P.O. Box 25275 Washington, DC 20027, USA
shb32@georgetown.edu
[3] Axon Connected, LLC, 2322 Blue Stone Hills Dr. Suite 20, Harrisonburg,
VA 22801, USA
{sven.brueckner,ravi.gupta}@axonconnected.com

Abstract. Computational Social Science (CSS) models are most commonly used to articulate theories and explore their implications. As they become more mature, they are also valuable in monitoring real-world situations. Such applications require models to be linked to dynamic real-world data in real time. This paper explores this distinction in a specific application that tracks crowd violence in an urban setting.

Keywords: Forecasting · Calibration · Apoptosis · Stigmergy

1 Introduction

On May 20, 2012, NATO held a summit in Chicago, IL. Protesters planned a demonstration. They registered with the authorities for a permit, which specified a route ending near the secure area where NATO delegates and heads of state would be meeting. The Cook's County Sheriff's office invited NEK Advanced Security Group to demonstrate the usefulness of social media in tracking unrest, and NEK invited us to demonstrate how agent-based modeling could help monitor the demonstration in real-time and give near-term forecasts of possible "hot spots" requiring additional police attention. In response, we constructed and demonstrated a prototype of CAVE (Crowd Analysis for Violence Estimation).

Crowd simulation is an important and fairly mature area of computational social science (CSS). We do not offer any theoretical advances over previous research, from which we borrow liberally. However, we do apply these techniques in a novel way. In a research setting, CSS models serve to articulate a theory in a precise way, and (calibrated with static input data) to test the theory against historical observations. CAVE must continuously update itself with real-world data to provide an ongoing estimate of the state of the world a short distance into the future. Our contribution is demonstrating practical techniques for tracking the real world with a computational model.

S.J. Alam and H. Van Dyke Parunak (Eds.): MABS 2013, LNAI 8235, pp. 3–16, 2014.
DOI: 10.1007/978-3-642-54783-6_1, © Springer-Verlag Berlin Heidelberg 2014

Section 2 of this paper distinguishes three applications of CSS: theory articulation, static prediction, and real-time monitoring and forecasting. Section 3 briefly reviews the particular CSS model that we adapt, summarizes its structure and operation (described more fully in a separate ODD specification [11]), and explains how we interface it with the real world. Section 4 reports the behavior of CAVE during the NATO summit, and Sect. 5 concludes.

2   CSS for Theory, Prediction, and Monitoring

CSS models can be applied in several different ways. We distinguish three.

2.1   Theory Articulation

A CSS model provides an unambiguous expression of the interaction of various causal influences within and among actors in a social scenario. It is a detailed embodiment of claims about factors and interactions that in a previous era could only be outlined verbally. A number of different formalisms for such models have been demonstrated [3]. We focus on agent-based models, which represent individuals (or small groups of individuals) as software agents [14]. Valuable insights concerning social phenomena can be gleaned from interview protocols (e.g., [15, 16]), but the resulting theories are difficult to test. A computational model is not only more precise than a verbal theory, but it also allows testing of hypotheses by executing the model. Even without external data, it can demonstrate testable qualitative trends and emergent behaviors that are not obvious from a verbal statement. For example, in the study on which CAVE is based [7], the tendency of groups to form as a function of crowd size is markedly different with two populations of different sizes than with balanced populations, and the emergence of violence depends on the size of the overall crowd.

2.2   Static Prediction

Qualitative agreement between simulation and observation is good, but accurate quantitative predictions (e.g., [1]) are even better, since their results are more directly comparable with observations from the real world, and they can support decisions that depend on a quantitative trade-off between cost and benefit. The first benefit is seen in an implementation that ingests live data at one point in time, then compares model outputs with subsequent observations. The second is clear in "what-if" exercises, in which the user runs the model off-line, then examines its results to guide a decision.

2.3   Real-Time Monitoring

Like static prediction models, CAVE seeks to align itself with data from the real world. However, it runs on-line, not off-line. It continuously ingests observed data and adjusts its configuration to give the user a continuously updated short-horizon forecast of the system being modeled.

Our approach is motivated by a fundamental limitation of predicting complex non-linear systems. The farther one seeks to project the dynamics of the system, the more random the projection becomes, resulting in a "prediction horizon" beyond which such a prediction is no better than random. We have demonstrated this horizon in simple agent-based models [12]. The limitation is fundamental in nature, not due to noise in the input data or shortcomings in model accuracy [17].

Abstractly, we can view the system as a vector differential equation,

$$\frac{d\vec{x}}{dt} = f(\vec{x})$$

When f is nonlinear, long-range prediction is impossible. However, it is often useful to anticipate the system's behavior a short distance into the future. A common technique is to fit a convenient low-order form for f to the system's trajectory in the recent past, and then extrapolate this fit into the future (Fig. 1, [8]). Iterating this process provides the user with a limited look-ahead into the system's future. The process is like walking through the woods on a moonless night. The traveler cannot see the other side of the forest, but her flashlight can show her the next few meters, and when she has covered that distance, it can show her the next few meters beyond that.

Realizing the program of Fig. 1 directly requires specifying the state space of the system explicitly, writing a set of differential equations that characterize it, and fitting an analytical function to recent observations. Agent-based modeling is attractive for social systems just because it is difficult to define the complete state space and express the system's behavior in terms of analytical functions. Thus it is difficult to use this technique to produce a fit. This paper shows how to approximate the strategy of Fig. 1 in an agent-based social simulation.

To motivate our approaches, let's look in more detail at local approximations to the system's state trajectory (Fig. 2). At time t_1, we fit a linear model a. At a subsequent time $t_2 > t_1$, we fit model b. These two models differ in two ways, each of which leads to errors. We can use observational data to correct both kinds of error.

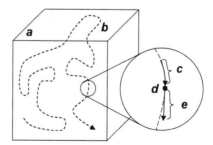

Fig. 1. Real-Time Monitoring of Complex Trajectories.—a: state space. b: system trajectory. c: recent observed system state. d: model update. e: short-range forecast

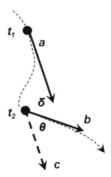

Fig. 2. Two adjustments in real-time monitoring.—Correcting system location (δ) and model fit (θ) at two time instances $t_1 < t_2$.

1. They differ in *direction*, which in this case corresponds to the internal structure and parameters of the model. The direction of the later fit b differs from that of a by θ.
2. They differ in *origin*. Model a, an approximation, experiences an error δ with respect to the real system.

The simplest use of observational data is simply to restart the (original) model at the new, observed location, yielding model c. If the model parameters are not completely off the mark, the model still moves in the same general direction as the system.

In addition to reinitializing the model, we can also retune its parameters. When analytical approaches are not applicable, we use synthetic evolution. Figure 3 illustrates the polyagent approach [13], representing each real-world entity by a single persistent *avatar* and a swarm of *ghosts*. The avatar continuously inserts a stream of simple agents in a faster-than-real-time model of the environment, a short distance in the past, and evolves their behavioral parameters until they correspond to observed behavior, then lets them run into the future to generate a prediction. The ghosts are apoptotic: they die after a specified period, so the system does not become clogged with an increasing number of agents.

We have demonstrated this approach in combat modeling [10]. While effective, it requires detailed observations of each entity being modeled in order to tune the ghosts' behaviors. In CAVE, we have aggregate observations of crowd size and composition, but not individual observations. So we do not evolve agents' behavioral models, and do not maintain the multiple representations of the world at different epochs required by the polyagent model. The CAVE approach resembles vector c in Fig. 2. Agent execution provides a short-range look-ahead into the future, while apoptosis (systematic removal of agents after a specified time limit) limits the depth of the look-ahead and allows us to reinitialize agents based on real-world data, shifting the origin (though not the parameters) of the agents.

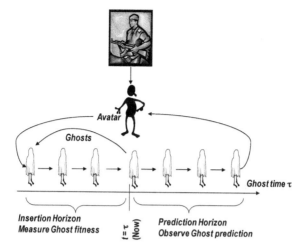

Fig. 3. Polyagent mechanism for dynamically learning agent behavioral parameters

3   The CAVE Model

CAVE draws on existing models of crowd psychology, using apoptosis and real-time data acquisition to adjust the model continuously.

3.1   Underlying CSS Theory

CAVE draws on two areas of research in crowd dynamics.

First, from the extensive literature on crowd psychology [21], we use the extended social identity model (ESIM) [7, 15, 16]. Unlike many other models, it is extensively supported by real-world evidence. While ESIM is not restricted to aggressiveness or violence, it has lent itself to several previous agent-based models of these behaviors [2, 7, 20] from which we draw inspiration. We adopt two conventions from [7].

1. Agents' aggressive behavior is driven largely by an internal state variable ([7]'s "aggression motivation") that in turn is influenced by events around them. In CAVE, this variable is called "Agitation."
2. Agents are not homogeneous, even within one side of a two-sided conflict, but differ in their degree of commitment to the cause.

Second, there is increasing anecdotal evidence that agitators in public events use network technology such as instant messaging and other social media in real-time to coordinate their activities [19], and that the contents of such media can be analyzed to track crowd sentiment [4].

An important feature of our work (like that of reference [7]) is that each agent is a simple rule-based entity without an elaborate model of individual cognition.

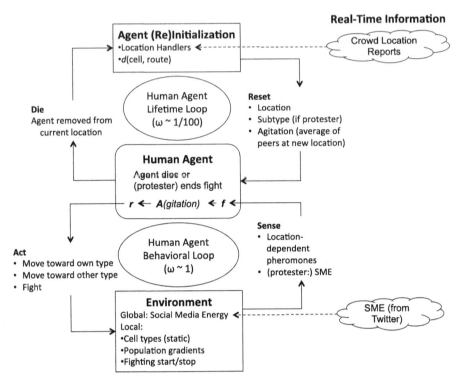

Fig. 4. Overall Information Flow in CAVE. The text discusses (in order) the environment (bottom of the figure), the human agent behavioral loop (bottom loop), the human agent lifetime loop (top loop), and real-time information (right side)

3.2   Model Structure

Figure 4 summarizes the overall information flow in CAVE. The following sections discuss the regions of the Figure. Further details about the implementation are provided in the standard ODD format [6] in a separate document [11].

The Environment.
The environment (bottom of Fig. 4) is a square lattice with cells 40 m on a side, representing downtown Chicago, derived from a GIS map.[1] We label each cell to indicate whether it contains a road, the approved protest route, the security zone within which the summit activities take place, and an extra-high security exclusion zone. The shading in Fig. 5 shows the cells corresponding to each of these categories. Agents are only created on roads. They can move off of roads, but their interactions are limited to roads, and in no case can they enter the Security or Exclusion zones.

---

[1] https://data.cityofchicago.org/browse?tags=shapefiles

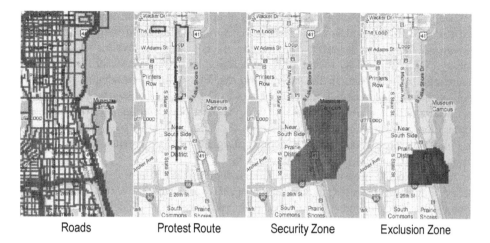

| Roads | Protest Route | Security Zone | Exclusion Zone |

Fig. 5. Coding of the CAVE environment

Human Agents: Behavioral Loop.

CAVE has two types of agents representing humans: protesters and police. These agents execute two loops. This section discusses the behavioral loop (at the bottom of Fig. 4), with a frequency ω of once per simulation step. The next section discusses the lifetime loop, which implements agent apoptosis.

Protesters are of three subtypes.

- *Leaders* aggressively seek to disrupt society, and energize their followers via social media. They can often be identified visually: they often wear bulky clothing to conceal hidden weapons, and also sometimes organize "black blocks," wearing black clothing and ski masks and moving cohesively to advertise their unified strength. Black blocks are known for engaging in violence and inciting clashes with the police.
- *Followers* accept the leader's agenda, but are not leaders.
- *Pacifists* are following the protesters out of curiosity more than ideology.

Police are of two types.

- *Patrol officers* are the usual cadre of an urban police force.
- *Riot police* have special training in dealing with unruly crowds, as well as specialized equipment such as riot shields and heavier padded armor.

The user initializes the total number of protesters and police, and the subtypes are allocated according to fixed proportions that are model parameters.

At the beginning of a run, the agents are distributed randomly on the roads in the environment that are outside the Security and Exclusion zones. Each road cell has a probability of receiving an agent that depends on how far the cell is from the protest route. The initialization function for protester agents concentrates them on the protest route, that for leaders lets them wander farther than pacifists, and that for police keeps them near the protest route but on it (so that they do not block traffic).

Each agent's behavior is determined by its level of Agitation, a variable that is defined by its drivers and its consequences. The *drivers* of an agent's Agitation are the presence of fighting in its cell, and (in the case of protesters) the level of Social Media Energy (SME) attested by tweets from the leaders. Increases in each of these lead to an increase in agitation. In the bottom loop of Fig. 4, an agent's input *f*(unction) translates the environmental state that it senses into a level of *A*(gitation), which is then translated via a *r*(ule) into one of three actions. The *consequences* of increased Agitation are that the agent first moves toward other agents of its own type (Protester or Police) for protection, then moves toward agents of the opposite type (in preparation for confrontation), and then engages in a fight.

Agents execute in random order, without replacement within a given simulation step. A single step corresponds to one min of real-world time; the actual elapsed time is much less, and depends on the speed of the processor.

Agents interact, not directly, but through a shared environment in which they are localized. The environment is not passive, but executes some processes that support the agent coordination. This pattern of coordination is called "stigmergy," a biological term that recalls the use of chemical markers (pheromones) by social insects [5, 9]. Agents interact only when they are on roads.

Each time an agent executes, it deposits digital pheromones on its cell in the environment, indicating its type, its presence, its level of Agitation, and whether it is engaged in Fight behavior. Similarly, agents sense a fight in the neighborhood by monitoring Fight pheromone, and move toward other agents of a specified type by climbing the gradient of the presence pheromone associated with agents of that type.

The environment supports pheromone-based interaction by evaporating all pheromones exponentially, thus removing obsolete information from the system. In AI terms, it provides basic truth maintenance (maintaining the consistency of a database), a task that is NP-complete in symbolic representations, with time complexity $O(1)$.

Human Agents: Lifetime Loop.
Apoptotic agents are central to CAVE's real-time updating. When an agent is created, it is assigned a lifetime is assigned from a uniform distribution on [50, 150]. When its lifetime is over, the agent is reinitialized to another location, based on real-time observations of the distribution of protesters and police. The top loop of Fig. 4 summarizes this life-cycle, whose frequency ω is on the order of $1/100$.

Apoptotic agents address two challenges facing an agent model that seeks to be aligned with the real world.

1. How does the model adjust its *internal state* to stay aligned with the real world (Fig. 2)?
2. How do we manage the relation between the simulation's *internal clock* (which depends on processor speed) and the dynamics of the real world?

The reassignment of agents to new locations at the end of their life addresses the first challenge, of state alignment. Each time CAVE receives an observation of a concentration of protesters or police, it instantiates a special agent (a "location handler") at the location of the observation. If the current population of agents at a location is greater than the location handler desires (that is, greater than the observation), it inhibits the assignment of reinitialized agents to that location, and apoptosis eventually reduces the population to the observed level. If the current population is too low, the location handler attracts reinitialized agents to its location. Thus, with a half-life of 100 min (the mean of the lifetime assignment distribution), population levels in the model adjust to match observed levels.

Apoptosis also mitigates the problem of varying execution speed. The mean agent lifetime is 100 min. Because lifetimes are randomized in [50, 100], agents are reborn at different times. After a few hundred steps, the average agent has been active for about 53 steps (Fig. 6), and the strength of the estimated violence reflects a lookahead about this distance into the future. With a modern computer, a single simulation step takes only a few milliseconds, so the view on the display is looking roughly 53 min into the future. Agent apoptosis keeps them from running indefinitely into the future and formulating an unjustified long-range forecast.

Data Sources.
CAVE is continuously updated with two real-world data sources, shown on the right-hand side of Fig. 4: an estimate of *SME* from Twitter feeds (modulating the behavioral loop), and estimates of crowd density from human observers (modulating the lifetime loop).

Leaders use social media such as Twitter to communicate with their followers. The effectiveness of this communication mechanism depends on their Twitter handles and relevant Twitter hashtags being known, so police can monitor their tweets. CAVE processes this stream of tweets through a simple natural language processor that computes the frequency of profanity and other indications of unrest. The higher the frequency of such traffic, the higher our estimate of *SME*.

Observers on the ground enter local observations of crowd density to CAVE via a web or smartphone interface. Figure 7 shows the web interface, and Fig. 8 the smartphone interface. The smartphone's geolocation capability provides the location of the observation automatically, allowing police and other observers to update location estimates easily from the ground, and its display of violence estimates provides them with immediate awareness of likely trouble locations.

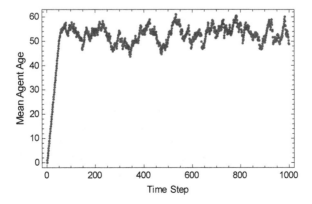

Fig. 6. Mean agent age = average lookahead

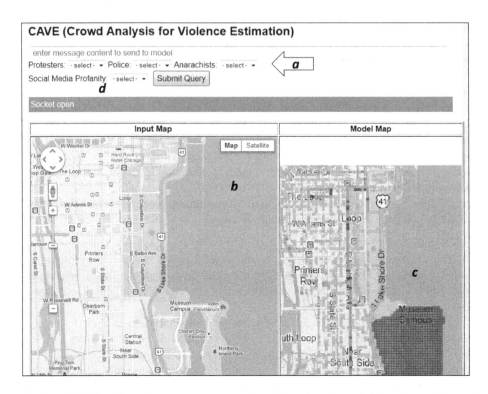

Fig. 7. CAVE interface. The operator enters estimated number of people of each type observed at a location (*a*), clicks on the left-hand map to show the location of the observation (*b*), and observes regions of high likelihood of violence on the right-hand map (*c*). In the prototype, *SME* is entered through this same interface (*d*), though the framework supports a direct feed from a NLP analysis program.

In the May 20 demonstration, SME estimates were entered by hand, based on manual monitoring of the Twitter feed. The smartphone interface was not deployed to observers on the ground, so crowd estimates were entered through the web interface based on real-time police reports and several streaming video feeds of the event recorded by protestors and journalists among the crowd.

4   Experience with the Model

The CAVE prototype shows the feasibility of integrating real-time data with an agent-based crowd simulation. The Cook County Sheriff's Department commented on the contribution of NEK's tool suite, "The intelligence we received from NEK was relayed to various law enforcement entities, such as the FBI, during the NATO event. The agencies were very appreciative of the information and it helped to enhance all of the intelligence information" [18].

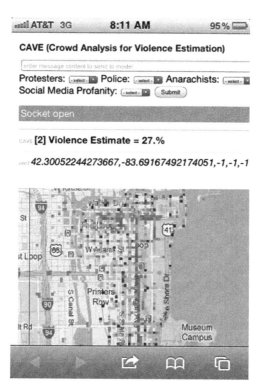

Fig. 8. Smartphone interface. The smartphone reports its location automatically.

Though the objective of our model is to integrate and present real-world information rather than to study crowd theory, its emergent behavior does provide interesting evidence for the impact of social media. Figure 9 shows distribution of the violence estimate for the same distribution of protesters and police, but in two different conditions. High *SME* (middle map) leads to numerous regions of elevated risk of violence, but with low *SME* (right map), only one location near the exclusion zone anticipates high violence.

The nature of our engagement with the Cook County Sheriff's Department did not permit detailed assessment of CAVE's accuracy in this prototype application. Such validation is possible in principle; the main obstacles are social and bureaucratic, not scientific. The purpose of the model is to give law enforcement personnel advance notice of geospatial locations where violence may break out. If the model is valid, one expects a higher than average correlation between outbreaks of violence and predicted violence, with outbreaks tending to occur at locations where the model predicts high violence, and at delays of 53 min or less after the prediction. Two details of implementing this program require attention: collecting the data, and quantifying the temporal dynamics.

Social and ethical considerations make it undesirable to stimulate riots in order to validate agent-based models. In some social settings, "war games" can be staged to evaluate predictive mechanisms (the approach we took in [10]), but the expense is

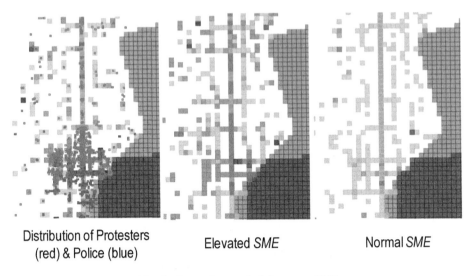

Distribution of Protesters
(red) & Police (blue)   Elevated *SME*   Normal *SME*

Fig. 9. Dependence of violence on *SME*

high, and questions remain about the fidelity of the reactions of actors who know that they are only playing a game. A more promising approach is to collect crowd observations and social media traffic during an actual event, then explore the correlation of CAVE's violence predictions with (say) the number of actual arrests for disorderly conduct as a function of place and time, after correcting for the number of officers available to conduct such arrests at each location in space-time. Government units will be reluctant to release such information for publication because of legal and privacy issues, but might conduct such an analysis in evaluating the technology for operational use.

The temporal dynamics are also problematic. In the current form of the model, the rates at which agitation builds up in the presence of violence or high SME, as well as the rate of its decay in the absence of stimulation and the threshold at which agitation turns into violence, are purely notional. They yield qualitatively coherent results. For the purpose of estimating areas at risk of violence anywhere within the 53 min lookahead of the model (as opposed to the actual time at which violence breaks out), these results may be very useful. But the lead time of our predictions depends on the actual values of agitation growth and decay and the violence threshold. In fact, observation of the time delay between prediction and the distribution of actual violence with greatest spatial correlation with the prediction may enable us to obtain more realistic estimates of these critical parameters.

5   Conclusion

Computational Social Science models have reached a level of maturity that allows them to be used in practical applications. Many such applications, such as crowd monitoring, require the simulation to be continually updated on the basis of real-time information from the domain. CAVE demonstrates how a stigmergic agent-based simulation with apoptotic agents can achieve this objective.

Our objective in this paper has been to describe mechanisms for updating a model continuously with real-world data, not to make claims about its predictive accuracy. We have outlined one approach to such validation for future research, but note that it is fraught with ethical and legal challenges.

References

1. Bert, F., Podesta, G., Rovere, S., North, M., Menendez, A., Laciana, C., Macal, C., Weber, E., Sydelko, P.: Agent-based modeling of land rental markets: comparison between simulated and observed prices in the Argentina Pampas. The Computational Social Science Society of the Americas (CSSSA 2011), Santa Fe, NM (2011)
2. Chao, W.M., Li, T.Y.: Simulating riot for virtual crowds with a social communication model. In: Jędrzejowicz, P., Nguyen, N.T., Hoang, K. (eds.) ICCCI 2011, Part I. LNCS, vol. 6922, pp. 419–427. Springer, Heidelberg (2011)
3. Gilbert, N., Troitzsch, K.G.: Simulation for the Social Scientist. Open University Press, Buckingham (1999)
4. Gonzalez-Bailon, S., Borge-Holthoefer, J., Rivero, A., Moreno, Y.: The dynamics of protest recruitment through an online network. Sci. Rep. 1(197) (2011). doi:10.1038/srep00197
5. Grassé, P.-P.: La Reconstruction du nid et les Coordinations Inter-Individuelles chez *Bellicositermes Natalensis et Cubitermes sp.* La théorie de la Stigmergie: Essai d'interprétation du Comportement des Termites Constructeurs. Insectes Sociaux **6**, 41–84 (1959)
6. Grimm, V., Berger, U., DeAngelis, D.L., Polhill, J.G., Giske, J., Railsback, S.F.: The ODD protocol: a review and first update. Ecol. Model. **221**(23), 2760–2768 (2010)
7. Jager, W., Popping, R., van de Sande, H.: Clustering and fighting in two-party crowds: simulating the approach-avoidance conflict. J. Artif. Soc. Soc. Simul. **4**(3) (2001)
8. Kantz, H., Schreiber, T.: Nonlinear Time Series Analysis. Cambridge University Press, Cambridge (1997)
9. Parunak, H.V.D.: 'Go to the Ant': engineering principles from natural agent systems. Ann. Oper. Res. **75**, 69–101 (1997)
10. Parunak, H.V.D.: Real-time agent characterization and prediction. International Joint Conference on Autonomous Agents and Multi-Agent Systems (AAMAS'07), Industrial Track, pp. 1421–1428. ACM, Honolulu, Hawaii (2007)
11. Parunak, H.V.D.: ODD Protocol for CAVE. Soar Technology. http://www.abcresearch.org/papers/ODD4CAVE.pdf (2013)
12. Parunak, H.V.D., Belding, T.C., Brueckner, S.A.: Prediction horizons in agent models. In: Weyns, D., Brueckner, S., Demazeau, Y. (eds.) EEMMAS 2007. LNCS (LNAI), vol. 5049, pp. 88–102. Springer, Heidelberg (2008)
13. Parunak, H.V.D., Brueckner, S.: Concurrent modeling of alternative Worlds with polyagents. In: Proceedings of the 7th International Workshop on Multi-Agent-Based Simulation (MABS06, at AAMAS06), pp. 128–141. Springer (2006)
14. Parunak, H.V.D., Savit, R., Riolo, R.L.: Agent-based modeling vs. equation-based modeling: a case study and users' guide. In: Gilbert, N., Conte, R., Sichman, J.S. (eds.) MABS 1998. LNCS (LNAI), vol. 1534, pp. 10–25. Springer, Heidelberg (1998)

15. Reicher, S.D.: The St. Pauls' riot: an explanation of the limits of crowd action in terms of a social identity model. Eur. J. Soc. Psychol. **14**, 1–21 (1984)
16. Stott, C., Hutchison, P., Drury, J.: 'Hooligans' abroad? Inter-group dynamics, social identity and participation in collective 'disorder' at the 1998 World Cup Finals. Brit. J. Soc. Psychol. **40**, 359–384 (2001)
17. Strogatz, S.H.: Nonlinear Dynamics and Chaos: with Applications to Physics, Biology, Chemistry, and Engineering. Addison-Wesley, Reading (1994)
18. Towne, B.: Letter from Cook County Sheriff's Dept. to NEK. Letter to Porterfield, T., 23 May (2012)
19. Wasik, B.: #Riot: Self-Organized, Hyper-Networked Revolts—Coming to a City Near You. http://www.wired.com/magazine/2011/12/ff_riots/ (2011)
20. Wijermans, N., Jorna, R., Jager, W., van Vliet, T.: Modelling crowd dynamics: influence factors related to the probability of a riot. In: Proceedings of The Fourth European Social Simulation Association Conference (ESSA 2007) (2007)
21. Zeitz, K.M., Tan, H.M., Zeitz, C.J: Crowd behavior at mass gatherings: a literature review. Prehospital Disaster Med. **24**(1), 32–38 (2009)

Large-Scale Multi-agent-Based Modeling and Simulation of Microblogging-Based Online Social Network

Maíra Gatti, Paulo Cavalin[✉], Samuel Barbosa Neto, Claudio Pinhanez,
Cícero dos Santos, Daniel Gribel, and Ana Paula Appel

IBM Research, Rio de Janeiro, Brazil
{mairacg,apappel,csantosp,cicerons,dlemes,pcavalin,
sbneto}@br.ibm.com

Abstract. Online Social Networks (OSN) are self-organized systems
with emergent behavior from the individual interactions. Microblogging
services in OSN, like Twitter and Facebook, became extremely popular
and are being used to target marketing campaigns. Key known issues on
this targeting is to be able to predict human behavior like posting, forwarding or replying a message with regard to topics and sentiments, and
to analyze the emergent behavior of such actions. To tackle this problem we present a method to model and simulate interactive behavior in
microblogging OSN taking into account the users sentiment. We make
use of a stochastic multi-agent based approach and we explore Barack
Obama's Twitter network as an egocentric network to present the experimental simulation results. We demonstrate that with this engineering
method it is possible to develop social media simulators using a bottom-
up approach (micro level) to evaluate the emergent behavior (macro
level) and our preliminary results show how to better tune the modeler
and the sampling and text classification impact on the simulation model.

Keywords: Online Social Network · Microblogging · Sentiment analysis · Modeling · Simulation

1 Introduction

Online social networks (OSNs) have become very popular in the last years, not
only for users but also for researchers. Twitter, for example, is just a few years
old, but has already attracted much attention from the research community [1,2].
Through an OSN, users connect with each other, share and find content, and
disseminate information. As example we can cite networks of professionals and
contacts (e.g., LinkedIn, Facebook, MySpace) and networks for content sharing
(e.g., Flickr, YouTube).

Information diffusion consists of a process in which a new idea or action
widely spreads through communication channels. OSNs are the most used means
for this nowadays [3]. This area is widely studied by sociologists, marketers, and

S.J. Alam and H. Van Dyke Parunak (Eds.): MABS 2013, LNAI 8235, pp. 17–33, 2014.
DOI: 10.1007/978-3-642-54783-6_2, © Springer-Verlag Berlin Heidelberg 2014

epidemiologists [4–6]. Large OSNs consist of a useful way for studying information diffusion as topic propagation. Blogspace [7], linking patterns in blog graphs [8], favorite photo marking in a social photo sharing service [9], and so forth, report on large OSNs. Besides, it is important to understanding how users behave when they connect to these sites for a number of reasons. For instance, in viral marketing one might want to exploit models of user interaction to spread their content or promotions quickly and widely. There are numerous models of influence spread in social networks that try to model the process of adoption of an idea or a product. However, it is still difficult to measure and predict how a market campaign will spread across an OSN if one or a set of users post, forward or reply a particular message, or if her or them don't post at all for a period of time about a particular topic, for instance. Agent-Based Simulation (ABS) provides a modeling paradigm that allows to perform what-if analysis to explore these kind of analysis.

ABS looks at agent behavior at a decentralized level, at the level of the individual agent, in order to explain the dynamic behavior of the system at macro-level. A multi-agent-based system is composed of many software agents interacting with one another and with the environment over time. The concept of an agent is more general than that of an individual, object or simulation process. An agent is an interactive computer system that is situated in some environment and is capable of accomplishing autonomous actions in order to meet the goals for which it has been designed [10]. Their collective behavior can be unpredictable, surprising, hence novel and emergent. In this way, this style of modeling is quite consistent with the sciences of complexity [11]. In addition, feedback loops can be achieved in ABS, since the result of agents actions stimulates other actions and eventually re-stimulate the first actions. Thus, a prerequisite for a multi-agent system to exhibit self-organization is feedback loops in which agents get feedback on their actions and stimulate or inhibit each other.

ABS has been successfully applied to a large number of works published in the literature [12]. However, to the best of our knowledge, this type of simulation has not yet been applied to information diffusion in large OSNs. Most works related to agent-based information diffusion models deal with synthetic networks for deriving the agents' behavior, making these works less realistic [13,14]. Nevertheless, there is plenty of OSNs from which we can gather real data to conduct this kind of investigation.

In the light of this, the main contribution of this work is to propose en engineering method to simulate user behavior using a real-world OSN. The ultimate main goal lies in modeling and simulating what users post on this OSN network, to analyze how information spreads across the network. Several challenges are faced: sampling the network from the real-world OSN, performing text classification (natural language processing) to predict topic and sentiment from the posts, modeling the user behavior to predict his/her actions (pattern recognition), and large-scale simulation - for $10,000$ seeds, it can easily reach 10^8 users in the network [15]. The proposed method makes use of a stochastic multi-agent based approach where each agent represents a user in the OSN. As a case-study, a political campaign in the Twitter microblogging service is examined, more specifically, Barack Obama's Twitter network during the 2012 United States presidential race. For doing so, we built an egocentric social network, i.e. Obama is considered as the central user (the seed) and only his immediate neighbors and their associated interconnections are examined, to help us model how individuals correspond with their connections within a social network. This paper is organized as follows. In Sect. 2 we describe the proposed method. Next, in Sect. 3 we present the experimental protocol and the results for some sensitive analysis we performed. Finally, in Sect. 4 we discuss our main remarks and point out the future work.

2 Proposed Method

The proposed method is based on a stochastic multi-agent based approach where each agent is modeled from the historical data of each user in the network as a Markov Chain process and a Monte Carlo simulation. The method has six phases and is iterative as illustrated in Fig. 1.

The first phase consists of sampling the OSN. After cleaning the data, the second phase consists of performing topic and sentiment classification on the posts extracted from the sampled data. Then in phase three, from the previously classified data we create sets of samples for each user. Each set contains the user's posts and the posts of whom he/she follows. We build each user behavior model (fourth phase) from these sets and the models are used as input for the stochastic simulator (fifth phase). The models are validated by running the simulation and applying the validation method. We performed this cycle several times until we found the modeling strategy presented in this paper. Once the model is accurate enough, forecast on information diffusion can be performed. Next, we describe these phases in greater detail (except the Dataset Partitioning phase which is quite straightforward).

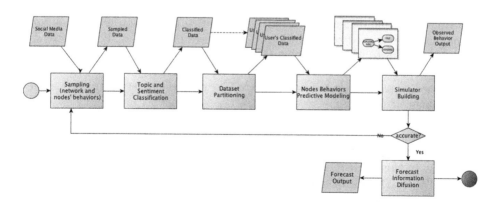

Fig. 1. Engineering method workflow.

2.1   Sampling

The sampling phase is the starting point of the method herein proposed and consists of crawling real data from an OSN. The crawling process must extract both network and user's actions. There are several network sampling methods: node sampling, link sampling, and snowball sampling [16]. In node or edge sampling, a fraction of nodes or edges is selected randomly. On the other hand, snowball sampling randomly selects one seed node and performs a breadth-first search (hence the name, snowball sampling), until the number of selected nodes reaches the desired sampling ratio. Only those links between selected nodes are included in the final sample network. The snowball sampling method is more feasible than node and edge sampling to crawl the OSN, since it is difficult to have access to node and edge randomly and also they have a high probability to produce a network with isolated clusters [17].

Depending on the OSN, the crawling method may vary due to constrains on the API or OSN policies. Twitter offers an Application Programming Interface (API) that is easy to crawl and collect data, being the OSN used in this work. However, it is not possible to retrieve the entire data from Twitters and our sample method needs to deal with the limits imposed by Twitter's API version 1.0 (the newest version of the API available when the data was extracted), such as the limited number of requests per hour that we could perform. Before we describe in detail how we collected users, tweets and the relationship among users, we defined some states of the nodes that are related to the information we have already obtained through the API.

We categorized the nodes depending on the type of information we have about them. For *Identified* nodes, the only information we have from these nodes are their IDs, a unique long value that identifies each user. Some of the these nodes where *Consulted*, which means that we have acquire metadata about these nodes, for instance the number of followers, user language and so on. For some of the consulted nodes we *Visited* them and acquired the IDs of some or all of its followers. For nodes we visited we also *Extracted* some or all of its tweets. The Twitter's API limited the number of consulted nodes by up to 100 nodes per request, the number of retrieved IDs by up to 5000 IDs per request and the number of retrieved tweets by up to 200 tweets per request. For tweets, we could retrieve up to 3200 of the latest tweets of a user using this process, that is, we repeat this process 16 times at most. We would stop when the API limit was reached, when all tweets were extracted or when the oldest extracted tweet reached a specific date.

The goal of this work is to analyze the diffusion of information having a unique node as its source. For analyses of this kind, we use an egocentric network, that is, a network that considers a node (person) as a focal point and its adjacency. In this context, we used Barack Obama's egocentric network. therefore we *Visited* Barack Obama's node and *Identified* all of its followers. Afterwards, we randomly *Consulted* 40 k of his followers (distance 1 from Obama), from which we randomly choose 10 k to *Visit* among the ones with English as a language. For each of these 10 k nodes, we *Identified* up to 5 k of its followers.

Among them there are nodes with distance 2 from Obama, from which we randomly *Consulted* up to 200 k. From these 200 k, we *Visited* up to 40 k randomly selected nodes whereas their profile language was set to English. In the end of this process, the network that we obtained contained approximately 32 million nodes and the extraction process took place in the week starting on October 26th 2012.

After that, we started extracting the tweets. Our threshold date was September 22nd and we started crawling after October 26th from 2012, therefore we tried to gather information from more than one month (sometimes the user did not have a whole month of tweets or tweeted so much that the API limit would not let us paginate further backwards before our threshold). We *Extracted* Obama's tweets and also the tweets from the 10 k *Visited* nodes with distance 1 and the 40 k *Visited* nodes with distance 2. In the end, we had approximately 5 million tweets and 24,526 users that posted in that period.

Previous work, known as "six degree of separation" [18], states that with 6 steps we are usually able to reach most of network's nodes starting in any node. On the other hand, it is reasonable to think that with distance 3 we are able to reach most of the network if we start at a high degree node. Since Obama has 23 millions of followers and the average number of followers in Twitter is around 100, performing a naive count without considering transitivity, we would have around 2 billion users in the second level (distance 2 from Obama), which is more than the number of Twitter users (1 billion). Thus, using distance 3 should be enough to analyze how information spread in this network, since it is reasonable to assume it should be possible to reach most of Twitter's users with 3 steps from Obama. Of course, if we choose other seed (user) for an egocentric network or if we use other OSN, this statistic may change a little, but it holds true in most cases for high degree seeds.

2.2   Topic and Sentiment Classification

We use text mining strategies to perform two important tasks of our modeling approach: topic classification and tweet sentiment analysis. The topic classification task consists in classifying a tweet as related to a certain topic or campaign (about politics, marketing, etc.). In the sentiment analysis task the objective is to classify a tweet as a positive or negative sentence. The *topic classification* task is performed using a keyword based approach. First, we select a list of keywords to represent each topic. Next, each tweet text is split into tokens using blank spaces and punctuation marks as separators. Then, the tokenized tweet is discarded or classified as belonging to one of the interesting topics, as follows:

- If the tweet contains keywords from more than one topic, it is discarded;
- If the tweet does not contain any keyword from any topic, it is classified as Other topic;
- If the tweet contains at least one keyword from a topic, it is classified as belonging to that topic.

The *sentiment classification* task is performed using a machine learning approach. We train a Naïve Bayes classifier using the training data created by Go et al. [1]. This training set contains examples of positive and negative tweets only. Therefore, the learned classifier predicts new tweets using these two classes only.

The first step when training or using the classifier is preprocessing. In preprocessing, we tokenize the tweet and perform the three strategies presented in [1] to reduce the feature space: (1) substitute all user names by the word USER-NAME; (2) substitute all urls (tokens starting with *http:*) by the word URL; and (3) replace any letter occurring more than two times in a token with two occurrences (e.g. *cooooool* is converted into *cool*). In order to train the Naïve Bayes classifier, we use a feature set composed of token unigrams and bigrams. The final classifier achieves 82 % accuracy when applied to Go et al.'s [1] test set.

2.3 Behaviors Predictive Modeling

The novelty of our approach consists of learning each user's behavior in order to explore the power of interactions. In a microblogging like Twitter there are several *actions* that we can observe in the data like *posting, forwarding, liking* or *replying* a message, for instance. For each action to be modeled, the sampling phase must take into account that the user to be replied or that will have his/her message forwarded must be in the sampled graph. In this paper we describe the most straightforward model that can be learned from the data, whereas only the *posting* action is modeled. Hence this modeling approach can be used as a foundation to create more complex behavior models.

To learn this behavior we designed the modeler which receives the list of users in the OSN as input and, for each user, a document containing his/her posts and the posts of whom he/she follows. From this merged document, the user's state change transitions are modeled as a Markov Chain, where the current state depends only on the previous state. Therefore the following assumptions are considered in the current version of the modeler:

- Time is discrete and we consider a Δt time interval to define action time windows;
- User actions like posting are performed on these time windows and states are attached to it. Therefore, current state on the modeler means what the user posted in the current time window, while previous state means that the user posted and/or read in the previous time window.
- Messages are interpreted as two vectors: a bit vector[1] which contains bits representing if the topic and sentiment appear in the message and an integer

---

[1] Suppose a user posted a positive message about *Obama*, a negative message about *Other* topic in the Δt time interval and there are only these two topics and two sentiments (positive and negative) being observed; if the first 2 positions of the vector are for positive and negative *Obama* index, and the other two for *Other* in that order; the vector is $[1, 0, 0, 1]$.

Table 1. List of observed states and transitions. Empty sets represent vectors not observed

Θ	Transitions	
1	$R_{t-\Delta t}, W_{t-\Delta t} \neq \emptyset$	$\rightarrow W_t \neq \emptyset$
2	$R_{t-\Delta t}, W_{t-\Delta t} \neq \emptyset$	$\rightarrow W_t = \emptyset$
3	$R_{t-\Delta t} = \emptyset, W_{t-\Delta t} \neq \emptyset$	$\rightarrow W_t \neq \emptyset$
4	$R_{t-\Delta t} = \emptyset, W_{t-\Delta t} \neq \emptyset$	$\rightarrow W_t = \emptyset$
5	$R_{t-\Delta t} \neq \emptyset, W_{t-\Delta t} = \emptyset$	$\rightarrow W_t \neq \emptyset$
6	$R_{t-\Delta t} \neq \emptyset, W_{t-\Delta t} = \emptyset$	$\rightarrow W_t = \emptyset$
7	$R_{t-\Delta t} = \emptyset, W_{t-\Delta t} = \emptyset$	$\rightarrow W_t \neq \emptyset$

vector containing the number of messages that appeared in the position where the bit has value 1.

We modeled two possible actions: reading and posting. Therefore, let R be the vector representing what the user read and W the vector representing what the user wrote, then $A_{t-\Delta t} = \{R_{t-\Delta t}, W_{t-\Delta t}\}$ and $A_t = \{W_t\}$. In this case $NT = 7$ and Table 1 describes the transitions and/or states that can be observed in the data and that will be used in the simulator. $R_{t-\Delta t} = \emptyset$, $W_{t-\Delta t} = \emptyset$ or $W_t = \emptyset$ represent non-observed data.

We compute the Maximum Likelihood Estimation (MLE) with smoothing to estimate the parameter for each $\theta_i \in \Theta$ transition type. Therefore, for each user's sampled data u we estimate L for:

- Observed transitions θ_1, θ_3, θ_5:

$$L(\theta | R_{t-\Delta t}, W_{t-\Delta t}, W_t) = \frac{count(\theta, R_{t-\Delta t}, W_{t-\Delta t}, W_t) + 1}{count(R_{t-\Delta t}, W_{t-\Delta t}, W_t) + |S|} \quad (1)$$

- Non-observed transitions θ_2, θ_4, θ_6 and θ_7:

$$L(\theta | R_{t-\Delta t}, W_{t-\Delta t}, W_t) = \frac{1}{count(R_{t-\Delta t}, W_{t-\Delta t}, W_t) + |S|} \quad (2)$$

Where $|S|$ is the number of states.

We take into account that the user may post a message related to a topic and a sentiment, which are grouped and stored in the set Ξ. For this reason, the aforementioned transitions are computed for each topic and sentiment $\xi_i \in \Xi$, so that the actions of the users are modeled according to the type of message that he/she is reading or writing.

In considering that the user might behave differently according to the period of the day, we compute the probability of posting a message at a given period $\phi_i \in \Phi$, where $1 \leq i \leq K$. This takes into account the total of messages m_i posted by the user at ϕ_i and the messages posted over all periods (the whole day), as in Eq. 3. In addition, we consider the following notation for each period ϕ_i. The corresponding starting time is denoted $\phi_i' \in \Phi'$, and its length (in hours) is denoted $|\phi_i|$.

$$L(\text{posting } |\phi_i|) = \frac{m_i}{\sum_{\phi_j \in \Phi} m_j} \tag{3}$$

The volume of messages posted by the user is saved in a vector containing integer values, where each position corresponds to the average number of messages written for an element in the set Ξ. Equation 4 describes how to compute the transitions volume, where N represents how many W_t vectors there are for the same θ transition, L denotes the total of topics/sentiments, i.e. $|\Xi|$, and w_{lj} corresponds to the number of messages written for $\xi_l \in \Xi$ and transition θ.

$$V_{W_t}(\theta) = [\frac{\sum_{j \in N} w_{1j}}{N}, \frac{\sum_{j \in N} w_{2j}}{N}, \ldots, \frac{\sum_{j \in N} w_{Lj}}{N}] \tag{4}$$

Volume vectors are computed for both transitions and periods. Equation 5 shows how to compute the average for periods:

$$V(\phi_i) = [\frac{\sum_{j \in M} w'_{1j}}{M}, \frac{\sum_{j \in M} w'_{2j}}{M}, \ldots, \frac{\sum_{j \in M} w'_{Lj}}{M}] \tag{5}$$

Where M represents how many different vectors there are for period ϕ_i, and w'_{lj} corresponds to the number of messages sent for the topic/sentiment $\xi_l \in \Xi$ at a period ϕ_i.

The volume vector $V(\phi_i)$, as we will explain further, is used by the simulator to set different weights to $V_{W_t}(\theta)$, according to the current period ϕ_i. For this reason, we divide each position of $V(\phi_i)$ by the mean observed volume over all periods. As a consequence, the periods where the user posted a larger volume of messages will have greater weights than periods where he/she posted less messages. In Eq. 6 we demonstrate how this division is done.

$$V'(\phi_i) = [\frac{v_{1i}}{\bar{v}_{1j}|_{\phi_j \in \Phi}}, \frac{v_{2i}}{\bar{v}_{2j}|_{\phi_j \in \Phi}}, \ldots, \frac{v_{Li}}{\bar{v}_{Lj}|_{\phi_j \in \Phi}}] \mid v_{li} \in V(\phi_i) \tag{6}$$

Where v_{li} denotes the volume for the topic/sentiment ξ_l and period ϕ_i.

2.4   Simulation

The SMSim simulator herein described is a stochastic agent-based simulator where each *agent* of the system encapsulates the social media network user behavior and the environment where the agents live and interact is the followers *Graph* extracted from the social media network. Since each user is an **agent** in the simulator, hence the corresponding graph notation is $G = (A, R)$ where A is the set of agents and R is the set of followers relationships.

The SMSim is modeled as a discrete-event simulation [19] where the operation of the system is represented as a chronological sequence of events. Each event occurs at an instant in time (which is called a *time step* or just *step*) and marks a change of state in the system. The step exists only as a hook on which the execution of events can be hung, ordering the execution of the events relative to each other. The agents and environment are events at the simulation core.

Therefore, the basic agent actions in the simulator are *To Read* or *To Post* and the agent states are *Idle* or *Posting* and in both states the agent reads the received messages from whom she follows and can write or not depending on the modeled behavior. When the agent is posting a message, at the simulator level, it is sending the message to all its followers. The message can have *positive* or *negative* sentiment about a *topic*. That's how the messages are propagated during simulation.

The agent behavior is determined by Markov Chain Monte Carlo simulation method. In the previous subsection we described how the user behavior is modeled as a Markov Chain into which we can call now the *UserModel* structure. During the SMSim initialization two important steps are performed: (i) the graph is loaded from the edges list file, and (ii) for each user in the graph, an agent instance is created and each *UserModel* file is deserialized into the agent model.

We implemented SMSim using Java and the second step is performed by translating the transitions saved in the *UserModel* by the modeler to a map where the key represents the source state id and the value is another map containing the probabilities to go from the source state id to the target state id, i.e., the key of the latter map is the target state id and the value is the *SimTransition* which contains the set of probability values. We defined these maps indexed by the states id to improve performance. Since each agent will have a set of transitions and there will be thousands of agents in the system interacting at the same time.

Every agent (user) is initialized in the *Idle* state. When the SMSim is started, each agent switches its behavior to *Posting* or *Idle* back depending on the activated transitions using Monte Carlo method. The transition will only be activated if the probability value calculated as described in Eq. 7 corresponds to a random value generated by the system, where $v_{w_t} \in V_{W_t}$.

$$\rho(\theta_i) = L(\theta_i | R_{t-1}, W_{t-1}, W_t) * L(posting | \phi_i) \tag{7}$$

In this case, once transition θ_i is picked, the volume of messages to be posted for each topic and sentiment ξ_l in the period ϕ_i of current time step is calculated using the weighted value of the corresponding average volume:

$$v(\theta, \phi_i, \xi_l) = v_{w_t}(\theta_i) * v'_{li}(\phi_i) \tag{8}$$

If no transition is activated, the system switches the user's state to *Idle*. Algorithm 1 describes these steps. We performed some experiments where instead of switching the state to *Idle* we switched to the most probable state according to the transitions Θ. However that approach did not result in a positive impact in the overall simulation results. The same happened if we create a uniform probability distribution for transitions where both previous and current state were not observed.

Algorithm 1 Agent states transition algorithm

```
1: if  State = Posting then
2:       for each subject do
3:           message ← new Message(subject)
4:           post(message)
5:       end for
6: else
7:       State ← getNextState()
8:       if State = Null then
9:           State ← Idle
10:      end if
11: end if

12: function GETNEXTSTATE( )
13:      value ← pseudoRandomGen.getNext(0.0,1.0)
14:      prevProbabilityValue ← 0.0
15:      for each stateId in TransitionsMap do
16:          probabilityValue ← TransitionsMap.get(stateId) * PeriodMap.get
                 (currPeriod)
17:          if prevProbabilityValue ≤ value and value ≤ (prevProbabilityValue +
                 probabilityValue) then
18:              return stateId
19:          end if
20:          prevProbabilityValue ← prevProbabilityValue + probabilityValue
21:      end for
22: end function
```

2.5   Validation

The Root Mean Square Error ($RMSE$) is frequently used to validate simulation models like weather predictions or to evaluate the differences between two time series. The formula to calculate this error is presented in Eq. 9.

$$RMSE(T) = \sqrt{\frac{\sum_{t=1}^{T}(y_t' - y_t)^2}{T}} \tag{9}$$

where y_t' represents the total of messages sent in the simulator at time t, and y_t denotes the total of messages sent at time t in the observed data.

The proposed models are validated using the Coefficient of Variation of the Root Mean Square Error CV_{RMSE} (Eq. 10), where the results of the simulator are compared with those computed from the observed data. Hence $RMSE$ is applied to compare the curve of the total of messages sent by the users in the simulator, up to a time T, with the curve plotted from the observed data used to estimate the parameters of the simulator; and the CV_{RMSE} normalizes to the mean of the observed data. With this metrics we can compare both pattern and volume.

$$CV_{RMSE}(T) = \frac{RMSE(T)}{\bar{y}|_{t=1}^{T}} \tag{10}$$

3 Experimental Results

In this section we present the experiments carried out to evaluate the simulator. The main goal is compare the total number of messages posted by the users in the simulator with the total number of messages sent by the real users. For this task it was considered a dataset consisting of tweets extracted from Barack Obama's Twitter network, posted during the 2012 United States presidential race. As a consequence, we modeled an egocentric network, centered on Obama, composed of 24,526 nodes. These nodes along with about 5.6 million tweets were sampled from the real network using the method described in Sect. 2.1. This dataset allows us to model and simulate the behavior of the users in the network when reading and posting messages related to the two main candidates of the 2012 elections: Barack Obama and Mitt Romney. For this reason, the topics/sentiments in Ξ are set to ('Obama Positive', 'Obama Negative', 'Romney Positive', 'Romney Negative', 'Other'), where the two main topics are 'Obama' and 'Romney' and the two main sentiments are 'Positive' and 'Negative'. Note that 'Other' corresponds to a message whose topic is neither Obama nor Romney, and whose sentiment is not relevant in this work. All tweets were then classified into a topic/sentiment of Ξ using the two-step procedure described in Sect. 2.2. In this case, 17,853 tweets were classified as 'Obama positive' and 8,766 as 'Obama negative'. Most of the remaining tweets were considered as 'Other'. More details about the sampled dataset are presented in Table 2.

Next, we describe in greater detail the topic and sentiment classification, the scenarios and results obtained in these experiments, and the performance of the simulator in terms of time.

3.1 Topic and Sentiment Classification

In our experiment, two topics are considered: Barack Obama and Mitt Romney. The keyword list used to the Obama's topic includes the words: *barack, barack2012, barackobama, biden, joebiden, josephbiden, mrpresident, obama, obama2012, potus*. For Romney, we considered the keywords: *mitt, romney, mittromney, paulryan, governorromney, mitt2012, romney2012*. Note that we also considered hashtags (e.g. *#obama, #romney, #gobama, #obamabiden2012, #goromney, #romneyryan2012*) and usernames (e.g. *@BarackObama, @MittRomney, @JoeBiden* and *@PaulRyanVP*). In addition, besides the cases considered for topic classification described in Sect. 2.2, we also considered a special

Table 2. Sampled data, topic and sentiment classification results

Tweets	Active users	Direct followers	Edges	Triangles	TS classification		
					Other	OB+	OB-
5.6M	24,526	3,594 (0.017 % of real amount)	160,738	83,751	5,564,170	17,853	8,766

treatment for messages originated by Obama. That is, if a tweet is generated by Obama himself, we also consider some personal pronouns (such as *I, me, my, mine*) and the keyword *president* to classify the main topic of the tweet as 'Obama'. According to this rule, retweets of Obama's messages also consider these additional terms. In this case, though, the *RT @username* text fragment is ignored for topic evaluation to avoid that a retweet of an original negative message is classified as a negative post about the candidate.

3.2 Sensitive Analysis

There are three types of sensitive analysis that we present here for the $24,526$ simulated users. First we analyze by periods, then by sliding windows time steps, and finally by sentiment . All of them we discuss on how the CV_RMSE varies throughout the simulation time. Recall, we are not stating that this is the only way of analyzing the results, though it gives tangible insights on the proposed method. For each scenario we run 10 simulation trials and computed the average.

3.2.1 Period Impact

We defined two distinct scenarios to consider:

Fixed: Modeler with 4 periods with equal durations: all periods $\Phi =$('Night', 'Morning', 'Afternoon', 'Evening') have the same length of hours, i.e. $|\phi_i| = 6, \forall \phi_i \in \Phi$, with the corresponding starting times defined as $\Phi' =$(12:00AM, 6:00AM, 12:00PM, 6:00PM).

Short Night: Modeler with 4 periods and short night: the same 4 periods in Φ as the other scenario but the 'Night' period is shorter with a duration of 4 h and starting later, the morning, afternoon and evening are shifted, and afternoon and evening have 1hr longer duration. The corresponding starting times are defined as $\Phi' =$(4:00AM, 8:00AM, 2:00PM, 9:00PM).

For both scenarios, $\Delta t = 15$ min. The 'Short Night' scenario was defined based on two observations: (i) the time observed in the data is UTC-3, Brasilia, Brazil time, however the majority of users are in the USA. Hence the minimum time zone difference is 3 h, and (ii) the night period in the observed data is shorter compared to the others periods.

In Fig. 2 the curves representing the volume of messages sent at each simulation step, for both scenarios, are shown along with the volume of messages plotted from the sampled data. In both scenarios the volume of messages results in a curve whose shape is similar to that computed from the real data. This shows that the proposed approach is promising towards an accurate modeling of users' behavior in social media networks. In Fig. 3 we show the validation with CV_{RMSE} as described in Sect. 2.5. It can be observed that the error rate of the simulator in the 'Short Night' scenario is generally lower than in the 'Fixed' scenario. This indicates that the proper setting of the length and the starting times of the periods may improve the overall modeling of the users' behavior.

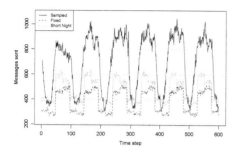

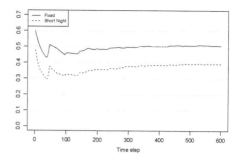

Fig. 2. Volume of messages per time step.

Fig. 3. CV_{RMSE} validation metric.

3.2.2 Sliding Window Time Step Impact

In our experiments, four different sliding window time steps (Δt) were applied through the simulation. The time steps were 5, 15, 30 and 60 min, and the whole simulation took place in a 9000 min time window, that corresponds to 6.25 days. By the end of each simulation, we plotted the curves corresponding to the simulated volume of messages that we sampled corresponding to the topic "Obama" and the simulated output. Also, we calculate the cumulative CV_{RMSE} of both curves and use it to analyze the quality of our simulation.

Figures 4, 5, 6 and 7 show the number of messages, simulated for 'Short Night' scenarios, and sampled in each time step. We can see that there is a higher agreement between the 5 min discretization and the sampled data than with the other discretizations. That is also verified when we look at the CV_{RMSE} in Fig. 8, that clearly shows lower cumulative error as time grows.

One possible interpretation for this behavior is that short time windows better capture the user behavior about a topic because there is less noisy data when considering a thinner granularity of our discretization. At the same time, we can imagine that Twitter users tend to react to stimulae from other users relatively fast, since the approach that presented the best results was the 5 min time step.

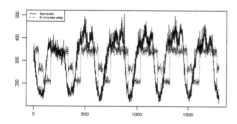

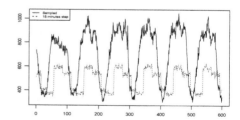

Fig. 4. Volume of messages per time step for a 5 min step.

Fig. 5. Volume of messages per time step for a 15 min step.

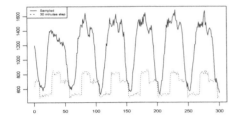
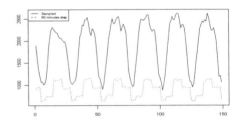

Fig. 6. Volume of messages per time step for a 30 min step.

Fig. 7. Volume of messages per time step for a 60 min step.

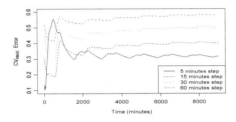

Fig. 8. Cumulative CV_{RMSE} error of the trials per time of the simulation.

It is also interesting to note how the error grows in the beginning of the simulation for the 5 min time step. It surpasses the errors of the other discretizations and then drops until it reaches the lowest error we observed. This indicates that, in spite of its higher error during the first simulation steps, the 5 min configuration can result in lower modeling error over longer simulation runs. The longer time window configurations, in contrast, might be more suitable for short simulation runs.

3.2.3 Sentiment Analysis

In Figs. 9 and 10, the CV_{RMSE} for each topic in $\varXi$ is shown, for 'Short Night' scenarios with sliding window (Δt) of 5 and 15 min time steps, respectively.

From these results we can observe that either the sampling would have to be increased with regard to the sentiment of the posts related to Obama and Romney topics or these sliding widows for considering the pair topic-sentiment are not well parametrized. First because the CV_{RMSE} should be minimized and second because we would expect the range scale in Fig. 9 to be lower than in Fig. 10, since it had better accuracy as showed in Figs. 4 and 5.

3.3 Performance

We run the experiments in a Red Hat x86_64 Linux with 256 GB memory size and 16 CPU cores. For the sample used, both the modeler and simulator scaled in a linear time. However we tested some scenarios with a complementary sample

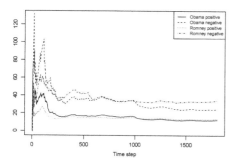

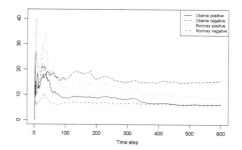

Fig. 9. CV_{RMSE} validation for each topic ('Short Night' - 5 min).

Fig. 10. CV_{RMSE} validation for each topic ('Short Night' - 15 min).

not used for the previous experiments described. If some users have more than 100 leaders the modeler was highly impacted, while the simulator had a lower increasing in the execution time. On the other hand the simulator execution time scales with the size of the network. Figure 11 shows the average simulation steps durations for 10 simulations trial with 602 steps and 24 k agents.

If we use the same host environment that we used, for instance, if we scale the network to 10^k agents, the average time would shift to 10^{k-1} ms through a naive induction.

4 Final Remarks

In this paper we proposed a method to simulate the behavior of users in a social media network, using Barack Obama's Twitter network as a case study. The data sampled from Twitter allowed us to build individual stochastic models to represent how each user behaves when posting messages related to two main topics, i.e. Barack Obama and Mitt Romney, and a positive or negative sentiment. Experiments considering different scenarios demonstrated that the proposed approach is promising for simulating the overall behavior of users in the social network. And the main contribution of using ABS technology is the possibility to explore what-if analysis where we tune user's behavior.

From the proposed method point of view, the future work is fourth fold. First, we need to enhance the modeling of the users. This might be achieved by using machine learning and optimization techniques to define both the architecture and the parameters of the models from data. Second, to re-evaluate the sampling of the data and to enlarge the dataset may help to better estimate the models. Third, by improving topic and sentiment classification the remaining phases of the simulator will be able to rely on a more accurate estimate of user opinions. And last but not least, the simulator does not scale with the sampling size. Therefore we need to address simulation distribution and parallelization in order to simulate larger samples. From the social network analysis point of view, we

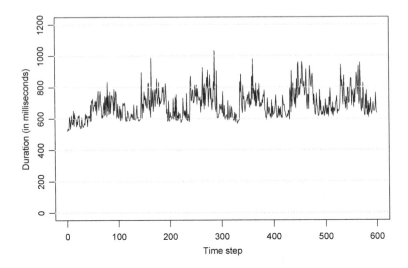

Fig. 11. Simulation steps durations.

are exploring scenarios where we change the behavior of highly influential users in order to understand their impact.

References

1. Go, A., Bhayani, R., Huang, L.: Twitter sentiment classification using distant supervision. Technical report CS224N, Stanford University (2009)
2. Kwak, H., Lee, C., Park, H., Moon, S.: What is twitter, a social network or a news media? In: Proceedings of the 19th International Conference on World Wide Web, WWW '10, pp. 591–600. ACM, New York (2010)
3. Rogers, E.M., Rogers, E.: Diffusion of Innovations, 5th edn. Free Press, New York (2003)
4. Kempe, D., Kleinberg, J., Tardos, E.: Maximizing the spread of influence through a social network. In: Proceedings of the Ninth ACM SIGKDD International Conference on Knowledge Discovery and Data Mining, KDD '03, pp. 137–146. ACM, New York (2003)
5. Leskovec, J., Adamic, L.A., Huberman, B.A.: The dynamics of viral marketing. In: Proceedings of the 7th ACM Conference on Electronic Commerce, EC '06, pp. 228–237. ACM, New York (2006)
6. Strang, D., Soule, S.A.: Diffusion in organizations and social movements: from hybrid corn to poison pills. Ann. Rev. Sociol. **24**(1), 265–290 (1998)
7. Gruhl, D., Guha, R., Liben-Nowell, D., Tomkins, A.: Information diffusion through blogspace. In: Proceedings of the 13th International Conference on World Wide Web, WWW '04, pp. 491–501. ACM, New York (2004)
8. Leskovec, J., Horvitz, E.: Planetary-scale views on a large instant-messaging network. In: Proceedings of the 17th International Conference on World Wide Web, WWW '08, pp. 915–924. ACM, New York (2008)

9. Cha, M., Mislove, A., Gummadi, K.P.: A measurement-driven analysis of information propagation in the flickr social network. In: Proceedings of the 18th International Conference on World Wide Web, WWW '09, pp. 721–730. ACM, New York (2009)

10. Wooldridge, M., Jennings, N.R.: Intelligent agents: theory and practice. Knowl. Eng. Rev. **10**(2), 115–152 (1995)

11. Jennings, N.R.: An agent-based approach for building complex software systems. Commun. ACM **44**(4), 35–41 (2001)

12. Macal, C.M., North, M.J.: Tutorial on agent-based modelling and simulation. J. Simul. **4**, 151–162 (2010)

13. Janssen, M.A., Jager, W.: Simulating market dynamics: interactions between consumer psychology and social networks. Artif. Life **9**(4), 343–356 (2003)

14. Wicker, A.W., Doyle, J.: Leveraging multiple mechanisms for information propagation. In: Dechesne, F., Hattori, H., ter Mors, A., Such, J.M., Weyns, D., Dignum, F. (eds.) AAMAS 2011 Workshops. LNCS (LNAI), vol. 7068, pp. 1–2. Springer, Heidelberg (2012)

15. Mislove, A., Marcon, M., Gummadi, K.P., Druschel, P., Bhattacharjee, B.: Measurement and analysis of online social networks. In: Proceedings of the 7th ACM SIGCOMM Conference on Internet Measurement, IMC '07, pp. 29–42. ACM, New York (2007)

16. Lee, S.H., Kim, P.J., Jeong, H.: Statistical properties of sampled networks. Phys. Rev. E **73** (2009)

17. Ahn, Y.Y., Han, S., Kwak, H., Moon, S., Jeong, H.: Analysis of topological characteristics of huge online social networking services. In: Proceedings of the 16th International Conference on World Wide Web, WWW '07, pp. 835–844. ACM, New York (2007)

18. Milgram, S.: The small world problem. Psychol. Today **2**, 60–67 (1967)

19. Fishman, G.S.: Discrete-Event Simulation: Modeling, Programming, and Analysis. Springer, New York (2001)

Formal Approaches in MABS:
Design and Validation

Dynamic Identity Model for Agents

Joana Dimas[(✉)] and Rui Prada

INESC-ID and Instituto Superior Técnico, University of Lisbon,
Av. Prof. Cavaco Silva, 2744-016 Porto Salvo, Portugal
joana.dimas@gaips.inesc-id.pt, rui.prada@ist.utl.pt

Abstract. Our identity plays an important role in our lives - it regulates our thoughts, feelings and behaviours. For that reason researchers have been focusing on identity and the way it can impact an agent's processes and make them more believable. Because identity is dynamic, people's behaviours will differ according to different contexts. The presence of others as well as several other social context's factors have an effect on the way someone is going to perceive oneself. Whether as part of a group with shared interests among its members, or as unique and distinctive individual, the perception of group membership is going to determine if one's behaviour is going to be influenced by one's social identity or personal identity. When a social identity is salient, people tend to cooperate more with members of their group even when the group's goals differ from their own personal goals. Due to that impact, we believe that a dynamic identity is especially important if the aim is to build believable agents with the ability to adjust their decisions to the social context they are in. In this paper, we present a Dynamic Identity Model for Agents that provides agents with an adaptive identity and behaviour that is adjustable to the social context.

Keywords: Context-situated agents · Dynamic identity · Identity · Socially intelligent agents · Social identity

1 Introduction

In virtual worlds research the importance of agent's identity has not been passed unnoticed. Because of its influence in thoughts, feelings and behaviours, many studies have been focusing on identity and the way it can impact the agent's processes and reactions.

Two of the currents focal points in building believable agents has been the development of the agent's identity, through the implementation of personalities and more recently culture's traits. While these approaches provide some consistent agent's behaviour, personality-driven or culture-based agents' identity remains unchanged across different social contexts [7,17,20,26,27,35], whereas in real life identity is not unchangeable and free of influences. Instead, a person's identity is dynamic as the expression of their individuality has a great dependence on the social situation the individual is in [13,19,30,31,40].

S.J. Alam and H. Van Dyke Parunak (Eds.): MABS 2013, LNAI 8235, pp. 37–52, 2014.
DOI: 10.1007/978-3-642-54783-6_3, © Springer-Verlag Berlin Heidelberg 2014

Building autonomous agents that are able to adapt their identity and behaviour to social contexts, however, still presents some challenges.

One of the processes that greatly influences a person's identity is how one sees oneself and others regarding each other's social groups. Seeing a person as a distinct individual or as member of a group that shares the same interests and norms with all its belonging members, not only have a great impact on how someone is going to perceive oneself and others, but also on one's behaviour [34, 40].

Those different approaches regarding oneself and others are dependent on several factors and many of them related to the social situation the person is in [19, 30, 40], but one of the most studied aspects is the presence of in-group or out-group members. When in the presence of members of a person's own in-group, that person becomes aware of each other's uniqueness and specific personal attributes, relating to others in an interpersonal manner dependent on their personality traits and close personal relationships with them. However, when in the presence of an out-group, the perception as group member strengthens, as a person tends to focus his or her perception on the shared features with other in-group members. That person sees itself as less distinctive from the rest of its own group and when that occurs there is a shift of their own motives and values from self-interest to group interests [34, 40].

How a person categorizes oneself and others is going to affect what type of identity that person is going to embrace and behave according to. When people refer themselves as "Me" and "I" their expressed self is being defined by the one's personal identity. When referring themselves as "We" or others as "You all" that is when a social identity became salient [33].

In virtual worlds several scenarios require agents to adapt their identity to their current social context and the agents should be prepared to behave in each of those situations. One of them being, for example, a social dilemma situation where individual interests were in conflict to the team's interests, since it has been shown that on those settings people can easily make decisions biased by their social identity [4, 15].

In this note we believe that in order to build agents that perform with more believable behaviour their own identity should be dynamic. In that direction, we propose a Dynamic Identity Model for Agents.

The paper is organized as follows. Section 2 presents some relevant related work. On Sect. 3 we present the Dynamic Identity Model. Section 4 describes a possible social dilemma scenario that uses this model. Finally, we present some conclusions on Sect. 5.

2   Related Work

Different approaches have been considered in order to create believable agents with human-like behaviour. In order to develop unique and distinct agents there has been a growing interest on the agent's identity and individuality aspects. Since a person's expressed identity can be determined by the distinct characteristics of the individual, or the shared ones with other members of a social category he or she belongs to, current studies have been developing those two components alongside.

One of these two approaches used to build identities in agents is through personality. Loyall [17] developed an architecture to support rich-personality expression on agents, called Hap. Rizzo et al. [27] presented a goals and plans-based model of personality for agents by attributing specific behaviour (personality) to the pursuit of each goal; Prada et al. [24] addressed the problem of creating better interactions by agents in small teamwork scenarios; and Tan and Cheng's [35] developed a framework which allows agents to adapt their behaviours to the player's personality, through a punishment-reward learning system.

To address the social side of identity, other studies tried to achieve human-like consistent behaviour through the implementation of cultural features. On that direction De Rosis et al. [7] proposed an embodied animated agent able to generate culturally appropriate behaviour, while Rehm and his colleagues [26] built a system where embodied conversational agents are capable of adjusting their expressive non-verbal behaviour to the user's culture. On Mascarenhas et al.'s work [20] it was developed an existing agent architecture, enabling agents to express different cultural behaviour through the use of rituals. Some other authors worked directly with social identity theories, implementing this concept on crowd behaviour [10] and opinion dynamics simulations [11,14,18,28]. But also like the research done on cultural agents these studies lack the agent's personal identity, which is one important component of one's identity dynamics.

Although some efforts have been taken in developing agent's own identity and individuality, these approaches have been taken separate ways and none of the systems address both concepts of identity together and working dynamically. When working with complex social virtual worlds we are dealing with dynamics that are difficult to predict. Yet, many of this works are context specific, and some even task specific without handling with the identity's ability to adjust to the social context, nor how these dynamics can impact the agent's thoughts, feelings and behaviours as a whole. As such, we are developing a new approach where both personal and social identities play a large role on the agent's decisions and behaviour.

3   Dynamic Identity Model

The Dynamic Identity Model for Agents (DIMA) aims at providing agents with a dynamic identity that is adaptive to the social situation they are in, while at the same time is also influenced by it. Although this model follows a psychological approach, it affects both individual and group level working from the individual and cognitive level of the agent without, however, disregarding the cultural influences on one's identity. For that we sought inspiration on Social Identity [33] and Self-Categorization [36,39] theories that we believe to explain very well how those two components (individual and social) work together on one's identity.

3.1 Agent's Identity

According to this approach, instead of showing a fixed personality, the agent features a sub-set of characteristics that represents the part of the self that is currently salient on the agent. So in DIMA each agent, besides its *name*, has a *salient identity* that will filter the characteristics that will determine the agent's decision, but also a set of social groups that it is known by the agent and kept in its *knowledge base*.

- **Name:** a label used to identify the agent;
- **Salient Identity:** representation of the agent's expressed identity that is going to influence the agent's decision making;
- **Social Groups' Knowledge Base:** representation of the agent's known social groups (aggregation of agents that share the same characteristics) and its prototypical characteristics and values (a set of characteristics that represents the typical agent of that group).

While *personal identity* is the part of the self-concept defined in terms of idiosyncrasies derived from the intra-group differentiation [9,33], *social identity* refers to the aspects of a person's self-concept that are derived from the knowledge and feelings about his or her in-group [33]. Following that, in DIMA an agent's salient identity can have two different levels: it can be social, if an agent's group memberships become salient through inter-group differentiation, or it can be personal when no social identity is salient. As such, the agent is not only going to be able to express its individual identity, but also for each social group it belongs, the agent will hold a social identity that can be expressed if the situation leads it. This way, the agent's salient identity can be:

- **Social:** a set of characteristics that the agent shares with the other members of the in-group;
- **Personal:** a set of characteristics that distinguishes the agent from it's in-group.

3.2 Characteristics

In order to represent these two levels, both social and personal identities are defined by characteristics that represent the agent's attributes or features that are going to be taken into consideration on the agent's decision making. When an agent's salient identity is personal the agent's decision will be determined by its personal identity characteristics, but when the salient identity is social, then the agent's expressed characteristics' values are going to shift towards the values of the prototypical characteristics of that specific social group.

Each characteristic is defined in DIMA by a *name*, a *type* and a *value*:

- **Name:** a label used to identify the characteristic;
- **Type:** a category that defines how a characteristic can be perceived;
- **Value:** an observed and measurable attribute or feature.

Characteristics can be one of the two types: explicit or implicit. Whereas *explicit characteristics* can be easily observed and obtained by other agents (for example: skin or clothes colour, symbols, skills and gender), *implicit characteristics* are gleaned indirectly by observing the agent's behaviour and expressions and requires agents with inferring mechanisms. Characteristics that are implicit can be *social values, norms, interests* or *goals* [12,29] and these four types of manifestations can be described as follows:

- **Social value:** indicates the degree to which something is considered good or bad. Values are related to norms, but tend to be more general and abstract. They are used as an evaluative criterion to assess specific desirability or repulsion of a certain behaviour. They can be orientations such as "I should be a good member to my group";
- **Norm:** is a socially and culturally situated standard for behaviour, which is also used as an evaluative criterion that specifies a rule of behaviour regarding what can and cannot be done in a given context, producing the feeling of obligation. Norms can be translated to rules such as "I cannot steal even if to help my group";
- **Interest:** is the direction of attention and action to a set of desired resources. An interest can be "I would like to gain status within my group";
- **Goal:** is a world state to be achieved, like "Having my team as a winner on this game".

All characteristics must have a numeric comparative function which returns the distance between two vectors ranging from 0 to 100, where 0 means the absence of that characteristic on the agent and 100 means that it highly represents the agent. Because of that, an interest cannot be for example "I want to gather resources", but instead should be represented as "How willing I am to gather resources" on a scale from 0 to 100.

3.3   Social Context

Like previously stated, the social context the agent is in will have a great influence on how the agent will perceive itself and others. It will increase the likelihood of the agent behave according to its personal identity or to its social identity, and also determine which type of identity is going to be salient and influence the agent's behaviour. Several important social and cognitive factors are known to influence the salience of an identity [2,3,30,32,38].

In DIMA, we represented these factors with a *theme*. When a specific theme is introduced on the social context, either by a place (e.g. a university), by a topic of a conversation (e.g. a discussion about politics) or by an event (e.g. a football match), the theme will bring out the characteristics that are relevant in that specific social context, and then this set of relevant characteristics is going to be processed by the agent. Because our current focus is the presence of in-group and out-group members, in the model, the social context is also going to be defined by the set of *agents present* in the current social situation. This way, the two aspects from the social context represented in DIMA are:

- **Theme:** the set of relevant characteristics manifested by a place, a talk or an event;
- **Agents Present:** the agents present in the social environment. They could be introduced in the environment through their physical presence, by being referenced in a conversation or by an event.

It is while looking at each other agents' characteristics, which the theme defines as relevant to the current situation, that the agent calculates and perceives if it is in the presence of members with which it shares the same social group (*in-group*) or not (*out-group*). If the agent perceives itself as in presence of only in-group members, its identity is going to be determined by its personal identity. But if the agent is in the presence of out-group members, its identity can be determined by a social identity, according to a formula that we will see next.

3.4 Identity Salience

Fundamentally, the identity the agent is going to take in account when processing its decision-making and to generate its behaviour, is going to be determined by the presence or not of the the out-group [6] but also by several other aspects inherent to the social identity itself.

According to Social Identity and Self-Categorization theories [33,36,39], the salience of a particular social identity (*SI*) is determined by the interaction between how accessible in memory that social identity is to an individual (*Accessibility*), as well as how well it fits the social context (*Fit*) [39,40]. Following Oakes [22], in this model a social identity salience is the product of fit and accessibility (see Eq. 1).

$$Salience_{(SI_i)} = Fit_{(SI_i)} \times Accessibility_{(SI_i)} \qquad (1)$$

The **fit** between a social identity and the context where the agent is situated is composed by two aspects: comparative fit and normative fit. Comparative fit is defined by the principles of the Meta-Contrast theory [39], which states that:

> "any collection of people will tend to be categorized into distinct groups to the degree that intra-group differences are perceived as smaller, on average, than inter group differences within the relevant comparative context", p.455, [40]

Normative fit refers to the content of that categorization and how well does it match with the characteristics of a social group from the agent's knowledge base.

In order to determine the fit of a social identity with DIMA, first the agent needs to define the social groups present in the context given the actual theme. To do that, all agents present in the social context are going to be clustered into categorizations, according to the relevant characteristics given by the theme. According to the clustering algorithm results, the agent might perceive as being in the presence of zero, one or more social groups. If the number of clusters is one or less, that means that the agent is in the presence of one social group. In this case, because of the absence of an out-group, the fit is zero. As such, the social identity is not salient and the agent will use its personal identity.

If in the presence of two or more groups, the agent will be able to determine if it is in the presence of a social group that it already knows and had experience with. So for all social groups in the agent's knowledge base that have those relevant characteristics, the normative fit is computed by comparing them to all the clusters resulted from the previous clustering process. If no match is found, its because the agent is in the presence of ad-hoc groups (groups who the agent does not have previous knowledge or past experiences with). In those situations the prototypical member, or centroid (Ct), of each social group that is going to be used later by the fit is going to be determined by the prototypical member of the present clusters. If there is actually a match between the social groups found by the clustering algorithm, the agent will use the centroid from the normative social groups that it already knows.

Calculating the fit of its social identity (SI_i) is going to be done according to the Eq. 2 where the distance between the agent's group and any other group is going to be calculated (inter group differences) and the dispersion of its own social group is measured (intra-group differences). Alfa (α) is a weighting value for both distance and dispersion, and since we want to attribute more weight to the distance than to the social group's dispersion, we set the default to 0,8.

$$Fit_{(SI_i)} = \alpha\left(\frac{Distance_{(SG_i,SG_o)}}{Kmd_{(SG_i,SG_o)}}\right) + 1 - \alpha\left(1 - \frac{Dispersion_{(SG_i)}}{Kmcw}\right) \qquad (2)$$

The *distance* between the agent's group and another group present in the social context is going to be measured by calculating the difference between the out-group centroids ($Ct_{(SG_o)}$), that represent the group's prototypical members, and the in-group centroids ($Ct_{(SG_i)}$) (see Eq. 3). If the agent recognizes the groups through the normative fit process then the group's centroids used will be the prototypical members' characteristics from the social groups from the agent's social group's knowledge base, if not, it will be the prototypical members' characteristics of the clusters found trough the clustering algorithm.

$$Distance_{(SG_i,SG_o)} = \left|Ct_{(SG_o)} - Ct_{(SG_i)}\right| \qquad (3)$$

The *dispersion* of the agent's social group is measured by calculating the average of absolute differences (MD) of all its members from the prototypical member of the social group (see 4).

$$Dispersion_{(SG_i)} = MD_{(SG_i)} \qquad (4)$$

Both distance and dispersion are normalized, using the constants Kmd and $Kmcw$, where:

- **Kmd:** is the maximum distance two clusters can hold, and can be calculated according to the Eq. 5, where $NChar$ is the number of characteristics used for clustering and $MAXChar$ is the maximum value a characteristic can have;

- **Kmcw:** is the maximum distance between the centroid member and another member for it to be considered as member of that group. It is a parametrizable value, that by default was set to 50.

$$Kmd_{(SG_i, SG_o)} = \sqrt{NChar} \times MAXChar \qquad (5)$$

Social groups with higher fit are the ones with less clustering dispersion and higher distance from the other social groups. Social groups with fit's values below a certain threshold are not strong enough to be acknowledged by the agent. As such, the agent will use its personal identity. Above that threshold, the social groups are strong enough to turn salient their corresponding social identity on that agent.

Accessibility of a particular social group, reflects a person's past experience, expectations, motives, values, goals and needs [40]. Identities have higher or lower accessibility depending on how accessible is that specific categorization in a person's memory. Identities that have been used more times and displace more emotional valence are more accessible. Accessibility is not applied to ad-hoc social groups, and will not be considered in order to determine the agent's social identity.

However, in the presence of normative groups the agent's social identity can have an accessibility value determined by the emotional memory and the easiness of bringing that social identity into the agent's mind [40]. The emotional valence of a memory is defined by the emotional impact of the actions taken by the agent supported by that identity. So, for example, if an agent from the social group "Blue Football Team fans", being in the presence of other agents from the out-group "Red Football Team fans" makes decisions using its social identity "Blue Football Team fan" and then he is punished for those decisions, its identity emotional valence will decrease the accessibility value. If the accessibility value is 0 that means that identity is not going to be remembered by the agent, and thus not used at all. This way, accessibility works as an stimulus to not use that specific social identity in later situations, but can in other cases increase the receptiveness of the agent to use a specific social identity in different settings.

For every time a social identity is salient its accessibility is updated according to the Eq. 6. The sum of all agent's identities is normalized so when one identity accessibility increases all the others suffer a decay.

$$Accessibility_{(SI)_{t+1}} = Accessibility_{(SI)_t} + Salience_{(SI)_t} \times EmotionalValence_{(SI)_t} \qquad (6)$$

The salience of a social identity will be highest if both accessibility and fit are high. The higher a social identity, more impact that will have on the agent's behaviour.

4   Example

Many times, agents are placed in situations where they should act rationally and try to maximize their expected utility according to their individual and social preferences, however, the perception of membership in humans leads many times to social bias in their decisions strategies [21]. In a social dilemma situation, for example, individuals rationality can be at conflict with social rationality [16].

One classic example of a social dilemma is the prisoner's dilemma [23] where two prisoners, being caught by the authorities, have been given the opportunity to testify against each other's partner or remain silent. Regardless of what the other decides, the prisoner gets a higher pay-off by betraying its partner, making this choice the most rational one in terms of utility. Still, several studies shown that social identity positively influence cooperation rates in these situations (e.g. [5, 15]) and our model recognizes those processes of social bias. With it is possible to achieve four effects besides the baseline:

- **Baseline:** from one agent's viewpoint is when all agents present are from the same social group and its decisions are made based on its personal identity;
- **Out-group effect**: from one agent's perspective is when some of the present agents are from another social group than its own and its decisions are made based on its social identity;
- **Social context effect:** it is when regrouping occurs due to changes in the social context. This effect happens when the presence of another agent leads to one agent, that was previously set in one group, to shift to another group;
- **Theme effect:** regrouping due to changes in the theme. Happens when changes on the theme leads to a new identifications.
- **Normative effect:** happens when the social groups found in the social context match the normative social groups known by the agent.

To demonstrate these processes let us imagine a scenario similar to the prisoner's dilemma. There are four agents, Adam, Brian, Chloe and Dave, but only Adam and Brian are playing the prisoner's dilemma game.

4.1   Baseline

In a simplified, but similar way to [32], all agents had to individually answer a question regarding their favourite colour and after that, Adam and Brian were allocated to a room, dressing a t-shirt of their favourite colour (see Table 1).

In that room Adam and Brian can see each other, but they are not allowed to talk according to the rules of the game. The theme of that social context is their colour preference, and because they are both using strong blue t-shirts

Table 1. Agents and the percentage of blue in their t-shirts.

	Blue Color on T-Shirt
Adam	90
Brian	100
Chloe	60
Dave	0

($Blue_{Adam} = 90$ and $Blue_{Brian} = 100$), looking through Adam's perspective, he knows which colour Brian prefers, and starts processing the clustering of all present members regarding those characteristics. From Adam's clustering calculation analysis, the result shows that he is in the presence of only one group, where everyone seems to like a strong blue colour. Because of that, Adam's social identity will not be salient and Adam is going to express his personal identity and focus on his personal goals on achieving is own personal welfare. Because the way the prisoner's dilemma was designed, this will result in Adam, and also Brian, defecting, ending up with the worst pay-out for them of the possible four.

4.2 Out-Group Effect

Another agent enters the room, Chloe, and because the social context has changed, Adam starts processing a new clustering taking into an account all the present members. Because Chloe's t-shirt has a lighter blue colour ($Blue_{Chloe} = 60$), the clustering will result in two different social groups and Chloe will be identified by Adam as belonging to the social group of agents that do not like a strong blue t-shirt.

Because now two groups were found, people who like strong blue and people who prefers light blue, Adam is going to start processing normative fit of its own social identity. Since these are ad-hoc groups, Adam does not have a previous knowledge of the prototypical characteristic of that social group, meaning that he does not have previous experience of how much preference a strong or light blue colour fan should be having. As such it is going to use the characteristic values of the present members to calculate it. So, following the Eqs. 7, 8, 9, 10 the fit in this situation is going to be low but present (see Eq. 11).

$$Centroid_{(SG_{Blue})} = \frac{90 + 100}{2} = 95 \tag{7}$$

$$Centroid_{(SG_{NotBlue})} = \frac{60}{1} = 60 \tag{8}$$

$$Distance_{(SG_{Blue}, SG_{NotBlue})} = |95 - 60| = 35 \tag{9}$$

$$Dispersion_{(SG_{Blue})} = \frac{|90 - 95| + |100 - 95|}{2} = 5 \tag{10}$$

$$Fit_{(SI_{Blue})} = (0.8 \times \tfrac{35}{100}) + 0.2 \times (1 - (\tfrac{5}{50})) = 0.28 + 0.18 = 0.46 \tag{11}$$

And since the accessibility is not considered in this situation, the salience is going to be the same as the fit value. With a threshold of 0.4 the agent's social identity becomes salient. Due to that, their own personal goals are going to be replaced by his social group goal, which is achieving their social group's welfare. Because of that, Adam will choose to cooperate, as well as Brian, because they now feel as part of a social group that represents them.

4.3   Social Context Effect

Now, someone mentions that Dave, which wears a white t-shirt ($Blue_{Dave} = 0$) is soon to be entering the room. Note that the agent Dave does not need to be physically present in order for Adam to reprocess a new social identity salience.

When the social context changes, a new clustering is processed by Adam, and because this time Dave does not present any shade of the colour blue in his t-shirt, the clustering will result again in two different social groups, but now Chloe will be identified by Adam as belonging to the same social group as him. At least she seems to like blue while Dave does not, Adam might think, since Chloe shares the same t-shirt colour while Dave does not even wear the colour at all (see Eqs. 12, 13, 14, 15 and 16).

$$Centroid_{(SG_{Blue})} = \frac{90 + 100 + 60}{3} = 83 \tag{12}$$

$$Centroid_{(SG_{NotBlue})} = 0 \tag{13}$$

$$Distance_{(SG_{Blue}, SG_{NotBlue})} = |83 - 0| = 83 \tag{14}$$

$$Dispersion_{(SG_{Blue})} = \frac{|90 - 83| + |100 - 83| + |60 - 83|}{3} = 15.6 \tag{15}$$

$$Fit_{(SG_{Blue})} = (0.8 \times \frac{83}{100}) + 0.2 \times (1 - (\frac{15.6}{50})) = 0.66 + 0.14 = 0.80 \tag{16}$$

Presenting a high fit value, the salience of Adam's social identity is going to be also high. Adam will continue to choose to cooperate because Brian is still perceived as part of its social group.

4.4   Theme Effect

After Dave's arriving, all four agents are asked to leave the room, and the theme is set to the outdoors. Imagining that now Adam and Dave share the same interesting in being outdoors, while Brian and Chloe do not, the changing of the theme will now allow for two different sets of social groups than seen previously (see Table 2).

Table 2. Agents and their interests in outdoors.

	Interest in outdoors
Adam	90
Brian	0
Chloe	10
Dave	100

Because now Adam's perception is that Brian belongs to an out-group, Adam would opt to defect in the prisoner's dilemma game in the case they were still playing it (see Eqs. 17, 18, 19, 20 and 21).

$$Centroid_{(SG_{Outdoors})} = \frac{90 + 100}{2} = 95 \tag{17}$$

$$Centroid_{(SG_{NotOutdoors})} = \frac{0 + 10}{2} = 5 \tag{18}$$

$$Distance_{(SG_{Outdoors}, SG_{NotOutdoors})} = |95 - 5| = 90 \tag{19}$$

$$Dispersion_{(SG_{Outdoors})} = \frac{|90 - 95| + |100 - 95|}{2} = 5 \tag{20}$$

$$Fit_{(SI_{Outdoors})} = (0.8 \times \frac{90}{100}) + 0.2 \times (1 - (\frac{5}{50})) = 0.72 + 0.18 = 0.90 \tag{21}$$

4.5   Normative Effect

Considering now that the previous social group does have a normative social group known by Adam, calculations would be different. So imagine this new situation. Adam determines, by clustering all four members, that he is in the presence of two groups. He then processes the normative process that shows that he is standing before a previously known social group with similar prototypical characteristic values, as the ones found in his social context (see Table 3).

Instead of using the prototypical characteristics of the present group to calculate the distance between both groups, he will use the ones from his knowledge base. The fit will be calculating according to the following Eqs. (22, 23 and 24) using the Centroids from the Table 3 and not from the Table 2.

$$Distance_{(SG_{Hikers}, SG_{NotHikers})} = \frac{|80 - 15| + |85 - 20|}{2} = 65 \tag{22}$$

$$Dispersion_{(SG_{Hikers})} = \frac{|95 - 65| + |100 - 65|}{2} = 17.5 \tag{23}$$

$$Fit_{(SI_{Hikers})} = (0.8 \times \frac{67.5}{141}) + 0.2 \times (1 - (\frac{17.5}{50})) = 0.38 + 0.13 = 0.51 \tag{24}$$

Table 3. Prototypical members of the social group Hikers and Non Hikers from Adams knowledge base

	Hikers	Non Hikers
Interest in outdoors	80	15
Interest in walking	85	20

Assuming that the Hikers social group accessibility on Adam is 0.8, and that the threshold is now 0.2 (because we are using two variables to determine the salience) Adam's social identity is going to be salient (see Eq. 25).

$$Salience_{(SI_{Hikers})} = 0.51 \times 0.8 = 0.41 \tag{25}$$

Because the prototypical characteristic values were not so extreme as presented by the members in Adam's social context, the fit will not be as high as in the previous example. But now, since this is not an ad-hoc social group, Adam would have had previous experiences with that social group before. Although the theme only made relevant the characteristic "Interest in Outdoors" because Adam recognized his group as the Hikers social group, he could now assume other characteristics values that were not first glanced by him before, such as "Interest in Walking", what could be important in helping Adam in his next decisions.

5   Conclusion and Future Work

With DIMA is possible to create interesting agents with a dynamic and contextual identity able to generate diverse behaviour and decision making and yet keeping the consistency found in humans. Because social identity has a positive impact on in-group cooperation and negative effect on out-group cooperation, it is our opinion that agents in social dilemmas scenarios could benefit from this model.

At the time of writing we have started with the implementation of DIMA on multi-player platform developed within the Project INVITE[1] (social Identity and partNership in VIrTual Environments) [1,8,25], but in the future we would also like to extend DIMA to include more features.

As future work, we would like to support degrees of importance regarding the characteristics given by the theme. Since that in some situations, in order to process the clustering of the present members, some characteristics are more important than others, this will introduce changes in the social group categorization and bringing not only different social bias, but also more uniqueness to each agent. This would allow scenarios where although two agents share the same characteristics (e.g. same nationality and history background), in a situation of war, the other one could be considered an out-group, because it belongs to a rival military group.

One other aspect that we would like to extend is the concept of identity levels. According to Turner and his colleagues [36,39], the self can be categorized at many different levels of inclusiveness [36] and self-categorization can exist at several different levels of abstraction that can be more or less inclusive than just personal and social identity, (e.g. individual, occupation, nation, gender and finally human being). The concept of multiple identity levels allows for the simulation of situations such as having two members belonging to two

---

[1] http://project-invite.eu/

different groups (e.g. a biologist and a computer scientist) which also share a more abstract identity (e.g. they are both scientists).

Another aspect that we think is important is to introduce multiple identity salience and relations among themselves (positive or negative). In many social situations it is possible to have factors that increase the salience of several identities, and some identities can have opposite forces between them. Either because there is a conflict between a personal and a social identity [37], or between two social identities that might occur for example when someone is a children of an intermarriage couple. Including relations between identities allows us to simulate situations where two or more identities work against each other.

Acknowledgements. This work was partially supported by the INVITE project (ref. UTA-Est/MAI/ 0008/2009) funded by FCT under the UT-Austin/Portugal cooperation agreement and by national funds through FCT - Fundação para a Ciência e a Tecnologia, under project PEst-OE/EEI/LA0021/2013, the PIDDAC Program funds.

References

1. Baptista, M., Dimas, J., Prada, R., Santos, P., Martinho, C.: A serious game based on a public goods experiment. In: 2013 ASE/IEEE International Conference on Economic Computing (2013)
2. Bem, S.: Gender schema theory: a cognitive account of sex typing. Psychol. Rev. **88**(4), 354 (1981)
3. Billig, M., Tajfel, H.: Social categorization and similarity in intergroup behaviour. Eur. J. Soc. Psychol. **3**(1), 27–52 (1973)
4. Bornstein, G.: Intergroup conflict: individual, group, and collective interests. Pers. Soc. Psychol. Rev. **7**(2), 129–145 (2003)
5. Bornstein, G., Ben-Yossef, M.: Cooperation in intergroup and single-group social dilemmas. J. Exp. Soc. Psychol. **30**(1), 52–67 (1994)
6. Brewer, M.: In-group bias in the minimal intergroup situation: a cognitive-motivational analysis. Psychol. Bull. **86**(2), 307 (1979)
7. De Rosis, F., Pelachaud, C., Poggi, I.: Transcultural believability in embodied agents: a matter of consistent adaptation. In: Payr, S., Trappl, R. (eds.) Agent Culture: Human-Agent Interaction in a Multicultural World, pp. 75–106. Lawrence Erlbaum Associates, New York (2004)
8. Dimas, J., Lopes, P., Pereira, G., Preto, G., Santos, P., Prada, R.: Social identity bias in agents rational decision. In: Intelligent Virtual Agents, p. 460. Springer (2013)
9. Festinger, L.: A theory of social comparison processes. Hum. Relat. **7**(2), 117–140 (1954)
10. Fridman, N., Kaminka, G.: Comparing human and synthetic group behaviors: a model based on social psychology. In: International Conference on Cognitive Modeling (ICCM-09). Citeseer (2009)
11. Grier, R., Skarin, B., Lubyansky, A., Wolpert, L.: Scipr: a computational model to simulate cultural identities for predicting reactions to events. In: Proceedings of the Second International Conference on Computational Cultural Dynamics, pp. 32–37 (2008)

12. Hofstede, G.H., Hofstede, G.: Culture Consequences: Comparing Values, Behaviors, Intitutions, and Organizations Across Nations. SAGE Publications, Incorporated (2001)

13. Hogg, M., Williams, K.: From i to we: social identity and the collective self. Group Dyn.: Theory, Res., Pract. 4(1), 81 (2000)

14. Kopecky, J., Bos, N., Greenberg, A.: Social identity modeling: past work and relevant issues for socio-cultural modeling. In: Proceedings of the 19th Conference on Behavior Representation in Modeling and Simulation, Charleston, SC, pp. 203–210 (2010)

15. Kramer, R., Brewer, M.: Social Group Identity and the Emergence of Cooperation in Resource Conservation Dilemmas. Graduate School of Business, Stanford University (1986)

16. Liebrand, W.: A classification of social dilemma games. Simul. Gaming 14(2), 123–138 (1983)

17. Loyall, A.: Believable agents: building interactive personalities. Ph.D. thesis, Stanford University (1997)

18. Lustick, I.: Ps-i: a user-friendly agent-based modeling platform for testing theories of political identity and political stability. J. Artif. Soc. Soc. Simul. 5(3), 7 (2002)

19. Markus, H., Kunda, Z.: Stability and malleability of the self-concept. J. Pers. Soc. Psychol. 51(4), 858 (1986)

20. Mascarenhas, S., Dias, J., Afonso, N., Enz, S., Paiva, A.: Using rituals to express cultural differences in synthetic characters. In: Proceedings of The 8th International Conference on Autonomous Agents and Multiagent Systems, vol. 1, pp. 305–312 (2009) (International Foundation for Autonomous Agents and Multiagent Systems)

21. McLeish, K., Oxoby, R.: Identity, cooperation, and punishment. IZA (2007)

22. Oakes, P.: The salience of social categories. In: Turner, J.C., Hogg, M.A., Oakes, P.J., Reicher, S.D., Wetherell, M.S. (eds.) Rediscovering the Social Group: A Self-Categorization Theory, pp. 117–141. Blackwell, Oxford (1987)

23. Poundstone, W.: Prisoner's Dilemma: John von Neuman, Game Theory, and the Puzzle of the Bomb. Oxford University, Oxford (1992)

24. Prada, R., Camilo, J., Nunes, M.A.S.N.: Introducing personality into team dynamics. In: ECAI, pp. 667–672 (2010)

25. Prada, R., Raimundo, G., Baptista, M., Dimas, J., Santos, P.A., Martinho, C., Pea, J., Ribeiro, L.L.: The role of social identity, rationality and anticipation in believable agents. In: Proceedings of AAMAS'2012 - 11th International Conference on Autonomous Agents and Multiagent Systems (AAMAS 2012), pp. 1175–1176 (2012) (International Foundation for Autonomous Agents and Multiagent Systems)

26. Rehm, M., Bee, N., Endrass, B., Wissner, M., André, E.: Too close for comfort?: adapting to the user's cultural background. In: Proceedings of the International Workshop on Human-Centered Multimedia, pp. 85–94. ACM (2007)

27. Rizzo, P., Veloso, M., Miceli, M., Cesta, A.: Personality-driven social behaviors in believable agents. In: Proceedings of the AAAI Fall Symposium on Socially Intelligent Agents, pp. 109–114 (1997)

28. Salzarulo, L.: A continuous opinion dynamics model based on the principle of meta-contrast. J. Artif. Soc. Soc. Simul. 9(1), 13 (2006)

29. Schwartz, S.H.: Universals in the content and structure of values: theoretical advances and empirical tests in 20 countries. Adv. Exp. Soc. Psychol. 25(1), 1–65 (1992)

30. Smith, E., Mackie, D.: Social Psychology. Psychology Pr (2000)

31. Swann, W., Bosson, J.: Self and identity. In: Fiske, S.T., Gilbert, D.T., Lindzey, G. (eds.) Handbook of Social Psychology, pp. 589–628. McGraw-Hill, New York (2010)
32. Tajfel, H.: Experiments in intergroup discrimination. Sci. Am. **223**(5), 96–102 (1970)
33. Tajfel, H.: La catégorisation sociale (social categorization). Introduction à la Psychologie Sociale **1**, 272–302 (1972)
34. Tajfel, H.: Differentiation between Social Groups. Academic Press, London (1978)
35. Tan, C., Cheng, H.: Personality-based adaptation for teamwork in game agents. In: Proceedings of the Third Conference on Artificial Intelligence and Interactive Digital Entertainment, vol. 37 (2007)
36. Turner, J.: Social categorization and the self-concept: a social cognitive theory of group behavior. Adv. Group Processes: Theory Res. **2**, 77–122 (1985)
37. Turner, J.: Some current issues in research on social identity and self-categorization theories. In: Ellemers, N., Spears, R., Doosje, B. (eds.) Social Identity: Context, Commitment, Content, pp. 6–34. Blackwell, Oxford (1999)
38. Turner, J., Brown, R., Tajfel, H.: Social comparison and group interest in ingroup favouritism. Eur. J. Soc. Psychol. **9**(2), 187–204 (1979)
39. Turner, J., Hogg, M., Oakes, P., Reicher, S., Wetherell, M.: Rediscovering the Social Group: A Social Categorization Theory. B. Blackwell, Oxford (1987)
40. Turner, J., Oakes, P., Haslam, S., McGarty, C.: Self and collective: cognition and social context. Pers. Soc. Psychol. Bull. **20**, 454–454 (1994)

Verification and Validation of Agent-Based Simulations Using Approximate Model Checking

Benjamin Herd[(⊠)], Simon Miles, Peter McBurney, and Michael Luck

Department of Informatics, King's College London, London, UK
benjamin.c.herd@kcl.ac.uk

Abstract. This paper focusses on the usefulness of approximate probabilistic model checking for the internal and external validation of large-scale agent-based simulations. We describe the translation of typical validation criteria into a variant of linear time logic. We further present a prototypical version of a highly customisable approximate model checker which we used in a range of experiments to verify properties of large scale models whose complexity prevents them from being amenable to conventional explicit or symbolic model checking.

Keywords: Agent-based simulation · Verification · Validation · Model checking

1 Introduction

Agent-based simulation (ABS) is rapidly emerging as a popular paradigm for the simulation of complex systems that exhibit a significant amount of non-linear and emergent behaviour. It is applied successfully to an ever-increasing number of real-world problems and could in many areas show advantages over traditional numerical and analytical approaches. Due to the high level of complexity, however, ABSs are difficult to understand, to verify and to validate. In order to deal with the large number of behaviours that a model can exhibit, random variance in the output and an often huge input parameter space, comprehensive experiments need to be conducted in all stages of the development process as well as during productive use. Insight into the dynamics is typically obtained by analysing the output (often by executing complex database queries), by statistical analysis and inductive reasoning. Similar to other software systems, correctness also plays a central role in agent-based simulation and questions of quality assurance become increasingly important [17]. In this context, it is important to distinguish between *verification* and *validation*. Whereas the former is targeted towards a system's correctness with respect to its specification, the latter ensures a sufficient level of accuracy with respect to the intended application domain, i.e. the real-world phenomenon in an ABS. Verification is typically associated with correctness of the *implementation* whereas validation is more targeted towards the system's *representativity*. The boundary between verification and validation

S.J. Alam and H. Van Dyke Parunak (Eds.): MABS 2013, LNAI 8235, pp. 53–70, 2014.
DOI: 10.1007/978-3-642-54783-6_4, © Springer-Verlag Berlin Heidelberg 2014

is often blurred, particularly in the context of simulation models. In this paper, we are not concerned with the actual implementation of an ABS but rather with its conceptual correctness. We will employ the following terminology: By *validation*, we refer to the general process of assessing the conceptual correctness of an ABS. In order to distinguish between correctness checks which concern the internal dynamics of the model only and those which include external (e.g. historical) data, we use the terms *internal* and *external validation*, respectively. By *verification* we refer to the technical process of answering a formalised question using a rigorous approach, i.e. a formal verification technique such as model checking. In short, we aim to use formal verification techniques for the purpose of ABS validation.

Due to their interconnected and emergent nature, ABSs typically exhibit a large semantic gap between their static (the code) and dynamic (the runtime behaviour) representation. In his seminal paper, Dijkstra points out a problem which will probably sound familiar to many of those working in agent-based modelling [6]: *"My second remark is that our intellectual powers are rather geared to master static relations and that our powers to visualize processes evolving in time are relatively poorly developed"*. Although he talks about the goto statement and its implications on code quality, the problem that we face in agent-based modelling is similar: what makes an ABS so hard to understand and control (and renders static analysis for its validation largely useless) is the fact that the global behaviour cannot easily be anticipated by scrutinising the behavioural logic of the individuals. Interaction between individual agents following simple (and well understood) behavioural rules may lead to positive or negative feedback loops which may either amplify, reduce or even cancel out certain effects entirely. It is exactly this element of surprise which makes ABSs powerful and complicated at the same time. Even the most experienced modeller will face situations in which the observed behaviour diverges significantly from what was intended or expected. It is the modeller's task to make sure that desired things happen and undesired things do not. It is of particular importance during this process to establish whether observed global behaviours are actually emerging from the individual's local rules or whether they are caused by an undesired mechanism, an *artefact* [10]. This, however, is a nontrivial task which requires deep understanding of the model's dynamics. The best way to understand the dynamics of an ABS is to build up a comprehensive set of validation criteria, i.e. a description of the desired behaviours, and test the system thoroughly and systematically against it. In order to accomplish that, we require two essential ingredients:

1. a language to describe validation criteria in a formal and unambiguous way
2. an automated mechanism to check if an ABS satisfies its validation criteria.

This paper addresses both points. Our contributions are (i) a demonstration of the usefulness of approximate model checking for ABS validation (Sect. 4); (ii) a description of how common ABS validation criteria can be formalised in a probabilistic variant of linear temporal logic (Sects. 5 and 6); and, (iii) the description of a prototype infrastructure for ABS validation with approximate model checking (Sect. 7).

The paper starts with a brief overview of related work on formal ABS analysis and verification and its limitations in Sect. 2 followed by some theoretical background in Sect. 3. Our ideas have been evaluated in a range of experiments which are described in Sect. 8. Here we demonstrate the application of approximate model checking to an ABS of considerable size and show its benefits for the analysis as well as its advantage over conventional model checking.

2 Related Work

In the following, we describe related work in the area of formal verification for probabilistic agent-based systems and simulations. A good overview of statistical validation techniques (which is omitted here) is given in Kleijnen's and Sargent's papers [14,18].

Despite the growing importance of ABS, dedicated formal verification techniques for their analysis are still largely missing. In recent years, probabilistic model checking has gained increasing importance for general multiagent systems (of which ABSs are a special type). An interesting approach to verify the emergent behaviour of robot swarms using probabilistic model checking has been presented by Konur *et al.* [15]. In order to tackle the combinatorial explosion of the state space, the authors exploit the high level of symmetry in the model and use *counter abstraction* [9]. In doing so, the authors manage to transform the problem which is originally exponential in the number of agents into one which is polynomial in the number of agents and exponential in the number of agent states. This is a significant improvement, yet it still remains limited to relatively small-scale systems.

Ballarini *et al.* [3] apply probabilistic model checking to a probabilistic variant of a negotiation game. They use PRISM [16], a probabilistic model checker, to verify PCTL (**P**robabilistic **C**omputation **T**ree **L**ogic) [2] properties referring to (i) the value at which an agreement between two agents bargaining over a single resource is reached and (ii) the delay for reaching an agreement. In this scenario, the overall state space is small and therefore combinatorial explosion is not an issue. According to the authors, probabilistic verification provides an interesting alternative to analytical and simulation methods and can provide further insight into the system's behaviour.

Dekhtyar *et al.* [5] describe a method to translate a multiagent system into a finite-state Markov chain and analyse the complexity of probabilistic model checking of its dynamic properties. Apart from mentioning the exponential complexity of both state space creation and verification, however, the authors do not present any ways to circumvent this problem. The verification of epistemic properties has also been addressed against the background of probabilistic agent-based systems.

Wan *et al.* [20] propose PCTLK, an epistemic, probabilistic branching-time logic which extends CTL (**C**omputation **T**ree **L**ogic) [2] with probabilistic and epistemic operators. In their paper, the focus of interest is rather on agent internals and thus complexity issues are not addressed.

A different formal approach to the analysis and verification of agent-based simulations has been proposed by Izquierdo *et al.* [13], who describe how simulations can be encoded into time-homogeneous Markov chains and analysed with respect to their transient and steady-state behaviour. Since the main focus of the paper is on the usefulness of Markov chain analysis for the understanding of complex simulation models, the authors do not provide any state space reduction techniques in order to circumvent the combinatorial explosion. However, they describe ways of analysing the limiting behaviour without having to represent the transition matrices by mere reasoning about the nature of the state space and deriving characteristics of the corresponding Markov chain. Despite advances, however, the verification of properties of large-scale ABSs with a focus on macro-level behaviour remains a largely unsolved problem.

3   Background

Probabilistic Transition Systems: A Probabilistic Transition System (PTS) is a tuple $\mathcal{M} = (S, P, I, AP, L)$ where S is a countable (but possibly infinite) set of states, $P : S \times S \to [0, 1]$ is a transition probability function such that for each $s \in S : \sum_{s' \in S} P(s, s') = 1$, $I \subseteq S$ is the set of initial states, AP is a set of atomic propositions and $L : S \to 2^{AP}$ is a labelling function. A path σ through a PTS is a finite or infinite sequence of states $(s_0, s_1, ...,)$ such that $P(s_i, s_{i+1}) > 0$ for all $i \geq 0$. By $\sigma[n]$ we refer to the n-th element of path σ and by $\sigma[j..]$ to the fragment of σ starting in $\sigma[j]$. The state space of an ABS can be modelled as a PTS in which each state represents a global state of the simulation. Due to the hierarchical nature of an ABS, each global state is itself comprised by n individual agent states plus the state of the environment. Each simulation run thus corresponds to one particular path σ through the underlying PTS.

Linear Temporal Logic: The treatment of time in temporal logic can be roughly subdivided into *branching time* (CTL, CTL*) and *linear temporal logic* (LTL) [2]. Branching time logics assume that there is a choice between different successor states at each time step and thus views time as an exponentially growing tree of 'possible worlds'. Linear time logic views time as a linear sequence of states. The approach described in this paper is based upon the analysis of individual finite paths representing simulation output. Since each path comprises a sequence of states, it is natural to assume linear temporal flow. We thus focus on LTL, the syntax of which is given below:

$$\phi ::= \mathrm{true} \mid a \mid \phi \wedge \phi \mid \phi \vee \phi \mid \neg \phi \mid \mathbf{X}\phi \mid \phi \, \mathbf{U} \, \phi \mid \phi \, \mathbf{U}^{\leq k} \, \phi \qquad (1)$$

The basic building blocks are atomic propositions $a \in AP$, the Boolean connectives $\wedge$ ('and'), $\vee$ ('or') and $\neg$ ('not') and the temporal connectives $\mathbf{X}$ ('next') and $\mathbf{U}$ ('until') including a bounded variant. LTL formulae are evaluated over paths. For formula ϕ and state s, true always holds, a holds iff $a \in L(s)$,

$\phi_1 \wedge \phi_2$ holds iff ϕ_1 holds and ϕ_2 holds, $\phi_1 \vee \phi_2$ holds iff either ϕ_1 or ϕ_2 holds, $\neg \phi$ holds iff ϕ does not hold and $\mathbf{X}\phi$ holds iff ϕ holds in the direct successor state of s. For formulae ϕ_1 and ϕ_2, $\phi_1 \mathbf{U} \phi_2$ holds in state s iff ϕ_1 holds in s and ϕ_2 holds at some point in the future. $\phi_1 \mathbf{U}^{\leq k} \phi_2$ holds iff ϕ_1 holds in s and ϕ_2 holds at some point within the next k time steps. Other logical connectives such as '$\Rightarrow$' or '$\Leftrightarrow$' can be derived in the usual manner: $\phi_1 \Rightarrow \phi_2 \equiv \neg \phi_1 \vee \phi_2$ and $\phi_1 \Leftrightarrow \phi_2 \equiv (\phi_1 \Rightarrow \phi_2) \wedge (\phi_2 \Rightarrow \phi_1)$. Additional temporal operators such as $\mathbf{F}$ ('finally','eventually'), $\mathbf{G}$ ('globally','always') and $\mathbf{W}$ ('weak until') can be derived as follows: $\mathbf{F}\phi \equiv$ true $\mathbf{U} \phi$ (ϕ *holds eventually*), $\mathbf{F}^{\leq k}\phi \equiv$ true $\mathbf{U}^{\leq k} \phi$ (ϕ *holds eventually within k time steps*), $\mathbf{G}\phi \equiv \neg \mathbf{F}(\neg \phi)$ (ϕ *holds always*) and $\phi_1 \mathbf{W} \phi_2 \equiv (\phi_1 \mathbf{U} \phi_2) \vee \mathbf{G}\phi_1$ (ϕ_1 *may be succeeded by* ϕ_2). It is often helpful to use certain combinations of operators. For example, $\mathbf{GF}\phi$ states that "ϕ *is satisfied infinitely often*"; $\mathbf{FG}\phi$ states that "ϕ *will eventually hold forever*".

Approximate Model Checking: Model checking [4] is a popular verification technique which uses a formal representation $\mathcal{M}$ of the system under consideration (usually a finite state model) together with a specification of the system's desired properties p, typically given in temporal logic. The verification of a system's correctness is then done by checking whether a given property p holds (formally $\mathcal{M} \models p$) by examining all possible execution paths. In the case of violation, the model checker can provide a counterexample. In order to deal with inherently random systems, probabilistic extensions to model checking have been developed [16]. Despite impressive advances made in recent years, exponential growth of the underlying finite-state model (the so-called *state space explosion*) remains a central problem which makes the verification of non-trivial real-world systems difficult or even impossible. Apart from symbolic model checking, a number of techniques have been developed in order to tackle this problem, such as reduction, abstraction, compositional verification and approximation. In this paper, we focus on the latter idea. Approximate (also *statistical*) model checking (AMC) is based on the following principle: n paths from the state space underlying the system under consideration $\mathcal{M}$ are obtained through random sampling. It is then checked for each path σ whether σ satisfies a given linear-time property ϕ, denoted $\sigma \models \phi$. The verification of ϕ on path σ can be considered a Bernoulli trial with either positive or negative outcome. Let A denote the number of successes in a sequence of N Bernoulli trials. The overall probability of $\mathcal{M}$ satisfying ϕ, denoted $Pr(\phi)$, can then be approximated by A/N. Clearly, the number of samples – i.e. paths verified – has a significant impact on the accuracy of the result. By varying it, the *confidence* with which the resulting probability reflects the actual probability can be adjusted. Several approaches to address this problem have been proposed. We follow the work by Hérault *et al.* [11] who provide a *probabilistic guarantee* on the accuracy of the approximate value generated by using *Chernoff-Hoeffding bounds* on the tail of the underlying distribution. According to this idea, $\ln\left(\frac{2}{\delta}\right)/2\epsilon^2$ samples need to be obtained in order to achieve a result Y that deviates from the real probability X by at most ϵ with probability $1 - \delta$, i.e. $Pr(|X - Y| \leq \epsilon) \geq 1 - \delta$. This results in the *Generic Approximation Algorithm* ($\mathcal{GAA}$) outlined in Alg. 1. It accepts four inputs: a path generator $pathGen$[1], an LTL property ϕ, the desired path length k, an approximation parameter ϵ and a confidence parameter δ. The algorithm obtains N samples where N is a function of ϵ and δ. Property ϕ is then evaluated separately for each path. Every successful evaluation increases a counter variable A. A/N then provides an estimation of the actual probability of ϕ.

Algorithm 1 Generic Approximation Algorithm $\mathcal{GAA}$

Input: $pathGen, \phi, k, \epsilon, \delta$
　$N := \ln\left(\frac{2}{\delta}\right) \cdot \frac{1}{2\epsilon^2}$
　$A := 0$
　for $i := 1$ to N **do**
　　1. Generate a random path σ of length k using $pathGen$
　　2. If ϕ is true on σ then $A := A + 1$
　end for
　return A/N

---

4   Agent-Based Simulation and Approximate Model Checking

In agent-based modelling, conventional statistical analysis is the predominant approach to validation. To this end, simulation output is often written to a relational database, extracted with SQL and analysed with statistical methods. This is convenient for exploratory analysis, i.e. for summarising the main statistical characteristics of the output or for comparing the simulation output with historical data. Formulating complex behavioural expectations including temporal relationships, however, can become a manual and time-consuming process. Consider, for example, the following statement about the desired behaviour of an agent in a transmission simulation: *"it should hold for the majority of agents that, whenever an agent is susceptible, it must become infected within t time steps, otherwise it must recover again"*. Translating such a statement into a statistical test is nontrivial. The situation is further complicated in the presence of randomness, i.e. if transitions only occur with a certain probability. As a consequence, the nature of any validation effort is typically highly tailored to the project and characterised by the development of custom validation scripts which exacerbates scalability and reusability.

On the opposite side of the spectrum of quality control, formal verification – particularly model checking – has been used successfully in safety critical areas such as air traffic control, nuclear reactor protection or railway signalling. The mathematical rigour of model checking as well as its exhaustive nature make it a powerful verification tool. On the other hand, its applicability is hampered by the high level of expertise required as well as by well-known scalability issues.

---

[1] In Hérault's paper, this parameter is referred to as *diagram* [11].

The high complexity of ABSs on one hand and their incompatibility with compositional verification techniques on the other hand renders conventional model checking unsuitable as a tool for their validation.

Approximate model checking (AMC) offers a nice balance between strict formal verification and statistical analysis. We believe it is of particular usefulness for ABS validation, for reasons given in the following. First, because of its non-exhaustive nature, AMC is interesting for systems whose complexity prevents the usage of conventional model checking. The parameters of the randomised algorithm can be used to approximate the actual verification result to an arbitrary degree of accuracy. Since the achievable accuracy is a function of the number of sample paths generated and this generation process may be expensive, AMC is particularly suitable for the verification of non-safety-critical systems for which an approximate result is sufficient. The vast majority of ABSs is extraordinarily complex but at the same time also non-safety-critical; a quick verification process that produces reasonably accurate results is thus mostly preferable over a highly precise, time-consuming one. Second, AMC allows for the separation of path creation (i.e. simulation) from actual verification. This makes it possible to verify blackbox systems from which only the output is available and whose logic cannot (or only with considerable effort) be translated into a more formal, lower-level language as required by conventional model checkers such as PRISM [16] or Spin [12]. The separation also allows for easy integration of the model checker into an existing simulation environment. Third, due to typically stochastic nature, repeated execution of an ABS provides a natural sampling of paths from the underlying probability space as required by AMC. Finally, the use of temporal logic allows for the formulation of complex behaviours in a succinct and descriptive way which makes it possible to formulate expectations about all observational levels (*micro*, *meso* and *macro*). Due to its approximate nature and in contrast to other model checking techniques which focus on individual or small groups of agents, AMC is perfectly capable of dealing with huge populations. This makes it a suitable candidate not only for the analysis of individual or organisational but also for global, emergent behaviours of arbitrarily large ABSs.

It is important to note that, due to its focus on finite paths, AMC is not able to analyse the steady-state behaviour of the underlying system. Given the time-bounded nature of most ABSs and the typical focus of validation on the temporal behaviour along individual paths, however, this is uncritical. The time-bounded nature of ABSs also eliminates the need for adjusting the maximum path length dynamically according to the result of the verification of an LTL formula (which can be hard) or, alternatively, the need for monotone LTL formulae [11]. AMC is also interesting from an engineering perspective since, due to the independence of individual path samples, verification can be easily parallelised.

The following section addresses the criteria formulation problem by describing PLTLa, a probabilistic variant of linear temporal logic, and its applicability for the formulation of ABS properties.

5   Towards a Temporal Logic for Agent-Based Simulations

In order to be verifiable by means of AMC, validation criteria need to be formulated in a linear temporal logic. In its basic form, LTL comprises only atomic propositions and temporal and Boolean operators. In order to verify statements like *"eventually the number of infected agents will exceed 100"*, it is thus necessary to introduce a 'helper property', e.g. $numInfGt100$, which is true in all states in which the number of infected agents is greater than 100. The statement can then be expressed by combining the atomic proposition with a temporal operator: $\phi = \mathbf{F}\,numInfGt100$. Although technically correct, this is not a very elegant solution. If we view the output of a simulation as a sequence of states, each of which is itself composed of multiple attribute-value pairs, it would be more convenient if we could refer to particular values in the simulation output and formulate arithmetic and comparison statements within the logic itself. Assuming the existence of a variable $numInfected$ in the output, the property above could then be reformulated as $\phi = \mathbf{F}(numInfected > 100)$ which is much closer to the statement in natural language.

The integration of numeric functions and simple arithmetic expressions into temporal logic is not new and has, for example, been investigated in the context of LTL with constraints (LTLc) [7]. Its usefulness for the verification of complex quantitative and qualitative properties involving external data in the domain of biochemical systems has been shown by Fages and Rizk [8]. We concentrate here on a subset of PLTLc (the probabilistic extension of LTLc) which is restricted to bound variables and thus releases the model checker from having to solve constraint satisfaction problems. We call this logic PLTLa (Probabilistic LTL with arithmetic expressions) and show how it can serve as a basic but powerful formal language for different types of typical ABS validation criteria in the following. The syntax of PLTLa is given below:

$$\phi ::= \text{true} \mid bFunc \mid \phi \wedge \phi \mid \phi \vee \phi \mid \neg\,\phi \mid val \trianglelefteq val \mid \mathbf{X}\phi \mid \phi \,\mathbf{U}\,\phi \mid \phi\,\mathbf{U}^{\leq k}\,\phi$$

$$val ::= val \oplus val \mid val^{val} \mid nFunc \mid \mathbb{R}$$

Here, $\trianglelefteq\, \in \{>, <, \geq, \leq, =, \neq\}$, $\oplus \in \{+, -, *, /\}$, val^{val} is the power function, $bFunc$ is a placeholder for a Boolean function $bFunc : S \times 2^{Args} \to \{\text{true}, \text{false}\}$ which accepts a finite number of arguments drawn from an arbitrary set $Args$ and returns true or false, $nFunc$ is a placeholder for a numeric function $nFunc : S \times 2^{Args} \to \mathbb{R}$ that accepts a finite set of arguments and returns a real number, and $\mathbb{R}$ is a numeric constant. Note the interpretation of atomic propositions as Boolean functions and number variables as numeric functions, the usefulness of which is described further below. As opposed to LTLc, we assume that all variables are bound, i.e. their values are determined by the underlying model. In terms of satisfaction, the LTL fragment of PLTLa is dealt with in the same way as in basic LTL. For the remaining fragment, let $Eval : S \times val \to \mathbb{R}$ be an evaluation function which accepts any state $s : S$ and any val as input, evaluates val on s and returns a real number. Then $val \trianglelefteq val$ holds in state s iff $Eval(s, val_1) \trianglelefteq Eval(s, val_2)$ holds. We further define $Last \equiv \neg\ \mathbf{X}\text{true}$

(which only holds in the final state of a trace) and $\mathbf{F}^L(\phi) \equiv \mathbf{F}(\phi \vee Last)$. This variant of the $\mathbf{F}$ operator will be important for preserving the semantics of nested temporal operators (see Sect. 6). For the same reason, we also need to redefine the semantics of the $\mathbf{G}$ operator as follows: $\mathbf{G}\phi \equiv \phi \mathbf{U} Last$. As described above, we aim to employ a Monte Carlo approach to estimate the likelihood of a formula ϕ, denoted $Pr(\phi)$. In order to refer to the probability of any PLTLa formula ϕ, we use the expression $\mathbb{P}_{\trianglelefteq p}(\phi)$ which is true iff $Pr(\phi) \trianglelefteq p$ is true. We further use $\mathbb{P}_{=?}(\phi)$ to refer to the value of $Pr(\phi)$ itself.

Boolean and numeric functions play a central role in PLTLa. They allow for the integration of custom logic which facilitates the formulation of complex, multi-level properties. An important requirement for an ABS validation framework is the formulation of properties over different levels: we may want to make statements about single agents, about groups of agents or about the whole population. We may also want to make statements about values which are not even part of the simulation output, e.g. aggregations such as *'the average number of healthy agents'*. Instead of manually transforming the output prior to validation, it would be more convenient to specify the mapping of output values to aggregations of interest within the validation framework itself. Functions can facilitate this process by offering a way to hide custom logic behind simple variables. In this way, frequently recurring computations can be integrated without unnecessarily cluttering the actual logical property. This is best illustrated with an example. Imagine an ABS in which all agents have an attribute *age* which we assume can take values in $[1, 100]$. In order to formulate individual properties, we can now define a numeric function $age : \mathbb{N} \times Att \to \mathbb{R}$ which accepts the ID of an agent and returns the current value of *age*. $age(x)$ can then be used just like any other numeric constant within the temporal logic. Let us now look at groups of agents. When dealing with group-level properties, we are mostly interested in some sort of aggregation. We may, for example, want to formulate properties about the *average* number of infected agents, about the *minimum* age of an infected agent or about the *sum* of all agents infected agents at time t. Again, all of these aggregations can be realised as numeric functions. For example, let $count : Att \times Value \to \mathbb{R}$ denote a function which accepts the name of an agent attribute $att : Att$ (e.g. *age*), a possible value $val : [1, 100]$ of the attribute and returns the number of agents for which $att = val$. Like the attribute access function defined above, $count$ can then be used just like any other numeric constant within the PLTLa formula. Boolean functions can be dealt with in the same way except that they are required to return a Boolean instead of a numeric value. The result of a Boolean function can thus be seen as a substitute for an atomic proposition in conventional logic.

The next section describes the formalisation of typical validation criteria in PLTLa.

6 Validation Properties for Agent-Based Simulations

An important part of the validation process is the formulation of a set of validation criteria, i.e. a description of the desired behaviours of the simulation. In conventional verification, it is common to classify different correctness questions as *reachability, safety* and *liveness properties* (among others which we shall not further discuss here). Since ABSs involve potentially large populations of heterogeneous agents, each equipped with arbitrarily complex internal behaviour, formulating a meaningful and sufficiently exhaustive set of criteria can be hard. It is helpful to use the aforementioned taxonomy as a means to guide and structure the formalisation process. In this section we show how the different property types correspond to typical ABS validation criteria. We further describe how basic questions that involve external (e.g. historical) reference data can also be formulated using the same technical framework. We give examples for each of these properties and show how they can be expressed in a formal way using PLTLa.

Reachability Properties: Reachability questions ask whether, starting from an initial state, a particular state s of interest *can eventually be reached*. In a probabilistic environment, this corresponds to the question whether the probability of eventually reaching s is greater than 0. Reachability forms an important basis for the verification of more complex properties as described below. Consider, for example, an ABS simulating the transmission of diseases. Possible reachability questions include: *"what is the probability of reaching a state in which all agents are infected?"* or *"the probability of all agents becoming infected within 10 time steps is less than p"*. The temporal aspect of both properties can easily be expressed using the (bounded) $\mathbf{F}$ ('finally') operator. In order to formalise the statements in PLTLa, we first need to find a way to extract the number of infected agents from a system state in order for this number to be usable within a PLTLa formula. To this end, we define a function $numInfected$ which returns the number of infected agents. Remember that, since functions are an integral part of PLTLa, $numInfected$ can then be used just like any other numeric constant. Further let $numAgents$ denote a function returning the overall number of agents. We can now define the first property above as $\mathbb{P}_{=?}(\mathbf{F}(numInfected = numAgents))$ and the second property as $\mathbb{P}_{<p}(\mathbf{F}^{\leq 10}(numInfected = numAgents))$.

Safety Properties: In addition to checking whether a *desired* state is reachable, we can also check *undesired* states for reachability. This leads to the definition of *unconditioned safety properties* which intuitively state that *"something bad will never happen"*. Unconditioned safety properties are *invariants* since they must hold for all reachable states in the system[2]. In an epidemiological ABS, we might, for example, expect that a situation in which all agents are infected should never occur. We can define a corresponding safety property using the $\mathbf{G}$ ('always') operator: $\mathbb{P}_{>(1-\epsilon)}(\mathbf{G}(numInfected < numAgents))$. An interesting application for safety properties is to check for correct state transitions. Imagine again an epidemiological ABS in which agents have an attribute $health : \{0, 1, 2\}^3$

---

[2] Note that, in the presence of finite traces, the duality between invariants and negated reachability properties does not hold.

[3] We assume the following mapping: $0 \rightarrow Susceptible, 1 \rightarrow Infected, 2 \rightarrow Recovered$.

and are only allowed to transition between those states in the following order: $S \rightarrow I \rightarrow R$. Assuming numerical function $health(x)$ which returns the value of attribute $health$ for agent x, we can now formulate the following safety property: '*if agent x is in state 0 (Susceptible) then it will never transition directly into state 2 (Infected)*'. In PLTLa, this property can be expressed as follows: $\mathbb{P}_{>(1-\epsilon)}(\mathbf{G}(\neg \ (health(x) = 0 \wedge \mathbf{X}(health(x) = 2))))$[4].

Conditioned Safety Properties impose restrictions on finite paths and thus cannot be considered invariants [2]. Using an example from a different domain, we could assert that *"the number of sales should never exceed a given threshold **unless** a marketing campaign has been started"*. This property can be expressed using the **W** operator. We first need to define a Boolean function $campaignStarted$ which is true in those states during which the campaign is running. We also need a numeric function $numSales$ which calculates and returns the overall number of sales in a particular state of the simulation. The corresponding PLTLa property is $\mathbb{P}_{\geq(1-\epsilon)}((numSales \leq t) \ \mathbf{W} \ campaignStarted)$.

Liveness Properties: Safety properties are always satisfied if the underlying system does nothing at all, which is clearly not a desirable situation. It is thus important to complement them with *liveness properties* which state that *"something good will eventually happen"*. An important subclass are *repeated reachability* or *progress properties* which state that something will *always eventually* happen – a pattern which is often used in validation criteria. In our example, we could, e.g., require that *"it is always possible to return to a state in which at most 10 % of the agents are infected"*. This corresponds with the expectation that, whatever happens, the population is always able to recover. In order to formulate this property in PLTLa, we can reuse the functions $numInfected$ and $numAgents$ defined above. Progress properties typically use the nested **GF** operator. However, the fact that we are dealing with finite traces has some implications on the semantics of nested temporal operators which, for space limitations, shall not be further described here. In order to ensure that the formal property correctly reflects our requirement, we thus need to use operator $\mathbf{F}^L$ instead of $\mathbf{F}$. This results in the following formula: $\mathbb{P}_{\leq p}(\mathbf{GF}^L(numInfected = (0.1 * numAgents)))$. Progress properties are particularly useful on the individual level. Imagine an ABS in which an agent is expected to perform regular actions, e.g. product purchases. Given a Boolean function $purchase(x)$ which returns $true$ whenever agent x made a purchase in a given tick, we can formalise the progress expectation as follows: $\mathbb{P}_{\geq p}(\mathbf{GF}^L(purchase(x)))$.

Comparing with a Reference Model: Many important and interesting internal validation questions can be formulated as reachability, liveness or safety properties. An important part of the validation of a simulation, however, is to assess external validity, i.e. how well the simulation output correlates with a given reference model, e.g. historical data. The reference model is often given in the form of *time series data*, i.e. sequences of time-stamped data points. The validation

---

[4] Alternatively, the property can also be expressed as follows: $\mathbb{P}_{=0}(\mathbf{F}(health(x) = 0 \wedge \mathbf{X}(health(x) = 2)))$

question then becomes to determine the correspondence between the reference model and the simulation output which is typically done using statistical analysis [14].

Fortunately, the same technical framework can be used to formulate properties that involve external data which fully integrates them into the model checking process. In order to exemplify that, let us consider two common metrics for time series comparison: *cumulative (CSE)* and *mean squared error (MSE)*. Let σ denote the simulation output and $\hat{\sigma}$ the reference model. We assume that both are of equal length. The CSE of state i describes the sum of all squared errors up to state i: $CSE(\sigma, \hat{\sigma}, i) = \sum_{i=1}^{n}(\sigma[i] - \sigma[\hat{i}])^2$. The MSE of state i is then calculated as follows: $MSE(\sigma, \hat{\sigma}, i) = 1/i \cdot CSE(\sigma, \hat{\sigma}, i)$. A typical validation property could be: "*The probability of the MSE w.r.t. the number of infected agents of any initial path fragment exceeding threshold t is less than or equal to p*". Since the MSE can be easily calculated from the CSE, all we need is a numeric function CSE which, given state $\sigma[i]$ as input, calculates and returns the CSE up to this state. We also need a function *tick* which returns the current time step. There are now several ways to formalise the property, one of which is $\mathbb{P}_{\leq p}(\mathbf{F}(((1/tick) * CSE) > t))$. Alternatively, we could wrap the entire calculation into a numeric function MSE which would then result in the following simplified version of the property: $\mathbb{P}_{\leq p}(\mathbf{F}(MSE > t))$.

7   (MC)²MABS: Monte Carlo Model Checker for ABS

In order to evaluate our ideas, we developed (MC)²MABS, an initial prototype of a Python-based Monte Carlo Model Checker for Multiagent-Based Simulations. It has full support for PLTLa and comprises the following components: (i) a PLTLa parser; (ii) an interface to a path generator; (iii) a labelling mechanism; and, (iv) a model checker. The PLTLa parser was implemented using the **pyparsing** library[5]. Properties can be formulated as conventional strings. Any property ϕ is parsed and translated into a tree structure which contains numerical values as well as Boolean and numeric functions as leaf nodes and ϕ as its root node. The interface to the path generator decouples the simulation

---

Algorithm 2 Outline of the function SAT

Input: Path σ, PLTLa formula ϕ
1: **if** ϕ is $bFunc$ **return** $\{\sigma[i] | \phi \models call(\phi)\}$
2: **if** ϕ is $\neg \phi_1$ **return** $\{\sigma[i] | \sigma[i] \notin \mathrm{SAT}(\sigma, \phi_1)\}$
3: **if** ϕ is $(\phi_1 \wedge \phi_2)$ **return** $\{\sigma[i] | \sigma[i] \in \mathrm{SAT}(\sigma, \phi_1) \wedge \sigma[i] \in \mathrm{SAT}(\sigma, \phi_2)$
4: **if** ϕ is $(\phi_1 \vee \phi_2)$ **return** $\{\sigma[i] | \sigma[i] \in \mathrm{SAT}(\sigma, \phi_1) \vee \sigma[i] \in \mathrm{SAT}(\sigma, \phi_2)$
5: **if** ϕ is $(\phi_1 \unlhd \phi_2)$ **return** $\{\sigma[i] | \sigma[i] \models \mathrm{Eval}(\sigma[i], \phi_1) \unlhd \mathrm{Eval}(\sigma[i], \phi_2)\}$
6: **if** ϕ is $\mathbf{X}\phi_1$ **return** $\{\sigma[i] | \sigma[i+1] \in \mathrm{SAT}(\sigma, \phi_1)\}$
7: **if** ϕ is $(\phi_1 \mathbf{U} \phi_2)$ **return** $\{\sigma[i] | \sigma[i] \in \mathrm{SAT}(\sigma, \phi_2) \vee (\sigma[i] \in \mathrm{SAT}(\sigma, \phi_1) \wedge \sigma[i] \in \mathrm{SAT}(\sigma, \mathbf{X}(\phi_1 \mathbf{U} \phi_2))\}$

---

[5] http://pyparsing.wikispaces.com

from the verification process and allows to plug in different path generators. This facilitates the integration of (MC)^{2}MABS into existing simulation environments. It is also possible to use (MC)^{2}MABS retrospectively, for example to analyse a set of paths that have been generated elsewhere. This is particularly useful if the creation of paths is expensive (e.g. due to time-consuming simulation) and cannot be done repeatedly and on demand.

Model checking of a single output path in (MC)^{2}MABS is based on a recursive labelling function SAT similar to those used in explicit state model checking [4]. A (simplified) outline of the algorithm is shown in Algorithm 2. Given path σ and PLTLa property ϕ, it performs a depth-first search through the parse tree of ϕ and, for each subformula ϕ_s of ϕ, returns all states that satisfy ϕ_s. Path σ can thus be said to satisfy property ϕ iff its initial state satisfies ϕ, i.e. iff $\sigma[i] \in \mathrm{SAT}(\sigma, \phi)$. Function names referenced in PLTLa formulae are expected to exist as callable functions (as indicated by line 1). Arithmetic expressions are evaluated using a special function Eval which was briefly mentioned in Sect. 5 and shall not be further explained here. The probability of ϕ being true in the entire state space is then approximated with the $\mathcal{GAA}$ algorithm proposed by Hérault et al. [11] and further described in Sect. 3.

Similar approximate model checkers have been implemented before, e.g. APMC / PRISM [11,16], and MC2(PLTLc) [7]. MC2(PLTLc) is closest to (MC)^{2}MABS. Our decision to build yet another tool was motivated by the following facts: First, both PRISM and APMC require the specification of the model in the Reactive Modules (RM) language. Despite the power of the language, the translation of an ABS written in a higher-level language like Java or even a domain-specific language like NetLogo [21] can be challenging, especially for modellers with a nontechnical background. RM was not designed as a general purpose language and data structures and helper functions typically found in other languages are thus largely missing. MC2(PLTLc) is more flexible in this respect and allows loading external simulation output. However, output parsing is hardcoded and can thus not be adapted. Second, RM puts a strong emphasis on states and transitions as opposed to the modelling of more complex behaviour which is the focus of higher level languages. Nontrivial conceptual preprocessing of the model prior to the actual implementation, i.e. translation into a state transition model, is thus necessary. Third, all three tools are closed systems, i.e. none of them allows for the integration of custom logic which complicates or renders impossible the formulation of more complex properties such as the MSE. Fourth, as opposed to communication protocols, distributed randomised algorithms or game-theoretic problems (typical application domains of PRISM), ABSs are characterised by a large number of individual constituents (hundreds or thousands). In this context, properties like "at least x % are in state y" become crucial. PRISM's labelling mechanism is restricted to expressions formulated over individual components. Because of that, the size of the textual description of such aggregate propositions grows exponentially with the number of agents and the formulation becomes cumbersome and error-prone. Finally, in PRISM each component (agent) progresses individually and simulation of the population update as an atomic step is thus not possible. As a consequence, properties need to be formulated in a less intuitive way and the path length to be analysed for bounded properties increases linearly with the size of the population. (MC)²MABS is intended to be as customisable as possible by allowing to 'plug in' external logic formulated in a high-level programming language in order to satisfy ABS-specific requirements. Encapsulating complex custom logic into simple Boolean propositions and numeric variables helps to decouple the interpretation of system states from the actual verification logic which increases modularity and reusability of both functions as building blocks and properties as templates in different validation scenarios. As mentioned above, the development of (MC)²MABS is still at a very early stage. Nevertheless, first experiments have shown promising results. As we shall describe below, we were able to verify properties for ABSs of considerable size efficiently.

8   Experiments

In order to assess the applicability of AMC to ABS validation, we designed two experiments. They were conducted on an Amazon EC2 [1] 64-bit instance with one virtual core comprising two EC2 computing units[6], 3.75 GB of memory and Ubuntu 12.10 Server as operating system.

The first experiment involved the comparison between AMC and conventional symbolic model checking. To this end, we wrote a simple (entirely unrealistic) epidemiological model in Python (see Algorithm 3). All agents are connected to each other and each agent can be in one of three states: *Susceptible*, *Infected* and *Recovered*. Transitions between states are probabilistic and partly dependent upon the number of infected neighbours. We also translated this model into PRISM's RM language. Due to the characteristics of RM discussed in Sect. 4 and the resulting complications in translation, we restricted our comparison to the

---

Algorithm 3 Outline of the agent update function

$p :=$ number of infected neighbours
$n :=$ total number of neighbours
if state $= Susceptible$ **then**
  move to state $Infected$ with probability p/n
  remain in state $Susceptible$ with probability $1 - (p/n)$
else {state $= Infected$}
  move to state $Recovered$ with probability 0.3
  remain in state $Infected$ with probability 0.7
else {state $= Recovered$}
  move to state $Susceptible$ with probability 0.5
  remain in state $Recovered$ with probability 0.5
end if

---

[6] At the time of writing, each computing unit is equivalent to a 1.0–1.2 GHz 2007 Opteron or 2007 Xeon processor.

Table 1. Runtime comparison between $(MC)^2MABS$ and PRISM's symbolic model checker (left) and time spent for the verification of NetLogo's Virus on a Network model (right). All times are given in seconds.

	$(MC)^2$MABS	PRISM		
#agents	Time	#states	#trans.	Time
10	0.08	$3.94 \cdot 10^4$	$2.93 \cdot 10^5$	0.13
15	0.09	$2.14 \cdot 10^6$	$1.76 \cdot 10^7$	7.80
20	0.09	$3.00 \cdot 10^8$	$3.23 \cdot 10^9$	o.o.m.
50	0.09	out of memory		
100	0.11	out of memory		

	Property									
	P1		P2		P3		P4		P5	
	#ticks		#ticks		#ticks		#ticks		#ticks	
#agents	50	100	50	100	50	100	50	100	50	100
100	0.09	0.17	0.10	0.23	0.65	1.33	0.4	0.78	3.7	13.72
500	0.09	0.17	0.09	0.17	0.64	1.25	0.4	0.76	3.73	13.67
1000	0.09	0.17	0.09	0.17	0.64	1.25	0.39	0.76	3.73	13.63

verification of a simple reachability property (**F***allInfected*) which states that eventually all agents will be in state *Infected*. We executed the Python model 1,000 times and checked the property on each path which results in $\delta = 0.01$ confidence at an approximation of $\epsilon \approx 0.05$. The population size was varied from 10 to 100. The results (see Table 1 left) indicate that $(MC)^2MABS$ outperforms PRISM's symbolic model checker for which the exponential growth of the underlying state space soon became a limiting bottleneck. All checks were performed 100 times. The coefficient of variation lies between 0.8 % and 3 %, suggesting little variance in runtime.

For the second experiment, we focussed on a more realistic and significantly larger example and used $(MC)^2MABS$ to verify properties of *Virus on a Network* [19], an epidemiological model from the NetLogo [21] model library. Using the BehaviourSpace feature which allows simulations to be run repeatedly, we created 1,000 sample paths. The size of the population was varied from 100 to 1,000. In each experiment, we obtained the approximate probability of the simple reachability property from above (referred to as **P1**) and the following properties:

P2: ($\mathbf{F}(numInfected = (numAgents * 0.3)))$): *"Eventually 30% of the agents will be infected"*
P3: ($\mathbf{FG}(numInfected \leq (numAgents * 0.01)))$): *"The population will always recover[7] "*
P4: ($\mathbf{G}(sqError \leq x)$): *"The SE btwn. the simulation and a ref. model is always < x "*
P5: ($meanSqError \leq x$): *"The MSE btwn. the simulation and a reference model is less than x"*

The results (see Table 1 right) indicate that properties of even large-scale models can be verified efficiently. Similar to the first experiment, each check was performed 100 times. The coefficient of variation lies between 0.6 % and 2.2 %, indicating little variance in runtime. The influence of the population size on the verification time is negligible which suggests good scalability. On the other hand, the path length has a significant impact. This is both due to the labelling process and to additional computation necessary, e.g. for **P5**. It needs to be taken into account, however, that $(MC)^2MABS$ is currently entirely unoptimised. We are confident that the numbers can be improved significantly by using more efficient

---

[7] By 'recovering' we mean returning to a state in which at most 1% are infected.

data structures, by avoiding unnecessary looping in the labelling process[8] or by examining paths in parallel.

9   Conclusions and Future Work

In this paper we discussed the usage of approximate probabilistic temporal logic model checking for large-scale ABS validation. We described how PLTLa, an extension of LTL that allows for the formulation of arithmetic expressions and the integration of external logic by means of numeric and Boolean functions, can be used to encode common internal and external multi-level validation criteria in a formal and rigorous way. By interpreting atomic propositions and numeric values as function calls, even complex properties that involve aggregation over individual agents can be formulated in a succinct way and verified automatically. We further presented our initial version of $(\text{MC})^2\text{MABS}$, an approximate probabilistic Monte Carlo model checker tailored to the verification of ABS validation criteria. Since $(\text{MC})^2\text{MABS}$ concentrates on the simulation output and treats the simulation itself as a blackbox, it can be integrated into existing simulation environments without much effort. Given the interdisciplinary nature of ABS which involves people from various domains often with non-technical backgrounds, the encapsulation of the technical verification process represents a critical advantage for its practical adoption. Preliminary experiments showed promising results. Because of its customisability with respect to both expressiveness and accuracy, $(\text{MC})^2\text{MABS}$ can be tailored to the characteristics of different types of ABSs and used for the verification of arbitrarily large systems.

There are a number of open problems that we are currently working on. Due to its focus on finite path fragments, the complexity in AMC is shifted from model construction and verification to the creation of a sufficiently large number of path samples in order to guarantee a sufficient level of accuracy. Against the background of large-scale real world systems, this aspect may represent a critical bottleneck. Depending on the complexity of the original simulation, a single run may take a long time, which renders the generation of thousands of traces impossible. A common idea followed by most existing verification tools is to offer a high-level description language in which the system logic can be formulated. The high-level description can then be translated automatically into a highly performant 'path generator' which is able to sample a large number of paths efficiently. Similar to simulation itself, this process is also easily parallelisable and can thus be engineered efficiently. We are currently working on a more expressive temporal logic in which ABS-specific features like aggregation, selection and quantification over groups of agents can be expressed more naturally within the logic itself. Finally, we are investigating the possibility of adding 'on-the-fly' verification capabilities to $(\text{MC})^2\text{MABS}$ which would allow it to run as a monitoring process in parallel to the simulation. In this way, violations of validation criteria could be detected immediately when they happen and cause the simulation to

---

[8] For example, a path could be labelled with multiple atomic propositions in a single iteration.

stop. Given the often significant running time, this has the potential to reduce the time needed for verification significantly.

References

1. Amazon Elastic Compute Cloud (EC2). http://aws.amazon.com/ec2/
2. Baier, C., Katoen, J.-P.: Principles of Model Checking. The MIT Press, Cambridge (2008)
3. Ballarini, P., Fisher, M., Wooldridge, M.: Uncertain agent verification through probabilistic model-checking. In: Barley, M., Mouratidis, H., Unruh, A., Spears, D., Scerri, P., Massacci, F. (eds.) SASEMAS 2004-2006. LNCS, vol. 4324, pp. 162–174. Springer, Heidelberg (2009)
4. Clarke, E., Grumberg, O., Peled, D.A.: Model Checking. MIT Press, Cambridge (1999)
5. Dekhtyar, M.I., Dikovsky, A.J., Valiev, M.K.: Temporal verification of probabilistic multi-agent systems. In: Avron, A., Dershowitz, N., Rabinovich, A. (eds.) Pillars of Computer Science. LNCS, vol. 4800, pp. 256–265. Springer, Heidelberg (2008)
6. Dijkstra, E.W.: Go to statement considered harmful. Commun. ACM **11**(3), 147–148 (1968)
7. Donaldson, R., Gilbert, N.: A monte carlo model checker for probabilistic LTL with numerical constraints. Technical report 282, Department of Computing Science, University of Glasgow (2008)
8. Fages, F., Rizk, A.: On the analysis of numerical data time series in temporal logic. In: Calder, M., Gilmore, S. (eds.) CMSB 2007. LNCS (LNBI), vol. 4695, pp. 48–63. Springer, Heidelberg (2007)
9. Fecher, H., Leucker, M., Wolf, V.: *Don't know* in probabilistic systems. In: Valmari, A. (ed.) SPIN 2006. LNCS, vol. 3925, pp. 71–88. Springer, Heidelberg (2006)
10. Galán, J.M., Izquierdo, L.R., Izquierdo, S.S., Santos, J.I., del Olmo, R., López-Paredes, A., Edmonds, B.: Errors and artefacts in agent-based modelling. J. Artif. Soc. Soc. Simul. **12**(1), 1 (2009)
11. Hérault, T., Lassaigne, R., Magniette, F., Peyronnet, S.: Approximate probabilistic model checking. In: Steffen, B., Levi, G. (eds.) VMCAI 2004. LNCS, vol. 2937, pp. 73–84. Springer, Heidelberg (2004)
12. Holzmann, G.: Spin Model Checker, The: Primer and Reference Manual, 1st edn. Addison-Wesley Professional, Reading (2003)
13. Izquierdo, L.R., Izquierdo, S.S., Galán, J.M., Santos, J.I.: Techniques to understand computer simulations: markov chain analysis. JASSS **12**(1), 6 (2009)
14. Kleijnen, J.P.C.: Validation of models: statistical techniques and data availability. In: Proceedings 31st Winter Simulation Conference, pp. 647–654. ACM (1999)
15. Konur, S., Dixon, C., Fisher, M.: Formal verification of probabilistic swarm behaviours. In: Dorigo, M., et al. (eds.) ANTS 2010. LNCS, vol. 6234, pp. 440–447. Springer, Heidelberg (2010)
16. Kwiatkowska, M., Norman, G., Parker, D.: Stochastic model checking. In: Bernardo, M., Hillston, J. (eds.) SFM 2007. LNCS, vol. 4486, pp. 220–270. Springer, Heidelberg (2007)
17. Midgley, D., Marks, R.E., Kunchamwar, D.: Building and assurance of agent-based models: an example and challenge to the field. J. Bus. Res. **60**(8), 884–893 (2007). (Complexities in Markets Special Issue.)

18. Sargent, R.G.: Verification and validation of simulation models. In: Proceedings of the 40th Conference on Winter Simulation, WSC '08, pp. 157–169. Winter Simulation Conference (2008)
19. Stonedahl, F., Wilensky, U.: NetLogo Virus on a Network model. Technical report, Center for Connected Learning and Computer-Based Modeling, Northwestern University, Evanston, IL (2008)
20. Wan, W., Bentahar, J., Ben Hamza, A.: Model checking epistemic and probabilistic properties of multi-agent systems. In: Mehrotra, K.G., Mohan, ChK, Oh, J.C., Varshney, P.K., Ali, M. (eds.) IEA/AIE 2011, Part II. LNCS(LNAI), vol. 6704, pp. 68–78. Springer, Heidelberg (2011)
21. Wilensky, U.: NetLogo. Technical report, Center for Connected Learning and Computer-Based Modeling, Northwestern University, Evanston, IL (1999)

Validating Simulated Networks: Some Lessons Learned

Shah Jamal Alam[1]([⊠]), S. M. Ali Abbas[2], and Bruce Edmonds[3]

[1] School of Geosciences, University of Edinburgh, Edinburgh, UK
sj.alam@ed.ac.uk
[2] Centre for Diet and Activity Research, University of Cambridge, Cambridge, UK
aa797@medschl.cam.ac.uk
[3] Center for Policy Modelling, Manchester Metropolitan University, Manchester, UK
bruce@edmonds.name

Abstract. Checking the network generated by a simulation against network data from the system being simulated holds out the promise of a fairly-strong validation. However, this poses some challenges. The nature of this task and its attended challenges are here discussed, and the outlines of a method for doing this sketched. This is illustrated using a synthetic and target network, applying increasingly detailed methods to elucidate the structure of these networks and hence make a tougher and more revealing comparison. We end with a discussion of the prospects and further challenges.

Keywords: Validation · Network analysis · Agent-based simulation

1 Introduction

This paper[1] proposes a scheme to validate simulated social networks. A vast majority of agent-based models of social phenomena simulate interactions among agents, usually, in a simulated social (and/or spatial) environment resulting in simulated (social) networks. Whether such interactions among the agents are instantaneous, long lasting or for some time, the process through which agents interact, and the duration of stay of agents in the system determine both the dynamics and stability of the simulated networks. Often data on real social networks is lacking, making the validation of the evolved simulated social networks hard. Even if the real social network data were available, the challenge for agent-based modellers is to select a suite of network analysis methods to compare the simulated networks that are generated under a variety of the model configurations against the available real data, which is often just a snapshot in time.

Extending our arguments put forward in Abbas et al. [1] and Alam et al. [3], we discuss in this paper, a series of steps taken to validate simulated friendship networks

---

[1] A companion paper by the authors has been published as part of the proceedings of the 2013 European Social Simulation Association Conference (ESSA 2013); see Abbas et al. [1].

S.J. Alam and H. Van Dyke Parunak (Eds.): MABS 2013, LNAI 8235, pp. 71–82, 2014.
DOI: 10.1007/978-3-642-54783-6_5, © Springer-Verlag Berlin Heidelberg 2014

against a real online social network data and reflect upon the lessons learned in carrying forward this exercise. Section 2 outlines some of the key challenges in validating simulated networks. It distinguishes some of the principal difficulties and complications involved in this task. Section 3 moves towards a method for comparing synthetic and target networks. Section 4 goes through an example comparison of a target and synthetic network to illustrate the process, and Sect. 5 concludes with a discussion.

2 Key Challenges in Validating Simulated Network

Consider a (agent-based) simulation generating a social network. Let us assume that we are only interested in the 'final' network(s) (i.e., we do not consider transient changes in a network that may have had occurred during a simulation run). The objective then is to compare this 'final' synthetic network with an empirical network that is obtained from a target social system as illustrated in Fig. 1 (right end). Most agent-based models will generate a class of synthetic networks, i.e., a different network each time a simulation is run, even with the same parameter settings due to stochastic elements in the model (for example, in the choices of nodes in the rules that build the network). Similarly, there are many judgments that are made each time one collects data about observed relationships between social actors, for example, respondents might give different answers at different times when asked about ties. For instance, Roth et al. [10] have shown that the selection of respondents and resource constraints in ethnographic fieldworks, even those that are well-known, can lead to strong structural biases in empirical kinship networks. Even when using detailed digital source data such as email or phone logs, one has to decide how many

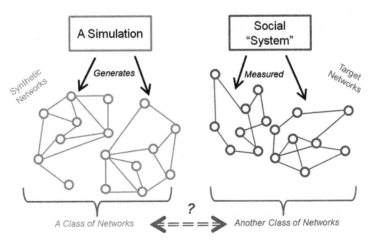

Fig. 1. An illustration of the problem of comparing and validating a class of simulated networks (left) to the available social networks of a target social system (right).

communication events over what period constitutes a link [11], with each possible decision likely to result in a different network. The fundamental task is not to compare a single synthetic network to a single target network but whether the simulation process is producing networks that are (in some sense) representative of the observed social processes, regardless of measurement variation of those processes. Thus, either implicitly or explicitly, one is comparing two classes of networks: the set that would be generated by the simulation if one ran it many times and the set of networks that one would obtain if one extracted social networks in different ways. The central task is thus to answer the question "are the two classes of networks 'equivalent' and to what extent?" We are faced with three key challenges (although not exhaustive) that are discussed below.

Challenge 1: implicitly or explicitly, we are not comparing every aspect of networks but only those that are not "accidental" (either in the synthetic or target networks).

Challenge 2: although, implicitly or explicitly, we are actually always comparing sets of networks, we usually only have a (small) sample of each (often only one).

As discussed in Abbas et al. [1], the problem of comparing networks is that the universe of the number of possible networks is huge. For example, there are $2^{n(n-1)/2}$ ways of connecting n nodes with undirected arcs[2] and thus the complexity of the problem grows more than exponentially with the size of a given network. A full comparison therefore remains infeasible for large networks. Figure 1 illustrates this problem: starting with a set of 25 nodes representing individuals, there are many ways through which some of the individuals may be linked as shown in the two candidate set of links that are generated by a simulation (Fig. 1; left). Such links reflect different patterns of relationship that may be possible for the same group of individuals. Thus, to illustrate the size of the problem there are more patterns of links between 25 such people than the number of atoms in the universe[3].

Permutations of a network that are structurally equivalent do reduce the size of the problem but it does not solve the problem per se that is raised here and in Abbas et al. [1]. This is because, first this problem scales anyway for large network sizes, and second, simplifications such as the concept of 'universality class' may only be useful when considering abstract individuals as nodes and thus ignoring named individuals and heterogeneity in behaviour in the population.

Challenge 3: the enormous number of possible networks makes it hard to distinguish between them and this probably calls for a combination of tests rather than a few simple measures.

Given that it is neither feasible nor relevant to identify exactly the same network or a set of networks, we are compelled to consider some abstraction from these, i.e., some set of characteristics that will stand in for the complete set. Thus, essentially, we are interested in what properties of the synthetic networks one would expect to

---

[2] Excluding links from a node to itself and multiple links between pairs of nodes.

[3] Since $2^{25 \times 24 \div 2} > 10^{80}$ (which is an estimate of the number of atoms in the universe http://en.wikipedia.org/wiki/Observable_universe).

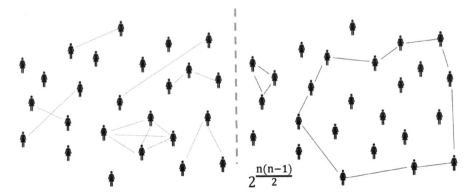

Fig. 2. Illustrating how the same cohort of individuals (nodes), having the same network density, may be linked in a different networks, and so have different characteristics.

observe given how the generating model has been constructed and which properties are 'significant' in terms of the intended processes incorporated in the model? Hence, the choice of network measures should be dependent upon the context, as illustrated in Fig. 2, of the real social network that is used to validate simulated networks. For example, Papadopoulos et al. [6] showed how the log-log plots of degree distribution versus of synthetic networks for two generative mechanisms, 'population x similarity' and the 'preferential attachment model' appeared identical when plotted against 'attraction probability' (the probability that an 'existing node of degree k attracts a new link'). However, when the 'connection probability' (the probability of 'connection between a pair of nodes') was plotted against the hyperbolic distance for the two generative mechanisms, the authors [6] found significant differences between the two. This illustrates that while a full-fledged comparison may be out of question, reliance on one or a few network analysis measures could be too restrictive and is likely to lead to incorrect inferences drawn from the model outputs: a middle-ground must be found.

Undoubtedly, the space of possible networks is vast but many networks will look similar because our brains cannot deal with them but automatically simplify them as part of perception. When restricted to only a sample of synthetic and target networks, it is hard to tell if the two classes match in respects that are important within the context of the research study. However, in principle, if synthetic and target networks do match (in some way) then this is potentially a step towards strong validation.

3   Towards a Method for Comparing Networks

As social network data become more and more prevalent, finding reliable and feasible tests for validity of simulated/synthetic networks becomes even more important in order to have confidence in the inferences drawn from the generating agent-based models [1, 4]. In this section, we propose an outline of an approach towards validating such networks as follows.

1. Explicitly describe the significant characteristics of the target networks that should be matched, even if these are only hypotheses and/or cannot be precisely described (by implication, scope out what characteristics of the target networks are not intended to be matched). For example, Geller et al. [12] took into account incest prohibition rules and a strong preference for endogamy when modelling kinship ties in the Swat valley, Pakistan. Elsewhere, Alam and Meyer [13] modelled dynamical social networks resulting from overlapping and multiple ties such as belonging to same-church, burial societies and same savings clubs in a Sub-Saharan village.

2. Decide which of (1) are intended to be somehow reproduced in the synthetic networks (and by implication, which aspects of the synthetic networks are essentially accidental for this purpose). For example, Geller and Moss [14] compared the simulated network of Afghan power nexus with an empirical network. They considered clustered caveman simulated networks [16] as one of the key network characteristics that were intended to be reproduced by their agent-based model.

3. Determine which measures or methods have the potential to distinguish between networks with the characteristics in class (2) (but calculated on the target networks), and ones without those characteristics. There are many such methods, see [1] for a survey of some of them. This includes one-dimensional network analysis measures such as the average degree, density and centrality [7], or as argued in [3], taking into account entire distribution for comparisons. Subgroup identification including triad census [8], function comparison and the use of exponential random graph models (ERGM) are also approaches to compare simulated and target networks and could be used for validation. Silo index, which is negative of E-I index [15], is another measure, which identifies the degree of inter-links between nodes with a particular attribute value in a network [1, 2]; the example model discussed in the next section demonstrates its use in comparing real and simulated networks.

4. Apply these measures and approaches to both target and synthetic networks.

5. Assess the significance of any differences (or lack of differences) indicated, in particular whether the methods found significant differences in terms of (2).

4 An example – A Model of Facebook Friendship Links

Abbas [2] developed an agent-based model of a Facebook friendship network of a college dormitory in the United States. Agents representing college students had attributes including age, year in college, major and dorm-id that corresponded to the reference data from Traud et al. [9]. Given the fact that the real network data was just a snapshot, i.e., taken at a single point in time, the agent-based model [2] was developed to explore four different mechanisms for agents to build their friendship networks: "Random", "Friend of a Friend" (FOAF), "Party" and "Hybrid" (a combination of the first three mechanisms). In the model, agents build new ties using these four mechanisms (depending upon the simulation configuration), taking into account their preferences for *same dorm, same major, same year* and whether a potential new friend had attended the *same high school*. The model was run for the above four mechanisms until the total number of links built by the agents became equal to those observed in the empirical network data. The simulated networks in each case were therefore 'cumulative networks' [17] and only the 'final outputs' were compared. Next, we report a comparison of the empirical social network data with one of the four simulated networks ("Hybrid" mode) in order to highlight the complementary nature of network measures, as simulated/synthetic networks are likely to score higher on some aspects than on others.

The purpose of the model was to investigate the kinds of friend-making strategy that people might use, and hence would be expected to reproduce some of the local clustering characteristics that would be found in a target network, but not reproduce the particular patterns of individuals [2]. It focussed upon the factors that were in the datasets to hand and did not include other factors, such as ethnicity.

4.1 An Overview of the Target Network

The target dataset [9] taken from Facebook includes both the attributes and social structure for 6575 students enrolled at the Princeton University. The dataset is completely anonymized, where both the identities and the attributes of students are represented by integer values. Missing values are represented by a special value, "0". The nodes are their Facebook pages and the links their Facebook "friends". In total, there are 293307 links – averaging to 89.2 per node. Each node has four attributes, which are characteristics of their owners, viz. major course of study (major); their place of living (dorm); year they joined the university, and their high school information. A summary of the data is shown in Table 1.

4.2 Generating Synthetic Networks

The simulation strategy was as follows: the exact number of nodes (in this case, *6575*) with the appropriate distributions of attributes was created and then these were subsequently connected using a given strategy as simulation proceeded. The process continued until the same number of links as in the real network data (in this case, *293307*) were created among the agents. The strategy that seemed to produce the 'best fit' to the real data was the "Hybrid" strategy, which was a combination of making some friends at random, meeting people at events which attract a similar kind of

Table 1. Basic characteristics of the Target Network (reported in [2])

Attributes	Dorm	Major	Year	High School
Missing (%)	33.76	24.86	11.77	20.7
Unique values	57	41	26	2235
Average population	115.72	160.88	244.30	2.95
Std. Dev. in population	293.06	268.68	399.13	29.21

person (e.g., those in the same dorm) and getting to know a friend of a friend. At every simulation step, a strategy between a random and the FOAF strategy was chosen with equal probability. The party strategy was run every 20th time step.

For ease of presentation, we will use report one network generated by the agent-based model and compare this against the target network. A description of the model and the simulation schedules are presented in Abbas [2].

4.3   A Comparison of the Target and Simulated Networks

We start with a comparison of local characteristics of the target (real) and simulated networks. Table 2 summarizes the basic measures on the networks such as the deviation in network degrees across the nodes, degree assortativity, transitivity and the respective fitted distributions' parameters. As mentioned before, we only report here measures from the 'Hybrid' new link formation strategy for illustration – the resulting here is referred to as the 'synthetic network'. Given the way synthetic networks are built in the agent-based model, the number of nodes, links and the average degree of the network are guaranteed to match the real social network.

As one can see from Table 2, the synthetic network had quite a good fit, especially, the dispersion of links across the entire network. It terms of clustering, the hybrid link forming strategy resulted in a lower transitivity indicating a lower level of local clustering than the observed empirical network. Next, we compute the same set of measures for several other synthetic networks including a random link formation model, which may be considered as the baseline model [2]. A higher clustering in the observed network suggests that more friend-of-a-friend (FOAF) linking might be introduced into the model. Notice that the here we are only reporting the best fitted model after exploring and fine-tuning a range of model parameters. A more challenging test is to look at the degree distributions of the two networks. As we can see from Fig. 3, qualitatively, the match between the degree distributions of the two networks is fairly good, however there is a "kink" – at degree 40, which shows the switch between preference based to friend-of-friend model in the synthetic distribution reflecting a transition between the dominance of different underlying processes in the "Hybrid" strategy at different scales This "kink" is found in many other observed social networks. The synthetic network over estimates the number of high degree nodes.

A slightly tougher test that probes deeper into the structure of the networks is a comparison based on degree assortativity [8], i.e., which degrees of nodes link to

Table 2. Basic Measures on the Target and the Synthetic Networks

Network	Std. Dev. degree	Assortativity	Transitivity	Best-fitted Distribution	Distribution parameter
Target	78.55	0.09	0.16	Exponential	$\alpha = 1.98$
Null	19.64	−0.002	0.03	Normal	$\mu = 89.21$, $\sigma = 19.64$
Synthetic	79.97	0.105	0.07	Exponential	$\alpha = 1.97$

Total Degree Distributions of Reference and Hybrid Networks

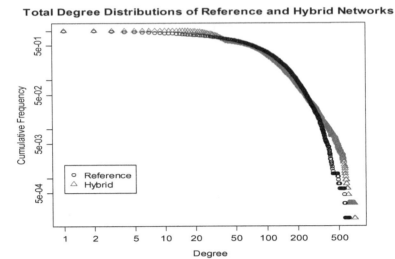

Fig. 3. Degree distributions of the target (reference) and synthetic ("Hybrid") networks [3]

which others It could be that high degree nodes tend to be connected to nodes of similar (high) degrees (assortative mixing) or lots of low degree nodes. We have plotted a degree mixing diagram for each network in Fig. 4. In lower degrees (<400), we find a high rate of similarities between the synthetic (Hybrid mode) and the reference dataset. On the other hand, for high degrees, the synthetic network is revealed as having a slightly different pattern of connectivity than that of the Target network. This suggests behaviour heterogeneity and we therefore focus on measures that incorporate individuals' attributes such as the Silo index [15].

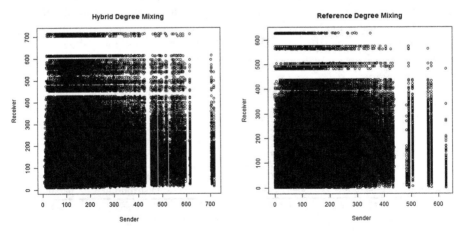

Fig. 4. A comparison of the synthetic "Hybrid" (left) and target network (right) showing assortative mixing in the two networks [3].

Our example agent-based model explicitly aimed to reproduce clustering based on agents' characteristics, so that a comparison of the clustering by attribute is appropriate. Figure 5 shows scatter plots for the Silo index for each of the four agents' attributes (and the unique values) for both the Hybrid and the reference dataset. The plusses in Fig. 5 represent the Hybrid Silo indices, whereas the triangles represent the reference dataset's Silo indices. Each panel in Fig. 5 shows the correlation between the two. It does show a remarkable correlation between the clusters achieved in the synthetic network and those in the target network.

To summarize, in this example, we have used several measures for structural and semantic comparison of a synthetic network with the real network. The underlying degree distribution helped us to identify how the overall network is structured, whereas the Silo index helped us to compare the two networks on the individual-based attributes. However, the role of transitivity, which determines the probability that adjacent vertices are connected, was found to be less significant. The reason being that we are not only developing an emergent interaction model (involving different node selection than the real network might have used), but also the interaction strategy is

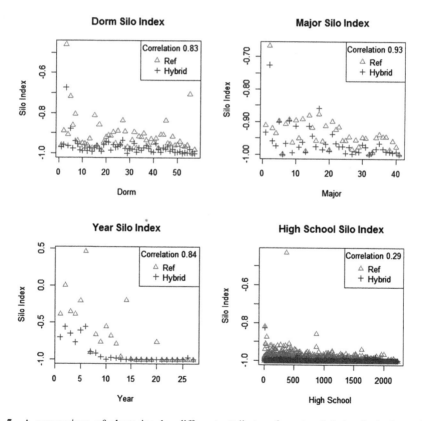

Fig. 5. A comparison of clustering by different attributes, from top left in clockwise order: *dorm, major, year, high school*. Each triangle represents the Silo Index for each unique value of each attribute of the reference dataset whereas a plus sign represents the Hybrid mode [3].

more complex than a FOAF network. Degree assortativity, however, makes sure that the end network has nodes connected with similar degrees and thus was found to be more significant for our research.

5 Discussion

Validation of synthetic social networks is hard and there are several key challenges in this regard. First, the number of possible ways in which two networks may be compared grows very fast with respect to the size of the networks under study. Second, papers presenting agent-based models are often unclear about what links in a synthetic network are supposed to represent and how that does relates to a real world case. This is partly because many (agent-based) social simulation models assume stereotypic networks structures such as the Watts-Strogatz small-world network [16] – either because of the lack of data or for 'simplicity' sake[4]. However, it is increasingly clear that the exact network structure matters (see e.g., Holzhauer et al. [5]) and resources must be invested to acquire network data for validation of agent-based models simulating networks. Even when there is a lack of available data about the target networks, some form of validation is still possible through crosschecking of the model's assumptions and processes generating networks through qualitative data and anecdotal evidence [18]. When network data is available, it is important to consider which aspects of the target network are subject to measurement error [10] (or otherwise judged not to be significant) and which should be reproduced by a synthetic network [3].

Identifying aspects of the synthetic network that are significant in terms of the generating process is important in order to filter those that are essentially accidental. For example, in comparing the simulated network with an empirical one in their model of power structures in Afghanistan, Geller and Moss [14] not only compare evolution of factions in their simulated network but also how different types of agents developed links within and across the factions. Likewise, simulating sexual networks in the model of a village in Sub-Saharan Africa, Alam and Meyer [13] reported two different sexual mixing schemes – both of which adhered to the same qualitative accounts from the stakeholders and what was reported in the literature. As the authors [13] showed, although the output time series for the prevalence of HIV/AIDS were similar at the population level, the two mixing schemes led to significantly different network structures requiring different intervention policies.

In continuation of the arguments presented in the companion paper [3], in this paper we present a concrete example of comparing an empirical social network with the generated one and discussed a set of network analysis measures that were used to compare the two networks. We have suggested a scheme that may lead to stronger validation of synthetic/simulated networks by appropriate choice of network analysis measures and approaches. This is important as the synthetic data may score higher on some measures than on others and therefore, it is important to deliberate on which measure are appropriate given the context and the research question. There is no

---

[4] See [19] for arguments against the Keep It Simple, Stupid (KISS) modelling approach.

single 'Golden Bullet' technique to validate synthetic/simulated networks. More thought and discussions are needed among the agent-based modellers and the social simulation community about what is significant about the synthetic and target classes of networks and of what form of measure is appropriate for what kind of use. A checklist comprising of a number of multiple approaches to validate such networks could be a start and one could evolve into an 'ODD like' [21] protocol in the future[5].

Acknowledgements. We are thankful to H. Van Dyke Parunak, the reviewers of this paper and the participants of the MABS 2013 workshop and the ESSA 2013 conference for their feedback and comments. This research was partially supported by the Engineering and Physical Sciences Research Council, grant number EP/H02171X/1 and also by the Economic and Social Research Council Secondary Data Analysis Initiative, grant number ES/K004549/1.

References

1. Abbas, S.M.A., Alam, S.J., Edmonds, B.: Towards validating social network simulations. In: Bogumił, K., Koloch, G. (eds.) Advances in Social Simulation – Proceedings of the 9th Conference of the European Social Simulation Association. Advances in Intelligent Systems and Computing, vol. 229, pp. 1–12. Springer, Heidelberg (2014)
2. Abbas, S.M.A.: Homophily, popularity and randomness: modelling growth of online social network. In: 12th International Conference on Autonomous Agents and Multiagent Systems (AAMAS 2013), pp. 135–142 (2013)
3. Alam, S.J., Edmonds, B., Meyer, R.: Identifying structural changes in networks generated from agent-based social simulation models. In: Ghose, A., Governatori, G., Sadananda, R. (eds.) PRIMA 2007. LNCS, vol. 5044, pp. 298–307. Springer, Heidelberg (2009)
4. Edmonds, B.: The use of models - making MABS more informative. In: Moss, S., Davidsson, P. (eds.) MABS 2000. LNCS (LNAI), vol. 1979, pp. 15–32. Springer, Heidelberg (2001)
5. Holzhauer, S., Krebs, F., Ernst, A.: Considering baseline homophily when generating spatial social networks for agent-based modelling. Comput. Math. Organ. Theor. **19**, 128–150 (2013)
6. Papadopoulos, F., et al.: Popularity versus similarity in growing networks. Nature **489**, 537–540 (2012)
7. Wasserman, S., Faust, K.: Social Network Analysis: Methods and Applications. Cambridge University Press, Cambridge (1994)
8. Newman, M.E.J.: Networks: An Introduction. Oxford University Press (2010)
9. Traud, A.L., Kelsic, E.D., Mucha, P.J., Porter, M.A.: Comparing community structure to characteristics in online collegiate social networks. SIAM Rev. **53**, 526–543 (2011)
10. Roth, C., Gargiulo, F., Bringe, A., Hamberger, K.: Random alliance networks. Soc. Netw. **35**, 394–405 (2013)
11. Kossinets, G., Watts, D.J.: Empirical analysis of an evolving social network. Science **311**, 88–90 (2006)
12. Geller, A., Harrison, J.F., Revelle, M.: Growing social structure: an empirical multiagent excursion into kinship in rural North-West Frontier Province. Struct. Dyn. eJ. Anthropol. Relat. Sci. 5, 1 (2011)

---

[5] There is already a growing interest in this regard, see e.g., [1, 3, 5, 10, 17, 20].

13. Alam, S.J., Meyer, R.: Comparing two sexual mixing schemes for modelling the spread of HIV/AIDS. In: Simulating Interacting Agents and Social Phenomena, pp. 65–76 (2010)

14. Geller, A., Moss, S.: Growing Qawm: an evidence-driven declarative model of Afghan power structures. Adv. Complex Syst. **11**, 321–335 (2007)

15. Krackhardt, D., Stern, R.N.: Informal networks and organizational crises : an experimental simulation. Soc. Psychol. **51**, 123–140 (2011)

16. Watts, D.J., Strogatz, S.: Collective dynamics of 'small world' networks. Nature **393**, 440–442 (1998)

17. Legendi, R.O., Gulyas, L.: Agent-based dynamic network models: validation on empirical data. In: Bogumił, K., Koloch, G. (eds.) Advances in Social Simulation – Proceedings of the 9th Conference of the European Social Simulation Association. Advances in Intelligent Systems and Computing, vol. 229, pp. 49–60. Springer, Heidelberg (2014)

18. Moss, S., Edmonds, B.: Sociology and simulation: statistical and qualitative cross-validation. Am. J. Sociol. **110**, 1095–1131 (2005)

19. Edmonds, B., Moss, S.: From KISS to KIDS – An 'Anti-simplistic' Modelling Approach. In: Davidsson, P., Logan, B., Takadama, K. (eds.) MABS 2004. LNCS (LNAI), vol. 3415, pp. 130–144. Springer, Heidelberg (2005)

20. Amblard, F., Quattrociocchi, W.: Social networks and spatial distribution. In: Edmonds, B., Meyer, R. (eds.) Simulating Social Complexity, pp. 401–430, Springer, Heidelberg (2013)

21. Grimm, V., Polhill, G., Touza, J.: Documenting social simulation models: the ODD protocol as a standard. In: Edmonds, B., Meyer, R. (eds.) Simulating Social Complexity, pp. 117–133. Springer, Heidelberg (2013)

MABS in Environmental Modeling

The MAELIA Multi-Agent Platform for Integrated Analysis of Interactions Between Agricultural Land-Use and Low-Water Management Strategies

Benoit Gaudou[1(✉)], Christophe Sibertin-Blanc[1(✉)],
Olivier Therond[2(✉)], Frédéric Amblard[1], Yves Auda[3],
Jean-Paul Arcangeli[1], Maud Balestrat[2,3],
Marie-Hélène Charron-Moirez[2], Etienne Gondet[3], Yi Hong[1,4,5],
Romain Lardy[2], Thomas Louail[1], Eunate Mayor[1], David Panzoli[6],
Sabine Sauvage[4,5], José-Miguel Sánchez-Pérez[4,5],
Patrick Taillandier[7], Nguyen Van Bai[3], Maroussia Vavasseur[1,2],
and Pierre Mazzega[3,8]

[1] UMR 5505 IRIT, CNRS, University of Toulouse, Toulouse, France
{benoit.gaudou,
Christophe.Sibertin-Blanc}@ut-capitole.fr
[2] UMR 1248 AGIR, INRA-INPT, Castanet-Tolosan, France
olivier.therond@toulouse.inra.fr
[3] UMR 5563 GET, IRD-UPS-CNRS-CNES, OMP, Toulouse, France
[4] INP, UPS; EcoLab, Université de Toulouse, 31326 Castanet Tolosan, France
[5] CNRS, EcoLab, 31062 Toulouse, France
[6] Centre Universitaire Jean-François Champollion, Albi, France
[7] UMR 6266 IDEES, CNRS, University of Rouen, Rouen, France
[8] Joint Mixt Laboratory OCE, UnB/IRD, LAGEQ, Universidade de Brasília,
Brasília, Brazil

Abstract. The MAELIA project is developing an agent-based modeling and simulation platform to study the environmental, economic and social impacts of various regulations regarding water use and water management in combination with climate change. It is applied to the case of the French Adour-Garonne Basin, which is the most concerned in France by water scarcity during the low-water period. An integrated approach has been chosen to model this social-ecological system: the model combines spatiotemporal models of ecologic (e.g. rainfall and temperature changes, water flow and plant growth) and socio-economic (e.g. farmer decision-making process, management of low-water flow, demography, land use and land cover changes) processes and sub-models of cognitive sharing among agents (e.g. weather forecast, normative constraints on behaviors).

Keywords: Social-ecological systems · Water management · Integrated assessment and modeling · Agent-based model

Benoit Gaudou, Christophe Sibertin-Blanc, Olivier Therond—These authors contributed equally to this work.

S.J. Alam and H. Van Dyke Parunak (Eds.): MABS 2013, LNAI 8235, pp. 85–100, 2014.
DOI: 10.1007/978-3-642-54783-6_6, © Springer-Verlag Berlin Heidelberg 2014

1 Introduction

Environmental and resource management problems are typically complex. They concern many actors with diverse and contrasting interests and objectives. They emerge into social-ecological systems (SES, i.e. coupled human-environment systems) in which four first-level core subsystems interact: two ecological ones (i) resource systems (e.g. water systems); (ii) resource units (e.g. water volume and flow) and two social ones (iii) governance systems (e.g., organizations that manage water resources and systems); and (iv) users (e.g. individuals and collectives who use water) [8]. Interactions within and between these subsystems give rises to emergent structures and functions at sub and whole system levels [11].

During the last decades, integrated assessment has been playing an increasing role to address sustainability issues and the associated environmental and resources management problems [9]. Integrated Assessment and Modelling (IAM) purpose is to assemble data and knowledge from a wide range of scientific disciplines and put them into a "policy oriented context" in order to analyse complex system responses to changes and design sound sustainable management and development strategies [9]. It is a model-based approach that combines representations of different multi-level subsystems into a cohesive framework [10]. The agent-based modelling and simulation approach is recognised as especially suited to deal with the understanding of SESs since it allows to represent interactions within and between the social and the ecological systems [1]. IAM approaches are frequently used for assessing scenarios. These "scenario exercises" allow decision-makers to explore and evaluate the potential consequences of different policy options or management strategies, in the context of socio-economic (e.g. demography, market, political framework), environmental (e.g. climate change) and technological (e.g. new cropping systems) changes [16].

Water resource management is typical of environmental management problems emerging from complex social-ecological systems. It deeply interacts with land use management and with global environmental and societal changes [5]. IAM is a way to model and simulate interacting ecological and socio-economic processes occurring at the catchment level in order to identify water and land management strategies allowing balancing water demands with supplies [4]. Water scarcity is a serious problem in the Adour-Garonne Basin (AGB, South-West France) with an annual deficit between demands and resources of 250 million m^3. In this basin, irrigated agriculture is the main consumer of water (about 80 %) during the low-water period. Despite important structural management arrangements being implemented to address this deficit, water flow rates under the compulsory thresholds set for the proper functioning of aquatic ecosystems are regularly found. To face such "water crises", the local government states irrigation withdrawal restrictions that may reduce crop yields and accordingly farmer' incomes. Due to implementation of the European Water Framework Directive (WFD) the French government is redesigning its water scarcity policy taking into account the expected effect of climate change (higher temperature and lower rainfall in the summer).

The MAELIA project aims at developing a simulation platform to assess the environmental, economic and social impacts of various management strategies and policies regarding the management and the uses of water resources while accounting for climate changes. This computational multi-agent platform is developed to provide information usable by institutions in charge of designing and implementing sustainable management strategies of water resources at watershed levels in the AGB.

This paper presents the IAM MAELIA platform. The second section sketches the water management problem to be handled with the platform. The third section presents the modelling conceptual and methodological framework and the software platform used to develop MAELIA. The fourth section describes the MAELIA model, i.e. how entities and processes are modelled within the platform. We conclude by highlighting the challenge regarding calibration of such an IAM platform.

2   The French Water Scarcity Management Issue

In the AGB, so far, French state services grant water withdrawal authorizations to farmers according to their requests without information to accurately estimate the consistency between the sum of farmers' requests and the available water resources in each watershed. As a consequence, very regularly local State services have to manage "water crises" i.e. to face with the risk that water flow rates pass under the compulsory water flow rates at given hydrological monitoring points. To avoid such illegal hydrological situations, when possible they release water from dams and if necessary they issue drought decrees that state irrigation withdrawal limitations or prohibitions. These restrictions are set up for specific locations (some districts) and durations (at least one week) and may cause significant crop yield reductions.

To overcome the recurrent water quantity management problems, the French Law on the Water and Aquatic Ecosystems (LWAE – French implementation of the WFD) institutes a new regulation of agricultural water withdrawals [3]. One of the objectives of this law is to prevent water crises, which should in average occur only one year in five in a given watershed. Its implementation, still in progress, led regional State services to determine for each elementary watershed the water volume that remains available for agriculture the driest hydrological year in a statistical 5-year period. This annual volume should be distributed between irrigated farmers of each Water Distribution Area (a coherent assembly of elementary watersheds) by a specific local organism representative of irrigated farmers. In many watersheds of the AGB, this volume is (much) under the water volume currently withdrawn by farmers during normal or even dry climatic years. This reduction of available water volumes for irrigation gives rise to vehement protests of farmers. They argue that such a water management leads to restrict agricultural water withdrawals, four years in five, much more than necessary to ensure a safe water flow in rivers. Farmers claim that the only way to manage water in river basins in order to ensure the viability of both existing farming systems and aquatic ecosystems is to manage the resource according to the actual water flow.

To identify strengths and weaknesses of different water management options, the MAELIA platform will assess the four following scenarios:

- *Management by rate of flow* (as asked by farmers): the daily management of low-waters relies on water releases and drought decrees;
- *Management by pluri-annual volume* (the management option that the French water law is trying to implement): farmers are assigned a predetermined annual volume that they may use at their discretion;
- *Management by annual volume* (a refined alternative of the previous solution): the volume for the next low-water period is defined during the spring according to the state of water resources and weather forecast;
- *Management by weekly or monthly volume* (a more refined option): available volumes for the next period are regularly defined and published according to the current water resources state and weather forecasts.

MAELIA will run simulations of these scenarios in combination with various climate change forecasts over the future twenty years. The assessment relies on environmental, economic and social outcomes such as water flow at the regulatory monitoring points, water releases, water drought decrees frequency and intensity (water crises), crop acreages, crop yields or farmer incomes.

3 Modeling Methodology and Tools

The MAELIA IAM platform development requires integration of knowledge from various disciplines (agronomics, hydrology…) and activities (farming, administering…). To this end, MAELIA developed a (conceptual) meta-model enabling collection and integration of heterogeneous knowledge into a coherent description of the system under consideration. This meta-model supports the elaboration of a conceptual model of the investigated SES shared by all participants of the modelling process [13].

3.1 The MAELIA Meta-model

The meta-model, shown in Fig. 1, considers SESs as double-faced: (i) a structure that constitutes the observable matter of the system where phenomena take place and (ii) a dynamics that produces the behavior of the system and generates the phenomena of interest. In addition, a SES suffers influences from its environment.

The *structure* of a system is composed of entities and relationships between them. *Entities* are lasting elements that may appear or disappear over time and experience changes. Each entity is characterized by *attributes*, whose values constitute its state, and is endowed with *operations* that process attribute values. We distinguish three types of entities, actors, material resources and cognitive resources:

- *Actors* are human agents that perform activities, be they an individual, a population of similar individuals or a group such as an organization, association or committee.
- *Material resources* are physical objects, spatially and temporally distributed such as a water body, a field plot or a dam.
- *Cognitive resources* stay in the minds of human beings; they are information, believes or expectations about facts, procedures or values that actors use or consider

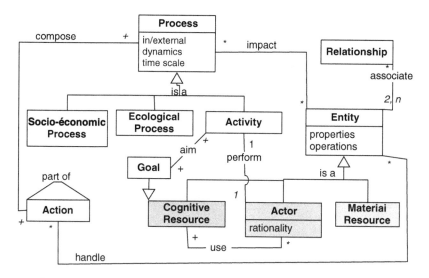

Fig. 1. The MAELIA meta-model represented as a UML Class diagram

in the performance of activities they undertake, in planning and decision making or in the formation of goals.

A *relationship* associates two entities due either to their very nature (e.g. each field plot has a soil type) or as a state of affairs resulting from a contingent action (e.g. a farmer owns a plot after he has bought it). At any moment, the *structure* of the system model is defined as the collection of its entities and necessary relationships, while its *state* is defined as the states of entities with their contingent relationships. The structure of the model is graphically represented as an *Actor-Resource Diagram* (ARD), or a set of such diagrams, that use the UML class diagram notation (see Fig. 2).

The *dynamics* of a system is the set of *processes* that modify the structure and the state of the system and so generate the phenomena of interest. Each execution of a process impacts some entities by changing their state or by creating or destroying entity instances or links. We distinguish three categories of processes, (human) activities, socio-economic processes and ecological processes:

- An **Activity** is a process executed by an actor intending to achieve some goals (e.g. to irrigate a field plot; to issue a drought decree); actors are endowed with a *rationality* to solve problems about the performance of enabled activities, since most activities may be carried out in several ways and conflicts between activities can occur.

- An **Ecological process** corresponds to the enactment of biophysical laws that determine the evolution of material resources (e.g. runoff of water; growth of crop, evapotranspiration…).

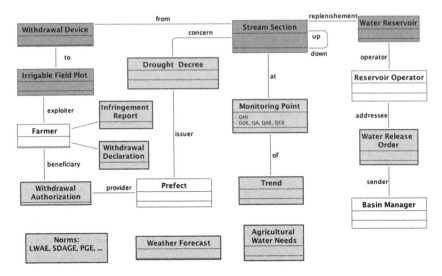

Fig. 2. An excerpt of the Actors-Resources Diagram of MAELIA regarding regulation issues. *Actors, material resources* and *cognitive resources* are figured as white, blue and green boxes respectively (Color figure online).

- A *Socio-economic process* generates phenomena resulting from the humans' economic and social activities (e.g. price evolution, urbanization). Only the effects of a socio-economic process are considered, without regarding how and by whom these effects are produced.

A process is broken down into *actions*. It is described by systems of equations, automata, algorithms or systems of (event-condition-action) rules, according to the most appropriate way. The *dynamics* of a process describes the scheduling of actions executions. Each process has its own *spatial, functional* and *temporal resolutions* that determine how it must be dealt with by the simulation engine.

The processes interact through entities. Indeed, at each time step of a system run, the current state determines the processes that are enabled and the processing they have to do, and the execution of these processes determines the system state at the next step. In an opposite view, entities are glued together by processes that make their evolution interdependent. Figure 3 is an *Interaction diagram* that shows the interweaving of processes and entities.

The behaviour of a system is influenced by its environment, so a simulation model must include the impact of the environment on the system. The *environment* of the system is defined as the set of processes that influence the system behaviour while their dynamics do not depend on its state or evolution. These processes are qualified as *external*. As examples, at the local level, the rain and the international price of corn are typically produced by external processes. Like any process, they impact the system through entities that are, from this fact, qualified as *interface entities*. Thus, an external process is described by a (spatio-) temporal series including, for each time step of a simulation, the new values (or the variations) of the state of interface entities.

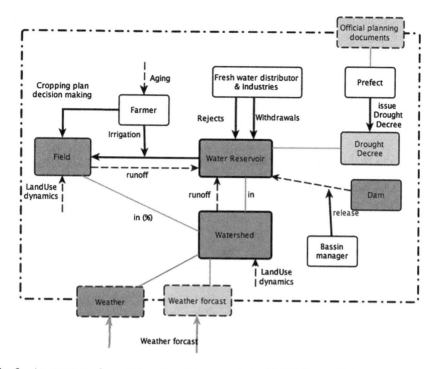

Fig. 3. An excerpt of one Interaction Diagram of the MAELIA model intended to outline interactions between processes and entities. *Actors, material resources* and *cognitive resources* are figured as white, blue and green boxes respectively. Thin lines between boxes are essential *associations* between entities. *Ecological* and *socio-economic processes* are represented as dashed arrows connected to the main entities they use or modify. Activities are represented as arrows from the performer actor to the main impacted entities. The dashed border points out interface entities and external processes (Color figure online)

3.2   The Modeling Process

Such a meta-model assists modellers in defining and designing the components of the model to be implemented, and thus the outcomes to be delivered by the modelling process. This process is guided by the question that originates the elaboration of the model and thus the definition of (1) *indexes*, in the form of the state of entities at the end of the simulation, a sampling of these states in the course of the simulation, or any expression calculated from these, susceptible to provide answers to the question and (2) *scenarios* enabling to test effects on indexes of different initial states or dynamics of interface or internal entities or even of different form of activities like farmer or dam manager strategies.

Regarding the construction of the model, this leads to identify on the one hand the entities that support the indexes and more generally the phenomena of interest and on the other hand the processes that influence the evolution of these entities. The model entities and processes are designed concurrently since an entity is relevant if and only if it is related to processes of interest and reciprocally. The progressive design of both the model and the question at hand is intimately and reflexively linked. Collective and progressive formalisation of Actors-Resources and Interaction Diagrams enables participants to the integrated modelling process to contribute to the design and share a common representation of the system. On other respects formal representation of dynamics of each process is the matter of each disciplinary team or even researcher. Each of them can choose the appropriate formal language to represent these dynamics according to their disciplinary and individual habits and specificities of the dynamics.

3.3   The GAMA Simulation Platform

The MAELIA simulation model is implemented with GAMA[1] [15], an open-source generic agent-based modeling and simulation platform. It provides an intuitive modeling language with high-level primitives to define agents and their environment. GAMA includes a powerful Integrated Development Environment to ease non-computer scientist to develop complex model with powerful features in terms of GIS integration and high-level tools (e.g. decision-making or clustering algorithms). In addition, both the language and the software have been designed to allow the development of big models with a huge number of agents (with various architectures from reflex-based to BDI architectures). It allows modelers to manage various kinds of complex environments such as square, hexagonal or irregular grids, networks or continuous environment linked to GIS data.

GAMA enables a hierarchical and dynamic organization of agents. Any agent is both a micro-agent (hosted in a macro-agent) and a macro one (hosting other agents). The platform is also easily extensible to add new features to models (e.g. to give the possibility to integrate equation-based (ODE) models into agents) or new agent architectures or features. GAMA has been successfully used to develop various large-scale applications that share the need of a strong integration and management of huge GIS data and of strong interactions between complex environment and agents.

4   The Model of the Integrated MAELIA Platform

The MAELIA platform simulates the ecological processes and human activities underpinning water scarcity issues at the relevant spatial, temporal and functional resolutions. To model processes, the main strategy was twofold. For ecological processes, given that many models of water flow and plant/soil dynamics exist we selected models (i) robust that can be applied on the wide range of biophysical conditions of the AGB, (ii) empirically founded to be likely to provide realistic outputs (iii) with space and time resolutions fitting with our modeling needs on the AGB and (iv) quite simple in terms of number of equations and parameters to be not too time-consuming in calibration, coding and computing. For human activities, specific models were developed in order to represent the decision-making processes of the key users and managers of water resources. In this section we describe how firstly

---

[1] http://code.google.com/p/gama-platform/

ecological processes and secondly human activities are considered and accordingly modeled within the MAELIA platform, without emphasizing the entities. Finally we present the way interactions between processes are managed in the platform.

4.1 Ecological Processes

To represent **water flow** we use the mathematical formalisms of hydrological cycle from the SWAT (Soil and Water Assessment Tool) model [6] because it quite well matches the requirements of the MAELIA project objectives as semi-empirical and semi-distributed model. The SWAT model has been applied in different watershed under contracted climatological and pedological conditions all over the world. SWAT has been developed to assess impact of land cover and use changes on water, sediments and agricultural yields. It is a semi distributed hydrological model in which the hydrological balance is estimated and spatially allocated into so called "sub-watersheds", i.e. elementary watersheds. These latter are subdivided into a spatial Hydrologic Response Units (HRUs) representing a unique combination of land cover, soil type and slope. The division into sub-watersheds allows the model to reflect the spatial organization of the hydrological network and reservoirs from where water is withdrawn. The subdivision into HRU is adapted to represent differences in evapo-transpiration for various plants and soils and in runoff, infiltration and subsurface water circulation. The possibility to define the size of sub-watersheds allows adapting the model to match requirements of the investigated agro-hydrological issues. This modeling approach avoids using a distributed hydrologic model often much more complicated and computing-time consuming. SWAT simulates agro-hydrologic cycle with a daily time step at least. In MAELIA we analyze, document and recode equations of SWAT for both (i) *the land phase* of the hydrologic cycle that controls the amount of water loadings to the main channel of each sub-watersheds (snow cover and melt, runoff with the curve number method, infiltration, redistribution in soil profile, evapotranspiration for non-crop plants, lateral sub-surface flow and percolation into shallow and deep aquifer) and (ii) *the routing phase* of the hydrologic cycle that controls the flow of water through the channel network of the watershed toward the outlet (transmission through the bed of the channel in and from runoff, sub-surface flow and shallow aquifer, evaporation and water routing through the channel with the Muskingum routing method [2]). The sub-watershed and HRU delineation has been made thanks to a GIS approach based on French georeferenced databases on water resources, topography and land use. The average size of the MAELIA sub-watersheds is about 2 to 6 km^2. It corresponds to the finest grain of the French watershed classification that is used to design and implement management strategies and policies.

To represent **plant growth** (and yield) we chose two strategies according the nature of plant. For non-crop plants (forest and grassland) we used the formalism of SWAT with the standard parameter values since MAELIA does not need to simulate biomass production. For crops we gave the priority to the capacity of the crop model to simulate realistic crop yields in the different situations of the ABG without great and often problematic calibration work. Accordingly we implement an empiric (vs. mechanistic) crop model developed by INRA (French national institute for agricultural research) in Toulouse (centre of the AGB). This model called "Jeu d'O" [7] has been developed step by step according results of agronomic experiments in the AGB during the last 20 years. It seeks to represent phenomena rather than mechanisms to ensure simplicity and robustness and accordingly large regional applicability. It represents effect of climate, soil and cropping system on yield for the eleven main crops of the AGB. The effect of water stress on yield is represented through an annual production function representing the relation between the coverage of crop water needs (ratio real to potential evapotranspiration) and effect on yield (ratio real to potential yield). This crop model simulates runoff given the effect of the crop above ground biomass development. It also represents effect on water soil dynamics of tillage (modification of soil layer depth that evaporates), sowing date (modification of the vegetation period) and irrigation.

The plant growth process simulates drainage and runoff of each sub-watershed fields and accordingly impacts shallow aquifer and river water states. This process interacts with the land phase of the hydrologic processes through this two water body types. Hence, as presented in Sect. 3, processes interact through entities.

4.2   Socio-economic Process and Human Activities

Since the MAELIA platform is intended to assess impacts of interactions between social and ecological processes, human activities and socio-economic processes need to be described. Socio-economics processes concern demography, land cover change and domestic and industrial water uses. Human activities concern farmer activities that determine their water withdrawals, management of dam water and implementation of water regulations that frames the fulfilment of the water demands.

Demography is treated as an external process using data provided by the French agency in charge of demography statistics.

In the AGB, urban and forest areas have been growing significantly during the last decades. In MAELIA, given the time horizon of the simulations (until 2030), we represent these **land cover changes** through the field plot disappearance[2]: each year some field plots disappear in favour of forest or urban areas. For this, we first computed the number of disappeared plots from 2006 to 2010 in each sub-watershed thank to the Corine Land Cover database[3] and second extrapolate the future yearly evolution until 2030. This time series is considered as an external process of the model (produced by a pre-treatment). Plots that disappear each year are randomly chosen next to urban or forest area (following the observed ratio).

The **domestic water use** is computed using the econometric equation developed in the MOGIRE model [12]. It takes the water price, the rate of houses that are used as main home, income, summer maximum temperature (external time series) and population density (provided by the demography process) as parameters. Three quarters of

---

[2] The most important cause of land use change related to our field of investigation is the field plot disappearance, evaluated to one French department par 10 years in France.

[3] Corine Land Cover France website: http://sd1878-2.sivit.org/ (as of 26/03/2012).

the yearly withdrawn volume for domestic use is rejected (it returns to the river). From this volume, we compute the daily withdrawn and rejected volumes in each withdrawn and rejection points, taking into account that daily withdrawn volume are higher during summer. The **industrial water use** is an external process based on withdrawal and rejection data for year 2010 from the dedicated database of the AGB water agency, which considers that the volume remains constant over years.

As irrigation is the most important process regarding management of low water periods, we developed a precise model for **farmer activities that underpin their water withdrawals**. The behaviour of the farmer agent is composed of two processes with different time scales. Yearly, the farmer makes cropping plan decisions: he gets a complete allocation of crop rotations to his fields. The choice of a rotation is carried out through a multi-criteria decision-making process based on Dempster-Shafer belief theory included in a BDI architecture [14]. This theory allows to make a decision even with incompleteness, uncertainty and imprecision of knowledge. From surveys, the four following criteria have been accounted: maximize the profit and the similarity to the last cropping plan and minimize financial risks and workload.

The farmer then applies the schedule of each cropping system through daily activities that are enabled by the state of soils and crops: sowing, irrigation and harvesting. He takes into account the workload (aggregation of the farm manpower) constraint. Each daily activity has a temporal window during which it can be done and a set of conditions (e.g. in terms of weather) that should be fulfilled. The activities performance is limited by the number of hours the farm manpower can work and by geographical constraints (distance between fields, field surfaces...). In addition, if the sowing activity is not possible, e.g. because of strong rains, the farmer will re-evaluate the cropping plan to find an alternative one. The model includes only one farmer actor per farm: he will take all the decisions and performs the activities for the sake of all the farm manpower. In addition, he uses a lot of cognitive resources: technical (possible crop rotations), economic (markets) and social (decrees). The instantiation of entities is based on the French Land Parcel Identification System that describes the spatial distribution of plots (including one or a small numbers of fields) of each French individual farm.

In the AGB, the strategy regarding **releases of water stored in dams and regulations of agricultural water withdrawals** during the low-water period determines to what extent both the compulsory water flow rates can be maintained and the agricultural needs can be satisfied (since the other needs have priority). This management is the result of complex multi-level regulatory and governance systems that extends from the European level to elementary watersheds where concrete actions dealing with water bodies take place. The MAELIA platform only includes the elements of the regulatory system that are involved in the concrete exercise of water management during low water periods. Elements that contribute to the emergence and deployment of the regulatory system itself are not represented. Accordingly we represent the activities of State services and commissioned associations regarding the management of water of dams and the setting of regulations of agricultural withdrawals.

Each year, a specified volume of water is purchased by State services to water reservoir managers that shall be preserved for release on demand in case of need.

During low-water periods, the flow rate of streams and rivers is daily measured (as Average Daily Flow, ADF) at so-called monitoring points. Four thresholds are associated with each monitoring point, from Objective Low-Water Flow (OLWF) to Crisis Flow, to evaluate the ecological state. Measures or visual checks are also taken at other given locations along the hydrological network. State services manage water uses and resources according to these daily measures.

In priority, when possible, they try to maintain water flow objective thanks to **water releases** from dams. In rivers that can be replenished by some dams, they try to compensate agricultural withdrawals when the flow rate passes under the OLWF. Accordingly, the MAELIA State service actor seeks to optimise releases according to these objectives and the dam constraints: reserved flow (minimum water flow at the exit of the dam), maximum flow due to dam and river characteristics, period of release (e.g. to maintain the water level of the lake high enough for touristic activities), transfer time between the dam and the targeted monitoring points, emptying curve of the reservoir (that indicates, given the date and the remaining amount of water, the probability to be able to satisfy the needs of release until the end of the low water period). Due to the transfer time of water between dams and associated monitoring points, water withdrawals have to be anticipated. However as information on irrigated area for the current year and farmer irrigation strategies for the time is lacking he has to estimate agricultural water needs day after day. For this he uses local references on irrigated crop areas and needs. Dam characteristics and these local references are cognitive resources for the actor. They enable to estimate the water flow needed to respect the compulsory flow at the monitoring points day after day.

When it is not possible to sustain water flow through water releases (no dams in an upstream watershed, no more available water in the dam) the State services might issue **Drought Decrees** that state withdrawal restrictions in some place and for some duration: 1 or 2 days a week (level 1), 3 or 4 days a week (level 2) or 7 days a week (level 3). The condition for the promulgation of a drought decree and its pattern (locations, durations and levels) are framed by a generic drought decree and several official planning documents. This is a daily process during the low-water period. A decree applies to one or several areas. Each area is linked to a downstream monitoring point and is divided in sectors determining, for the decrees of level 1 or 2, which days a prohibition applies. The level of restriction applicable to an area depends on the position of ADF3 (the average of ADF on the 3 last days) with regard to the thresholds of its monitoring point and the possibility to replenish the stream from an upstream reservoir. The decision to apply this restriction is constrained by principles regarding temporal continuity – an ongoing restriction cannot be upgraded before at least 3 days and downgraded before at least 7 days – and spatial solidarity – an upstream area must be a in restriction level greater or equal.

Farmers may be given a ticket for violation of drought decrees by certified civil servants. MAELIA implements the **control of compliance and sanctioning** in the following way: when drought decrees apply, each week hundred randomly chosen farmers are checked for the respect of restrictions. Infringements are just recorded, because the effective consequences of overtaking are still doubtful. The same holds for the annual quantity of abstracted water that should not overpass the granted quantity.

4.3 Interactions Between Processes Through Entities

One of the main features of the MAELIA model is the fact that processes do not interact directly but only via resources. The best example in our model is the interactions between processes around the water resource at the watershed level. As presented above and summarized in Fig. 3, the sub-watershed is the key entity of the water flow model. It aggregates the water computed by the land phase and gets and provides water from upstream and to downstream watersheds through the routing phase. This water quantity computed at the sub-watershed level, is considered as a water reservoir in which various water users withdraw water for irrigation, consumption or industrial uses and reject water used for industry or for domestic consumption. In addition, withdrawals restrictions apply to sub-watershed water reservoirs.

As mentioned above, actors interact only via resources. For example, the prefect does not interact directly with farmers to prohibit irrigation, but via the creation of cognitive resources, that can be drought decrees and withdrawal restrictions.

4.4 Running the Simulation Model

The generation and the running of the simulation model require a lot of datasets, that supposes a (very) good empirical knowledge of the studied system.

Structural data are necessary to instantiate the model entities and relationships into a concrete model. This latter describes all the actual constitutive elements of the modelled system and serves as the initial state of simulations.

Dynamic data are temporal data series that describe dynamics of the state of the interface resources. Dynamic data are also needed for the calibration-validation of internal processes.

In the first version of the MAELIA platform, more than 250 structure and dynamics datasets are used. Most datasets require pre-processing to solve heterogeneity, compatibility and consistency issues and be put at the required temporal and spatial resolutions. Indeed, while there is a great number of data, most of them are collected in a specific context and purpose, without concern for a wider use[4] and particularly an integrated modelling. Some of these pre-processing require expert knowledge to compensate the lack or incompleteness of data.

5 Ongoing Work

The current version of MAELIA implements all the presented processes on the Garonne upstream watershed (125×100 km) using the GAMA platform. Figure 4 shows a synopsis of key results of a MAELIA simulation on the 2002-2008 period

---

[4] Within the French context, some incoming projects intend to solve these issues, which are also related to difficulties about the availability of data.

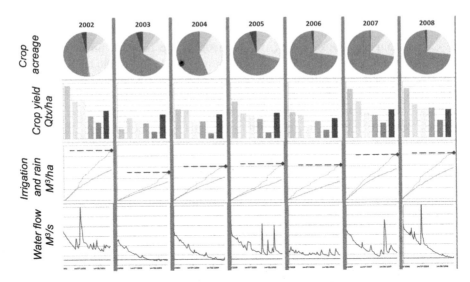

Fig. 4. Synopsis of keys results of a MAELIA simulation on the 2002-2008 period : crop acreage at the river basin level, crop yields for the main irrigated (blue = corn) and rainfed crops (yellow to green : wheat, sunflower, pea, rapseed...), average cumulated water irrigation and rain in irrigated crop fields, water flow at the outlet of the river basin (yellow and red lines represent compulsory Objective low-water flow and Crisis flow) (Color figure online).

(with a day step). It shows the evolution of (i) crop acreage at the river basin level, (ii) crop yield for the main crops (depending on the water stress level), (iii) average cumulated water irrigation and rain level in irrigated crop fields and (iv) water flow at the river basin outlet. When the river flow drops below the crisis flow (the red line) drought decrees prohibit irrigation. This leads to increase water stress of irrigated crops and in turn to the decrease of crop yields. During the year 2003, the more intense drought over the fifteen last years, drought decrees and so prohibition of irrigation, and natural drought have strongly affected irrigated as well as rainfed crop yields.

Figure 5 shows a synopsis of the key processes simulated in the MAELIA platform at a given day: precipitation level (external process) in meteorological pixels, spatial position of farmers, in crop fields irrigation level in irrigated fields, crop growth stage in crop fields, rotation in crop fields, irrigation restriction level (due to drought decrees) in restriction zones, water flow at the outlet of each sub-watershed and air temperature (external process) in meteorological pixels.

We are currently working on calibration and evaluation of each process. Some processes can be validated in isolation, for example the farmers' cropping plan decision-making process (it gives very good results much better than other existing models [14]). One of the main issues regarding calibration stems from the reciprocal dependence between processes. For example, to calibrate hydrologic models, we only have observed data of water flow that take into account all the field processes impacting the water flow (weather, irrigation and other withdrawals, releases, regulations, etc.). We thus should rely on computed "natural" flow to calibrate separately the hydrologic model.

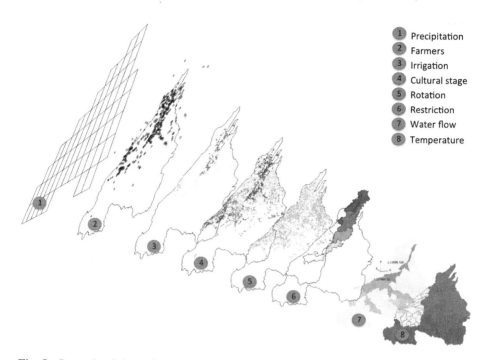

Fig. 5. Synopsis of the main processes simulated in the MAELIA platform (at a given day): precipitation level in meteorological pixels, spatial position of farmers, in crop fields irrigation level in irrigated fields, crop growth stage in crop fields, rotation in crop fields, irrigation restriction level in restriction zones, water flow at the outlet of each sub-watershed and air temperature in meteorological pixels

Acknowledgement. The MAELIA Project "Multi-Agents for EnvironmentaL norm Impact Assessment" (http://maelia1.wordpress.com/) is funded by the French "Sciences & Technologies for Aeronautics and Space" Foundation (http://www.fondationstae.net/).

References

1. Bousquet, F., Page, C.L.: Multi-agent simulations and ecosystem management: a review. Ecol. Model. **176**, 313–332 (2004)
2. Chow, V.T., Maidment, D.R., Mays, L.W.: Applied Hydrology. Tata McGraw-Hill Education, New York (1988)
3. Debril, T., Therond, O.: Les difficultés associées à la gestion quantitative de l'eau et à la mise en oeuvre de la réforme des volumes prélevables : le cas du bassin Adour-Garonne. Agronomie, Environnement & Sociétés **2**(10), 127–138 (2012)
4. Leenhardt, D., Therond, O., Cordier, M.-O., Gascuel-Odoux, C., Reynaud, A., Durand, P., Bergez, J.-E., Clavel, L., Masson, V., Moreau, P.: A generic framework for scenario exercises using models applied to water-resource management. Environ. Model Softw. **37**, 125–133 (2012)

5. March, H., Therond, O., Leenhardt, D.: Water futures: reviewing water-scenario analyses through an original interpretative framework. Ecol. Econ. **82**, 126–137 (2012)
6. Arnold, J.G., Srinivasan, R., Muttiah, R.S., Williams, J.R.: Large area hydrologic modeling and assessment. I. Model development. J. Am. Water Resour. Assoc. **34**(1), 73–89 (1998)
7. Nolot, J., Debaeke, P.: Principes et outils de conception, conduite et évaluation de systèmes de culture. Cah. Agric. **12**, 387–400 (2003)
8. Ostrom, E.: A general framework for analyzing sustainability of social-ecological systems. Science **325**, 419–422 (2009)
9. Pahl-Wostl, C., Schlumpf, C., Büssenschütt, M., Schönborn, A., Burse, J.: Models at the interface between science and society: impacts and options. Integr. Assess. **1**, 267–280 (2000)
10. Parker, P., Letcher, R., Jakeman, A., Beck, M., Harris, G., et al.: Progress in integrated assessment and modelling. Environ. Model Softw. **17**(3), 209–217 (2002)
11. Parrot, L.: Hybrid modelling of complex ecological systems for decision support: Recent success and future perspectives. Ecol. Inform. **6**(1), 44–49 (2011)
12. Reynaud, A., Leenhardt, D.: Mogire: a model for integrated water management. In: International Environmental Modelling and Software Society (iEMSs), Barcelona, Spain (2008)
13. Sibertin-Blanc, C., Thérond, O., Monteil, C., Mazzega, P.: Formal modeling of social-ecological systems. In: European Social Simulation Association Conference, Cemagref (2011)
14. Taillandier, P., Therond, O., Gaudou, B.: A new BDI agent architecture based on the belief theory. Application to the modelling of cropping plan decision-making. In: International Environmental Modelling and Software Society (iEMSs), Leipzig, Germany, pp. 1–5 (2012)
15. Taillandier, P., Vo, D.-A., Amouroux, E., Drogoul, A.: GAMA: a simulation platform that integrates geographical information data, agent-based modeling and multi-scale control. In: Desai, N., Liu, A., Winikoff, M. (eds.) PRIMA 2010. LNCS, vol. 7057, pp. 242–258. Springer, Heidelberg (2012)
16. Therond, O., Belhouchette, H., Janssen, S., et al.: Methodology to translate policy assessment problems into scenarios: the example of the seamless integrated framework. Environ. Sci. Policy **12**(5), 619–630 (2009)

Globalisation, Regionalisation and Behavioural Responses of Land Use Agents

Calum Brown[1(✉)], Dave Murray-Rust[1], Jasper van Vliet[2],
Shah Jamal Alam[1], Peter H. Verburg[2], and Mark D. Rounsevell[1]

[1] School of Geosciences, University of Edinburgh, Edinburgh EH8 9XP, UK
{Calum.Brown, D.Murray-Rust, SJ.Alam,
Mark.Rounsevell}@ed.ac.uk
[2] Institute for Environmental Studies and Amsterdam Global Change Institute,
Vrije Universiteit Amsterdam, Amsterdam, The Netherlands
{Jasper.van.Vliet, Peter.Verburg}@vu.nl

Abstract. The global land system is under intense pressure from human demands for a range of different services. Neo-classical economic theory suggests that globalised free trade is the most efficient way of handling these demands, allowing maximum productivity and specialisation of supply. However, political responses are often protectionist in nature, designed to ensure continuity of land uses and the regional production of multiple services. We investigate the implications of both globalisation and regionalisation of demand for the efficiency and productivity of land uses and, using an agent-based model of land use change, how realistic forms of human behaviour can strengthen, weaken or alter these implications. We show that 'rational' productive agents tend towards optimal land use configurations under globalised systems, but that 'irrational' behaviour yields superior results under regionalisation. Finally, the adoption of multifunctional land uses is found to be a strong and effective emergent property of agent populations under regional demand.

Keywords: Globalization · Regionalization · Land use · Agent-based modelling · Supply and demand

1 Introduction

Land across the globe is under intense pressure from the demands of an increasing, and increasingly affluent, human population. Meanwhile, wealth inequalities and economic liberalisation drive globalisation of demand and supply, and lead to dramatic land use transitions, especially in the developing world (Lambin *et al.* 2001; Lambin and Meyfroidt 2011). Neo-classical economic theory suggests that this will result in an 'optimal' distribution of land uses that maximises productivity, productive efficiency, the land area available to different land uses, and the value of production that occurs in each country or region (McKenzie 1953; Pingali 2007).

Governments and international bodies sometimes pursue policies to this end (e.g. Burfisher *et al.* 2001; Kose *et al.* 2004; Subramanian and Wei 2007), but more often

S.J. Alam and H. Van Dyke Parunak (Eds.): MABS 2013, LNAI 8235, pp. 101–114, 2014.
DOI: 10.1007/978-3-642-54783-6_7, © Springer-Verlag Berlin Heidelberg 2014

attempt to protect particular land users and to maintain stability in land systems (e.g. Potter and Burney 2002; Dibden and Cocklin 2009). They also increasingly promote 'multifunctional' land uses(Wiggering *et al.* 2006; Piorr *et al.* 2009). In contrast to globalisation, policies of this kind should lead to relatively inefficient land uses distributed via policy mechanisms rather than optimal allocation (Lambin *et al.* 2001) - although neither extreme can be reliably linked with true efficiency because of other externalities (e.g. Robertson and Swinton 2005; Godfray *et al.* 2010).

In reality, the behaviour and decisions of individual land managers can have strong and complex effects on policies concerning land use change (Starr and Adams 2003; Walford 2003; Potter and Tilzey 2005). These effects are extremely difficult to assess, depending upon a host of personal and cultural characteristics that may act and interact in unpredictable ways. However, the few quantitative analyses that have been undertaken suggest that human behaviour can entirely confound a policy or trend, and is certainly capable of altering its course (e.g. Weisbuch and Boudjema 1999). Despite this, the implications of individual behaviour for land use changes caused by globalisation or regional protectionism have not been fully investigated.

Agent-based models (ABMs) allow examination of how particular behaviours affect land use dynamics (e.g. Matthews *et al.* 2007; Rounsevell *et al.* 2012) and so are ideally suited to confronting the theoretical implications of globalisation with realistic behavioural responses. Nevertheless, while multifunctional land use and density gradients have been explored for urban land uses (Van Vliet et al. 2012), we are not aware of any application that comprehensively includes multifunctional land uses or gradients of land use intensity, both of which are important in this context and common in the real world (Lambin *et al.* 2000). The ability to include these is one of the significant advantages of the ABM presented in this paper.

We use a newly-developed ABM framework, the CRAFTY model (Competition for Resources between Agent Functional Types; Murray-Rust *et al.* (2014) in review), to investigate the implications of globalization and regionalisation of demand for land use productivities and competition, and how these change under modelled human behaviours. The ABM applies exogenous demand levels which agents attempt to meet according to behavioural rules and service productivity. Where individual behaviour is absent, agents effectively optimise their land uses according to supply and demand levels, but as the variety and strength of behaviours increase, these become a dominant factor in determining land use change. Our framework allows the adoption of different land uses, variations in the intensity of land uses, diversification into multifunctional land uses, land abandonment and competition for available land. In this study we investigate the effects of these in a simulation setting designed to isolate particular processes, according to a number of hypotheses concerning processes and drivers of land use change. These are:

- That demand expressed at global scale encourages optimisation of land uses and that deviation from this is driven only by local agent behaviour;
  - That behaviour that constrains sensitivity to competition delays the establishment of this optimal configuration;
  - That behaviour that limits sensitivity to demand levels can prevent establishment of an optimal configuration;

- That demand expressed at regional scales leads to (globally) sub-optimal production and leaves the most productive land at risk of abandonment;

  - That behaviour that constrains sensitivity to competition or demand levels delays establishment of an optimal configuration but may also produce configurations that are globally more efficient;
- That varying land use intensity will lead to sub-optimal production at the global scale, but will allow agents to match land uses to regional characteristics more effectively, so increasing efficiency of production;
- That allowing agents to adopt multifunctional land uses will similarly allow agents to match land uses to regional characteristics, and may increase global production above other regional cases.

2 Methods

2.1 An Overview of the Agent-Based Model

The CRAFTY model used here is designed to work at large (e.g. European) scale, and is described in detail in Murray-Rust et al. (2014) (in review). Forming part of the EU FP7 'Visions of Land Use Transitions in Europe' (VOLANTE) project, the model will be used to investigate the effects of human behaviour on land use transitions in Europe under a range of socio-economic and environmental scenarios.

The model is based on demand and supply of services; demand is defined exogenously whereas supply is a function of agent behaviours and productive abilities, and location characteristics. Both are expressed in abstract 'units' of production representing the maximum possible yield of a service from a piece of land. We define productivity as the quantity of a service produced in a given area (agent productivity is the quantity that agents are capable of producing), and productive efficiency as the average productivity per unit of land. Land units are formed by the division of the modelled landscape into grid cells, and each is assigned values for the levels of capitals (e.g. economic, natural productivity, infrastructure) at that location. Agents use these capitals to produce services according to a production function that can apply at the individual or typological level. The model is intended to operate with an agent typology based on the Human Functional Type concept (Rounsevell et al. 2012).

At each modelled timestep (used to represent a single year, but practically representing the timescale at which agents respond to demand levels) the level of service production achieved by an agent is given a utility value that depends on unmet demand. Agents compete for land on the basis of these utility values, and this competition is also affected by individual or typological behaviour. Behaviour can be modelled via a number of parameters that control agents' productivities, sensitivities to demand and utility, and abilities to search for new land. Especially important are 'giving-up' and 'giving-in' thresholds that describe the minimum utility level an agent will accept before abandoning land, and the minimum value by which a competitor's utility must exceed an agent's own before that agent relinquishes its land (this is

Table 1. Basic simulation schedule showing the role of the giving-up and giving-in thresholds. Timestep actions occur at every modelled timestep, and the Allocate Land actions follow from one of these. Capitalised terms refer to a complete set, and parameters n and m are given in Table 2.

Timestep	Allocate Land

1. For each agent ∈ Agents
   a. Update competitiveness based on
     residual demand
   b. If competitiveness
     < giving-up threshold, leave system
2. For each region ∈ Regions
   allocate-land
3. For each agent ∈ Agents
   Update supply of services
4. For each region ∈ Regions
   Update supply and demand
	1. For each agent type t ∈ Agent Types,
	   undertake n search iterations of m cells
	2. For every searched cell, calculate t's
	   competitiveness
	3. If t's competitiveness > cell owner's giving-
	   in threshold, owner relinquishes cell
	4. Agent of type t takes cell over

equivalent to an agent changing land uses) (Table 1). Behavioural parameters are all subject to random or systematic variation at individual or typological level, and we do not attempt here to accurately parameterise them for any particular system.

2.2   Experimental Setup

We begin with a simple modelled world to investigate the effects of regionalisation in the absence of any confounding processes, and gradually add complexity to this world. In all experiments, the world is represented by a 50 by 50 cell grid, where each cell may be managed by a single agent and each agent may manage only one cell. Agents are distributed randomly across the world at the start of the simulation, and are allowed to compete for land over the course of 25 timesteps. In each case, we keep track of the distribution of agents relative to capital levels and the supply and average productivity of services. We run 30 realisations of each basic model configuration and a single realisation of each configuration that includes agent behaviour, to see whether this falls within the envelope of results from the equivalent basic model. Parameter settings used in each case are given in Table 2.

Experiment 1

Initially, we model only two agent types – farmers and foresters, producing only food and timber respectively – competing to satisfy demands expressed at the global level. We include crop and forest productivity capitals that take perpendicular gradients across the world, with forest productivity being maximised along the top of the arena and crop productivity along the right. We make farmer agents sensitive to crop productivity and forester agents sensitive to forest productivity. These agent types are chosen only to represent producers of distinct services; their identities are otherwise arbitrary.

At first, agent behaviour is kept to a minimum, so that the dynamics of the system resemble a process of optimisation. Each agent type undertakes 5,000 search iterations at every timestep, in each of which the types' competitiveness scores on 10

Table 2. Parameter settings used in Experiments 1 and 2. Settings that are altered relative to Experiment 1 in each case are in bold. Experiments *a.2b* and *a.3b* follow a similar pattern for 4 and 9 regions. Productivities are the units of service produced under perfect conditions (capital levels). N(y;z) denotes a Gaussian distribution with mean y and standard deviation z.

Ex.	Farmer GU; GI	Forester GU; GI	Farmer Prod.	Forester Prod.	Search its.	Cells/search it.	Utility function	Agent types
1.1	0.0; 0.0	0.0; 0.0	1.0	1.0	5000	10	$y=3x$	2
2.12	**0.2**; 0.0	0.0; 0.0	1.0	1.0	5000	10	$y=3x$	2
2.17	0.0; **0.1**	0.0; 0.0	1.0	1.0	5000	10	$y=3x$	2
2.19	**0.2**; 0.0	**0.2**; 0.0	1.0	1.0	5000	10	$y=3x$	2
2.110	**N(0.2, 0.0)**; 0.0	0.0; 0.0	1.0	1.0	5000	10	$y=3x$	2
2.111	0.0; **N(0.1, 0.0)**	0.0; 0.0	1.0	1.0	5000	10	$y=3x$	2
2.112	0.0; 0.0	0.0; 0.0	**N(1.0, 0.1)**	1.0	5000	10	$y=3x$	2
2.114	0.0; 0.0	0.0; 0.0	**N(1.0, 0.1)**	**N(1.0, 0.1)**	5000	10	$y=3x$	2
2.115	0.0; 0.0	0.0; 0.0	1.0	1.0	5000	10	$y=3x$	2
2.116	0.0; 0.0	0.0; 0.0	1.0	1.0	**100**	**1**	$y=3x$	2
2.119	0.0; 0.0	0.0; 0.0	1.0	1.0	5000	10	$y=e^x$ **(farmer)**	2
2.120	0.0; 0.0	0.0; 0.0	1.0	1.0	5000	10	$y=e^x$ **(both)**	2
2.121	0.0; 0.0	0.0; 0.0	1.0	1.0	5000	10	$y=3x$	**4**
2.122	0.0; 0.0	0.0; 0.0	1.0	1.0	5000	10	$y=3x$	**3**

randomly-selected cells are calculated. Agents of that type then attempt to take these cells over, and succeed if they are currently unoccupied or if the current occupiers relinquish the cells (Table 1). Agents abandon cells when their giving-up threshold is not met and relinquish cells when their giving-in threshold is exceeded. Both thresholds are here initially set to 0.0, so that agents abandon a cell when they do not have a positive competitiveness score, or when another agent has a higher competitiveness score. Therefore, for each agent type, 50,000 cells are sampled with replacement at every timestep and assigned to the most competitive agent type, making it unlikely that inferior agents would persist.

Agent competitiveness is calculated on the basis of a utility function that relates supplies produced to residual (unmet) demand levels. In this case, utility functions for food and timber are identical, being linear functions of the form $y = x$, with negative values set to zero. The form of these functions ensures that when demand for a service is met an agent gains no competitiveness from further production of that service, but as unmet demand for a service increases, the competitive value of providing that service grows rapidly. Using these settings, the model is run with demand applied at the global level, and subsequently divided equally between four and nine regions that together cover the entire modelled world.

Experiment 2

We now introduce variation between agents to the model used in Experiment 1. We include heterogeneity in giving-up and giving-in thresholds between and within agent types (which is systematic and stochastic in form, respectively, and used to capture the effect rather than the magnitude of real behaviour), in productivities within types, in agents' abilities to search and compete for cells, and in the service utility functions (to represent real-world utility, which may remain positive even where overproduction occurs). Finally, we divide the agent typology further by land use intensity and introduce an additional, multifunctional agent type (see Tables 2 and 3). Our objective is to identify the general effect of broad variations in individual behavior. Because stochastic variation within types may provide a more robust description of real-world behaviours than a complex model requiring detailed calibration (Bell 1974; Siebert et al. 2006; Helbing 2010), we investigate behavioural trends through inter-type variations, and individual divergence through intra-type variations.

Table 3. Capital sensitivities and production levels of each agent type used in the experiments

Agent type	Sensitivity to CROP PRODUCTIVITY	Sensitivity to FOREST PRODUCTIVITY	Food production	Timber production
Farmer	1.0	0.0	1.0	0.0
LIFarmer	0.9	0.0	0.9	0.0
Forester	0.0	1.0	0.0	1.0
LIForester	0.0	0.9	0.0	0.9
AgroForester	0.5	0.5	0.5	0.5

3   Results

3.1   Experiment 1

In the globalised case, the two agent types rapidly achieve an equilibrium distribution, both specialising to areas of high productivity for the service that they produce (Fig. 1a). This distribution is near-optimal and allows supply levels for the two services to be equally close to overall demand levels. Under regionalisation, however, agents attempt to meet demands separately in each region and therefore are forced to use less productive land (Fig. 1b). In regions that are generally less productive (containing the lower ends of the productivity gradients), areas occupied by the different agent types remain distinct, but in highly productive areas they are less so, with some land left unmanaged as regional demands can be met using fewer cells. Productivities decline sharply as a result (Fig 1c).

3.2   Experiment 2

Giving-up and Giving-in Thresholds

When the giving-up threshold of a single agent type is increased, agents of that type abandon less productive land, which is then occupied by agents of the other type until demand for their service is satisfied (Fig. 2a). Under regionalisation, much of this abandoned land is located in the most productive regions of the arena (Fig. 2b). When both giving-up thresholds are increased together, a larger portion of the arena remains unmanaged, but this is predominantly located in the less productive areas of each region (Fig. 2c). As a result, the increase in the giving-up threshold of a single agent type leads to dramatic drops in overall production of that type's service relative to Experiment 1, and an increase in both types' thresholds produces further drops in production because both agent types compete more strongly for areas of high productivity (Fig. 2d).

Giving-in thresholds have a different effect, preventing the development of superior land use configurations as agents fail to relinquish land on which another type is more competitive. This decreases overall production of both services in the global case because agents that persist in unproductive areas cause others to abandon land in more productive areas when demand is met. However, it slightly increases production (and efficiency) of agents with the higher threshold under regionalisation, as regional demand is difficult to meet in all but the most productive regions, and land abandonment therefore occurs less frequently (Fig. 2e).

Introducing random variation to the thresholds alters the equilibrium distribution of land uses, with agents persisting or relinquishing land where they otherwise would not. Production by agents with randomly varying giving-up thresholds increases slightly, presumably because agents of the same type (with different thresholds) tend to keep taking over productive land when it is abandoned, while land that is less productive for that agent type is more likely to be taken over by the other agent type.

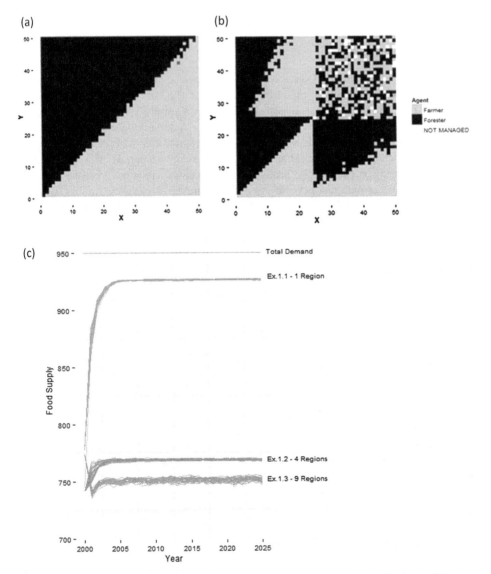

Fig. 1. Map of the simulated world after 25 timesteps with demand at global level (a) and divided across four regions (b). The overall levels of demand and supply for food in all three regionalisations (1, 4 and 9 regions) are shown in (c) (data for all realisations are shown, giving 30 curves for each regionalisation).

Random variation in giving-in thresholds has a similar effect because land that is relinquished will tend to be re-taken by the original type when it holds a competitive advantage there, while land that is retained may be at any point along the relevant capital gradient.

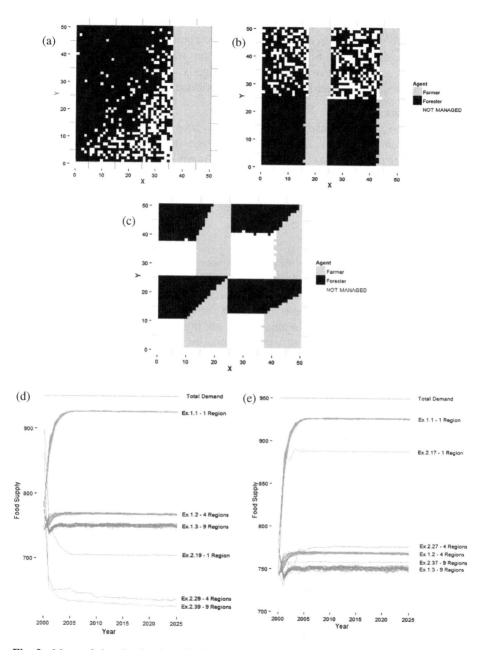

Fig. 2. Maps of the simulated world for experiments 2.12 (a), 2.22 (b), and 2.29 (c), food demand and supply for all 2.x9 regionalisations where both agent types have higher giving-up thresholds (d), and food demand and supply for all 2.x7 regionalisations where farmer agents have a higher giving-in threshold (e). Demand and supply plots include Experiment 1 runs for comparison.

Productivities
Where random variation in agent productivities applies only to one agent type, unproductive agents tend to be lost from the system, while highly productive agents can retain land and increase overall production slightly. Where both types are subject to variation, however, neither receives a net benefit and production does not change.

Search Abilities
Decreasing the number of search iterations at each timestep delays but does not alter the eventual configuration of land uses, and average and total production gradually rises to its level in Experiment 1. Decreasing the number of cells considered at each search iteration means that agents of a single type that do not already 'own' a cell will often compete for the same cells (through increased proportional resampling) rather than finding other cells which they may be able to take over, which also delays the development of the equilibrium configuration.

Utility Functions
Switching one of the two utility functions to an exponential curve, in which over-production of a service still provides a positive utility, benefits the agents that produce that service. This leads to substantial overproduction of that service and corresponding underproduction of the other. It also means that the overproducing agent type is more competitive in areas where both capital levels are high, and that type's average productivity increases dramatically as a result, while the other type's declines.

When both utility functions are exponential, the dynamics under global demand are similar to those in Experiment 1, but the system converges to a near-optimal configuration more quickly. Under regionalisation, however, the system converges to a point that balances regional and global (total) demands because agents in particularly productive land still benefit from competitive advantage even where they are regionally overproducing. As a result, average and total production are both considerably higher in the system as a whole than under linear utility functions.

Land Use Intensities and Multifunctionality
Allowing the intensity of land use to vary by introducing lower intensity foresters and farmers to the simulation prevents a clear convergence from occurring. In each regionalisation, the four agent types remain mixed across the arena, but low intensity agents clearly dominate in the areas of lowest capital. Outside these areas, land changes hands repeatedly as low- and high-intensity producers compete, giving productivity a cyclical form that rarely achieves the levels seen with two agent types. Nevertheless, less of the highly productive land is abandoned in this case.

Introducing multifunctional 'AgroForester' agents (Table 3) has a similar effect in preventing a stable equilibrium arrangement of land uses from developing. However, the multifunctional agents clearly dominate in less productive areas, especially under regionalisation (Fig. 3a). Productivities fluctuate under competition, but are similar to those without multifunctional agents in the global case. Under regionalisation, however, the presence of multifunctional agents dramatically increases production of both services (Fig. 3b).

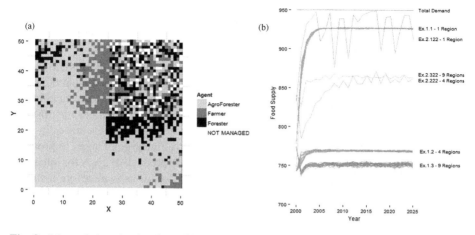

Fig. 3. Map of the simulated world after 25 timesteps with multifunctional AgroForester agents included, in four regions (a), and the resulting changes in food supply and demand in all regionalisations, with Experiment 1 results for comparison (b).

4 Discussion

Our results clearly demonstrate that expression of demands at the global scale does, in principle, allow an optimal configuration of land uses to develop, with services produced to mutually maximal levels using the most productive land. Regionalisation of demand, in contrast, encourages land users to produce services inefficiently, using unproductive land and abandoning the most productive areas. As a result, fully 'rational' and equivalent land use agents that compete on the basis of their ability to satisfy regional demand create a markedly sup-optimal land system. Instead, behavioural agents that are (partially) insensitive to demand levels may be preferable.

Human behaviour causes substantial deviations from economic or productive rationality in the real world, and has the potential to confound drivers of land use change (Weisbuch and Boudjema 1999; Potter and Tilzey 2005). We investigated several forms of behaviour through their effects on agents' productivities, sensitivities to demand, and abilities to compete for land and to intensify or diversify land uses. We found that some of these had dramatic effects on land uses and, while none were capable of entirely masking the consequences of regionalisation (at the strengths we modelled them), they did substantially alter them.

Among the strongest effects were those of altering agents' willingness to abandon or relinquish land, and the utility functions of different land uses. Agent types with lower sensitivities to demand or competition were able to maximise production levels at the expense of the other type. Random variation within types (which may provide an accurate description of real-world variation) did not produce a clear effect unless it led to a systematic difference between types. Utility functions that rewarded overproduction of a service were, unsurprisingly, found to favour that service at regional and global levels. However, where both services had functions of this form, the effects of regionalisation were dampened, with productive efficiency and overall production levels both increased at global scale.

We also found that varying the intensities and specialization of land uses had strong effects on the system as a whole. Disequilibrium followed, as intermediately productive land changed hands between equally-competitive land users. This limited land abandonment in productive areas, but also caused fluctuations and, sometimes, declines in productivity. Multifunctional land uses, though, generated dramatic increases in productivity. These can be attributed to the efficiency of using marginal areas to produce small quantities of multiple services and reserving highly productive areas for intensive use. We conclude that the adoption of multifunctional land uses is therefore a strong emergent trend of a system dedicated to matching supply to demand levels.

Although we investigated these processes in a simple, theoretical setting, it is unlikely that the complexity of the real world entirely confounds the effects we identify. Much of the human behaviour identified as important in the literature is expressible through the parameters that we use in this model, as detailed above. In particular, land managers are known to be very unwilling to convert to different land uses (e.g. Siebert et al. 2006), suggesting that the small variations we model in giving in thresholds understate the effects of real behavior. Processes of intensification and diversification of land uses are also apparent throughout the world's land systems, and numerous policies have been enacted to encourage or discourage these (e.g. Piorr et al. 2009). Overproduction does occur, and leads to regional over-supply even as global shortages persist (e.g. Stoate et al. 2001); regional demand can cause the abandonment of productive land in the same context (Bouma et al. 1998).

These results underline the difficulty of applying theoretical principles to the land system. A tenet of classical economics is that free trade and globalisation leads to specialisation and maximisation of production (McKenzie 1953). In reality, demand is not and cannot be truly globalised. Pressure for regional production may originate with governments or institutions (e.g. Potter and Burney 2002), or may emerge from the population, particularly where the effects of globalisation are thought to be disadvantageous (Mughan et al. 2003; Starr and Adams 2003). Under such circumstances, free trade between rational agents does not produce the best result in terms of production levels or efficiency. Instead, human behaviour that limits apparent 'rationality' may be preferable at regional and global scales.

It is also apparent that rising food demands pose a serious challenge to terrestrial and aquatic ecosystems (Godfray et al. 2010), and that globalisation leads to job insecurity in the developed world (e.g. Burfisher et al. 2001), and may have considerable negative effects in under-developed countries (e.g. Fujita and Hu 2001; Pingali 2007). An important recent response to these issues is the promotion of multifunctional land uses (Robertson and Swinton 2005; Pretty 2008). We find that these can increase productivity and respond more effectively than intensification to regional demand. Global markets are of course highly complex, containing, for example, numerous demands at different levels and 'spaghetti bowls' of (restricted) free trade between specific partners (e.g. Baldwin 2006), and being a mix of ideologically dominant free trade and practical protectionism. Nevertheless, our findings suggest that human characteristics have strong and sometimes counter-intuitive effects at the global scale, and that agent-based modelling is a highly relevant and useful tool for their investigation.

References

Baldwin, R.E.: Multilateralising regionalism: Spaghetti bowls as building blocks on the path to global free trade. World Econ. **29**, 1451–1518 (2006)

Bell, E.J.: Markov analysis of land use change—an application of stochastic processes to remotely sensed data. Socio-Econ. Plann. Sci. **8**, 311–316 (1974)

Bouma, J., Varallyay, G., Batjes, N.: Principal land use changes anticipated in Europe. Agric. Ecosyst. Environ. **67**, 103–119 (1998)

Burfisher, M.E., Robinson, S., Thierfelder, K.: The impact of NAFTA on the United States. J. Econ. Perspect. **15**, 125–144 (2001)

Dibden, J., Cocklin, C.: "Multifunctionality": trade protectionism or a new way forward? Environ. Plann. A **41**, 163–182 (2009)

Fujita, M., Hu, D.: Regional disparity in China 1985-1994: the effects of globalization and economic liberalization. Ann. Reg. Sci. **35**, 3–37 (2001)

Godfray, H.C.J., Beddington, J.R., Crute, I.R., Haddad, L., Lawrence, D., Muir, J.F., Pretty, J., Robinson, S., Thomas, S.M., Toulmin, C.: Food security: the challenge of feeding 9 billion people. Science **327**, 812–818 (2010)

Helbing, D.: Quantitative sociodynamics: stochastic methods and models of social interaction processes. Springer, Heidelberg (2010)

Kose, M.A., Meredith, G., Towe, C.M.: How has NAFTA affected the Mexican economy? Review and Evidence (2004)

Lambin, E., Rounsevell, M.D., Geist, H.: Are agricultural land-use models able to predict changes in land-use intensity? Agric. Ecosyst. Environ. **82**, 321–331 (2000)

Lambin, E.F., Meyfroidt, P.: Global land use change, economic globalization, and the looming land scarcity. Proc. Nat. Acad. Sci. USA **108**, 3465–3472 (2011)

Lambin, E.F., Turner, B.L., Geist, H.J., Agbola, S.B., Angelsen, A., Bruce, J.W., Coomes, O.T., Dirzo, R., Fischer, G., Folke, C., George, P.S., Homewood, K., Imbernon, J., Leemans, R., Li, X., Moran, E.F., Mortimore, M., Ramakrishnan, P.S., Richards, J.F., Skånes, H., Steffen, W., Stone, G.D., Svedin, U., Veldkamp, T.A., Vogel, C., Xu, J.: The causes of land-use and land-cover change: moving beyond the myths. Glob. Environ. Change **11**, 261–269 (2001)

Matthews, R.B., Gilbert, N.G., Roach, A., Polhill, J.G., Gotts, N.M.: Agent-based land-use models: a review of applications. Landscape Ecol. **22**, 1447–1459 (2007)

McKenzie, L.W.: Specialisation and efficiency in world production. Rev. Econ. Stud. **21**, 165–180 (1953)

Mughan, A., Bean, C., McAllister, I.: Economic globalization, job insecurity and the populist reaction. Electoral Stud. **22**, 617–633 (2003)

Murray-Rust, D., Brown, C., van Vliet, J., Alam, S.J., Verburg, P.H., Rounsevell, M. Combining agent functional types, capitals and services to model land use dynamics. In review (2014)

Pingali, P.: Agricultural growth and economic development: a view through the globalization lens. Agric. Econ. **37**, 1–12 (2007)

Piorr, A., Ungaro, F., Ciancaglini, A., Happe, K., Sahrbacher, A., Sattler, C., Uthes, S., Zander, P.: Integrated assessment of future CAP policies: land use changes, spatial patterns and targeting. Environ. Sci. Policy **12**, 1122–1136 (2009)

Potter, C., Burney, J.: Agricultural multifunctionality in the WTO—legitimate non-trade concern or disguised protectionism? J. Rural Stud. **18**, 35–47 (2002)

Potter, C., Tilzey, M.: Agricultural policy discourses in the European post-Fordist transition: neoliberalism, neomercantilism and multifunctionality. Prog. Human Geogr. **29**, 581–600 (2005)

Pretty, J.: Agricultural sustainability: concepts, principles and evidence. Philos. Trans. R. Soc. Lond. B Biol. Sci. **363**, 447–465 (2008)

Robertson, G.P., Swinton, S.M.: Reconciling agricultural productivity and environmental integrity: a grand challenge for agriculture. Front. Ecol. Environ. **3**, 38–46 (2005)

Rounsevell, M.D.A., Pedroli, B., Erb, K.-H., Gramberger, M., Busck, A.G., Haberl, H., Kristensen, S., Kuemmerle, T., Lavorel, S., Lindner, M., Lotze-Campen, H., Metzger, M.J., Murray-Rust, D., Popp, A., Pérez-Soba, M., Reenberg, A., Vadineanu, A., Verburg, P.H., Wolfslehner, B.: Challenges for land system science. Land Use Policy **29**, 899–910 (2012)

Siebert, R., Toogood, M., Knierim, A.: Factors affecting European farmers' participation in biodiversity policies. Sociologia Ruralis **46**, 318–340 (2006)

Starr, A., Adams, J.: Anti-globalization: the global fight for local autonomy. New Polit. Sci. **25**, 19–42 (2003)

Stoate, C., Boatman, N., Borralho, R., Carvalho, C.R., de Snoo, G.R., de Eden, P.: Ecological impacts of arable intensification in Europe. J. Environ. Manage. **63**, 337–365 (2001)

Subramanian, A., Wei, S.-J.: The WTO promotes trade, strongly but unevenly. J. Int. Econ. **72**, 151–175 (2007)

Van Vliet, J., Hurkens, J., White, R., Van Delden, H.: An activity based cellular automaton model to simulate land use dynamics. Environ. Plann. B **39**, 198–212 (2012)

VOLANTE Project. http://www.volante-project.eu/. (2013)

Walford, N.: Productivism is allegedly dead, long live productivism. Evidence of continued productivist attitudes and decision-making in South-East England. J. Rural Stud. **19**, 491–502 (2003)

Weisbuch, G., Boudjema, G.: Dynamical aspects in the adoption of agri-environmental measures. Adv. Complex Syst. **02**, 11–36 (1999)

Wiggering, H., Dalchow, C., Glemnitz, M., Helming, K., Müller, K., Schultz, A., Stachow, U., Zander, P.: Indicators for multifunctional land use—linking socio-economic requirements with landscape potentials. Ecol. Ind. **6**, 238–249 (2006)

Simulating the Expansion of Large-Sized Farms in Rural Netherlands: A Land Exchange Model

Shah Jamal Alam[1]([⊠]), Martha M. Bakker[2], Eleni Karali[1],
Jerry van Dijk[3], and Mark D. Rounsevell[1]

[1] School of Geosciences, University of Edinburgh, Edinburgh, UK
{SJ.Alam,Mark.Rounsevell}@ed.ac.uk,
ekarali@staffmail.ed.ac.uk
[2] Chair of Land Use Planning, Wageningen University, Wageningen,
The Netherlands
Martha.Bakker@wur.nl
[3] Faculty of Geosciences, Utrecht University, Utrecht, The Netherlands
J.vanDijk2@uu.nl

Abstract. This paper introduces a data-driven agent-based simulation model of rural land exchange in the Netherlands. The model development process is part of an ongoing research program aiming at understanding the effects of climate change and socioeconomic drivers on agriculture land use and nature conservation. The first model version reported in this paper, is being developed for the Baakse Beek region in the Netherlands and is empirically grounded. The general framework described in this paper will be applied to another case study area in the Netherlands in the second phase of our research program and compare the projected land use patterns in the two case studies region.

Keywords: Agent-based model · Land exchange · Spatially explicit · Data-driven

1 Introduction

Agriculture is one of the most important land uses in Europe [1, 2]. Farming activities utilize about half of the surface of the European Union (EU) and are largely responsible for the past and current landscape patterns in rural areas [3, 4]. The Netherlands comprises an exemplar of a country with a dynamic agricultural sector. Agriculture is the largest land use, covering about 70 % of the country's terrestrial surface [5]. During the last decades, it has experienced rapid and extensive changes including decrease in the total number of farms, dominance of dairy farms, dwindling of the pig and poultry sectors, and rise in the number of owner over tenant farmers [5]. Further changes have resulted from the dynamic interactions between agriculture and other land uses. The proximity of rural areas to urban centers [6] for example, has stimulated urbanization at the expense of farmland. Additionally, the implementation of nature management policies along with the development of recreation areas and woodland has led to annual exemptions of farmland from agricultural activities [7].

S.J. Alam and H. Van Dyke Parunak (Eds.): MABS 2013, LNAI 8235, pp. 115–128, 2014.
DOI: 10.1007/978-3-642-54783-6_8, © Springer-Verlag Berlin Heidelberg 2014

The aforementioned processes alone decrease farmland surface by about 0.5 % every year [7]. Unavoidably, land transactions are accompanied by modification of the use and/or the management land, provoking changes not only in the landscape structure, but also in the range and flow of ecosystem services that they provide [8–10]. Hence, the importance of land tenure as a driver of land use/management decisions increases [11, 12]; along with the need to better understand land exchange processes and their implications.

Land use models can be used as tools to simulate land exchange processes and explore their outcomes under the assumptions of alternative future scenarios. Agent-based models simulating land market have largely focused mostly on urban (e.g., [13–15, 19]) rather than rural areas. Although some of these models are quite sophisticated, they have so far, not been used to explore land use change since they require records on land prices and budgets of potential buyers; details that are not likely to be available on the temporal and spatial scales at which land use change becomes manifest. In order to simulate land use change evolving from land transactions a more rigorous approximation of likely transactions needs to be made.

In this paper, we introduce the first version of the RUral Land EXchange (RULEX) model developed in the context of the Climate Adaptation for Rural arEas (CARE) project. This research program, funded by the Dutch government, is designed to generate knowledge that is necessary for the design and evaluation of adaptation strategies to climate change in rural areas in the Netherlands. The RULEX model simulates the process of parcels' evaluation as conducted by agents that represent individual land managers/farmers and land exchange between them. The purpose for developing the model is to generate future land use maps and the development of farm sizes under different socioeconomic and climate change scenarios. A roadmap describing the development and validation cycles for the model is presented. We present preliminary results concerning the expansion of large-sized farms as well as the reduction in the number of small farms under different simulation settings.

2   The Baakse Beek Case Study Region

The Baakse Beek region, shown in Fig. 1, is located in the Province of Gelderland, in the eastern part of the Netherlands, defined by the boundaries of a watershed. This is a strategic action area according to the provincial water management plan[1]. The integration of rural development processes related to the nature, agriculture and water management play a key role in climate change adaptation strategy.

The introduction of fertilizers and the Common Agricultural Policy (CAP)[2] have resulted in significant changes in farmland management, namely the heavy cultivation of farmland and the resulting nutrient surplus. Furthermore, intense land use changes have taken place such as the replacement of mixed (arable and some cattle) farms by either arable farms, dairy farms or pig farms, or their purchase by private companies

---

[1] http://www.baaksebeek.nl/

[2] http://ec.europa.eu/agriculture/index_en.htm

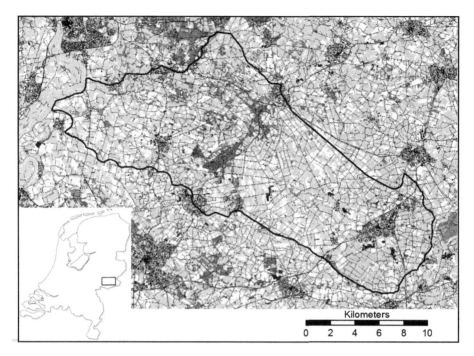

Fig. 1. An map of the Baakse Beek region in the Netherlands (courtesy: Utrecht University)

when farmers were not able to find a successor. The current trend involves the dominance of livestock (usually, pigs and dairy are combined) over arable farms. 'Natura 2000' sites are located in proximity to the study area, enhancing the ecological value of the area. Disappearance of semi-natural habitats, desiccation and acidification of wet nature areas, increased sensitivity of flood pulses and flooding are some of the issues that land managers and policy-makers are expected to confront with.

One of the important issues concerning the Baakse Beek region is an ever-increasing size of expanding farms resulting in the loss of small farm elements. Currently, dairy farmers constitute about 70 % of the farmers in Baakse Beek while the rest of the farmers use their land for intensive pigs and poultry, arable, mixed and horticulture. Land parcels with mixed land use tend to be replaced by dairy, arable and pigs/poultry farm. Several other important social and environmental issues exist e.g., whether farmers' would be willing to participate in schemes such as the 'Green-Blue' corridors, or whether the ongoing trend of increasing farm sizes would result in a loss of social cohesion. These issues are addressed elsewhere (in preparation).

3   Materials and Methods

The Rural Land EXchange (RULEX) model incorporates data of different types from different sources following the evidence-driven modeling approach [16, 17]. In RU-LEX, we have used real land parcel and farm delineations, historical transactions and the available census data. The spatial data of landownership in the Baakse Beek region comes in the form of land parcel ESRI shapefiles and farmers' locations in the region. The agricultural census data from the Gelderland province gives details about the farmers' age, land uses, economic size and other demographic information. Shapefiles inform land ownerships, land uses and delineation of the National Ecological Network (NEN). Dairy income loss and soil maps generated from biophysical models that have been developed by our project partners, inform equations that are used to calculate the perceived values of land parcels of the farmer agents.

The RULEX model is developed using Repast Simphony 2.0[3] and uses the Java JTS[4] and Geotools[5] Java libraries. The model runs on an annual time scale. By default, simulation runs for 40 years and the starting year is assumed to be 2009 following the most recent agricultural census data available to us. Next, we present an overview of the model entities, state variables and the simulation schedule.

3.1   Land Use Categories

The basic assumption of the model, consistent with respect to our case study, is that land use change is brought about through land exchange, i.e., a land parcel's current land use depends upon the land use category of its owner. Land use is an input characteristic for farmer agents and an output characteristic for parcels in RULEX. For the first version of the model, we reclassify the existing land use categories (based on the census data) into six broad categories, viz., arable, dairy, pigs-and-poultry, horticulture, mixed and 'nature'. Each farmer agent is assigned exactly one of the above land use categories except 'nature'. The 'nature' land use category concerns with the nature managers (another type of actors) and the National Ecological Network (NEN) policy, which will be incorporated in the next model version.

3.2   Typification of Farmers' Strategies for Land Exchange

A first step to model exchanges of parcels between farmers is to identify which farmers are likely to buy land, which are likely to sell land, and which are not likely to participate in the land exchange process at all. Using the panel agriculture census data of 1999 and 2009, we classified farmers in the case study region into four types: expanders, shrinkers, intensifiers and stable. Those farmers whose area increased at least 10 % in the past 10 years were identified as expanders; those whose area decreased by more than 10 % were identified as shrinkers. Farmers whose economic size increased during this time were identified as intensifiers while the rest were identified as stable farmers. Farmer agents initialized based on 2009 census data are then initialized strategy probabilistically based on their existing profile that is updated

---

[3] http://repast.sourceforge.net/

[4] http://www.vividsolutions.com/jts/JTSHome.htm

[5] http://www.geotools.org/

Table 1. Attributes and description of agents representing farmers in the Baakse Beek region; the last column indciates whether an attribute changes during a simulation.

Agent attribute	Description	Updated?
BRS_ID	A farmer's registration number as in the agriculture census	No
Land use type	{Arable, dairy, pigs-and-poultry, horticulture, mixed}	No
Area in BB	Total area in hectares owned in the Baakse Beek region	Yes
Age	Initialized from 2009 census	Yes
Economic size	Farmer agent's total economic size (NGE) in Baakse Beek	Yes
Strategy	{Expand, Shrink, Intensify, Remain stable}	Yes

at each time step (see Sect. 3.4). In our model, we use the Dutch equivalent of the European economic size, called Nederlandse Grootte Eenheid (NGE)[6].

3.3 Agents Representing Farmers in Baakse Beek

Agents in the first version of the model represent existing farmers in the Baakse Beek region. As of 2012, analysis of the land parcels ownership data identified 1259 farmers in Baakse Beek who own at least one land parcel. We use the land parcels delineation and the ownership data to match it with the most recent census data (for the year 2009) of these farmers in the region. In our model, simulation starts with each agent representing the existing owners of the agriculture land parcels in the case study region. Each agent is assigned land parcels ownership, land use category, age and the calculated economic size. Agents are assigned geographical locations in the region: for corresponding resident farmers, for whom a geographical location is available, a position is assigned in the geometry. For farmers whose location is missing, we assume that they live outside and hence a random location is assigned outside the region. Table 1 summarizes the attributes of farmer agents in the model.

In the first version, we assume that no new agents representing land managers enter the system during a simulation run. On the other hand, shrinking farmer agents who have sold away all of their parcels leave the system. Thus, we observe a decrease in the number of farmers; a trend that has been observed in the case study region and informed by the domain experts.

3.4 Agents' Methods

Updating Attributes. At each time step, a farmer agent is assigned one of the four strategies (see Table 1). The probabilities for the four strategies are calculated from equations that are estimated using multinomial regressions on the agriculture census data for 1999 and 2009. Based on our analysis (in preparation), the factors taken into account were: age, dairy {Boolean}, area, economic size and whether the farmer agent

---

[6] http://epp.eurostat.ec.europa.eu/statistics_explained/index.php/Farm_structure_in_the_Netherlands

had an expanding strategy in the previous time step {Boolean}. In our model, a farmer agent's land use type is the only static attribute besides its BRS_ID. At each time step, age is incremented. The total area, in hectares, of a farmer agent changes over time when they buy or sell land parcels as expanding or shrinking agents respectively. While the expanding and shrinking farmer agents buy and sell land parcels respectively, intensifiers augment their NGE each year (default: 0.19 per ha.), whereas stable farmer agents currently do nothing in the model (unless they change strategy in subsequent time steps).

Price-Prepared-to-Pay (PPP) aka Perceived-Value of a Land Parcel. Estimating the price that an expanding farmer would be willing to pay is difficult. For the Baakse Beek case study, data is available on sale transactions and the prices paid, however, the actual price paid is not the same as the price that a potential buyer would be willing to pay. In our model, we consider PPP as the value of a piece of land that a land manager, in our case, a farmer agent would perceive or would be willing to pay. In order to estimate that, it is important to know which parcels are more likely to be placed in the market by shrinking farmers and which parcels are more attractive to the potential buyers (in this case, the expanding farmers). We have used regression analysis (to be reported elsewhere) on the land transactions data to estimate parameters of the equation used by farmer agents in our model, in Eq. 1 below.

$$\begin{aligned} \text{PPP}_{\text{farmer}} = {} & 40670 - 12.224 * \text{distance}_{\text{parcel}} + 5747749 * \text{distance}_{\text{village}}^{-1} \\ & - 883356.7 * \text{distance}_{\text{NEN}}^{-1} + 209.5\text{incomeloss}_{\text{dairy}} - 9760.1 \end{aligned} \tag{1}$$

Figure 2 highlights the factors taken into account to estimate farmer agents' perceived value of land parcels. Proximity to a land parcel is the most dominant factor in determining its desirability; we observe a sharp decline in the trend of purchasing

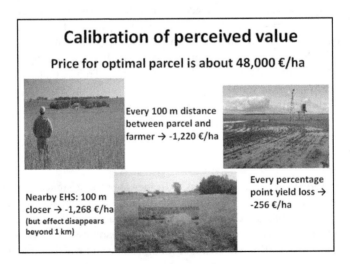

Fig. 2. Calibration of perceived value by farmer agents in the RULEX models taking into account the shortest distances to a given land parcel, the National Ecological Network and the nearest village (also, a possible loss of income due to climate change).

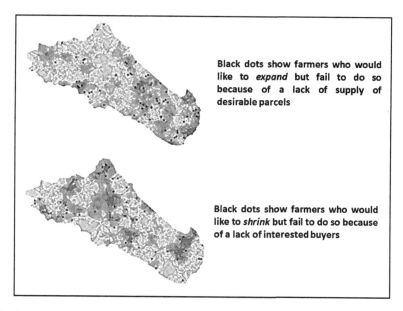

Black dots show farmers who would like to *expand* but fail to do so because of a lack of supply of desirable parcels

Black dots show farmers who would like to *shrink* but fail to do so because of a lack of interested buyers

Fig. 3. Right: Two cases depicting sellers' and buyers' market scenarios respectively.

parcels that are distant and almost no purchases observed beyond 5 km distance. Other factors also contribute to a farmer agent's perceived value. For instance, the distance to the National Ecological Network (NEN) – due to the government's NEN policy, a parcel that lies within NEN or is near, has of little desirability to expanding farmers and thus as seen in Eq. 1, a parcel's proximity to NEN decreases its price that a potential buyer (expanding farmer) may be willing to pay. While the factors included in Eq. 1 give a good fit for the land transactions in Baakse Beek, we are currently conducting sensitivity analysis for these estimates on the model's outputs. As Fig. 3 illustrates, determination of farmers' perceived values of land parcels based on the parcels' location and biophysical features, may result in a situation where expansion of existing farms are limited by the lack of desirable land parcels for sale (a sellers' market case); or when shrinking farmers are left with unsold parcels because of a lack of interested buyers in the vicinity (a buyers' market case).

Succession of Farms. In Baakse Beek, succession of farms occurs when a farmer dies or retires from farming. In RULEX, a farmer agent retires when a farmer attains a retirement age (default: 67 years) and has an economic size >8.2 (estimated). Otherwise, a farmer agent stays until it dies. If a farmer agent retires or dies, we assume that its successor takes over. This we do by resetting the age (age ← age − 35 years). Notice that age is one of the factors that determine an agent's strategy that is updated each year. In our model, agents die based on the probabilities reported in the WHO life expectancy tables for the Netherlands[7]. Model assumptions concerning

---

[7] http://apps.who.int/gho/data/view.main.61160?lang=en

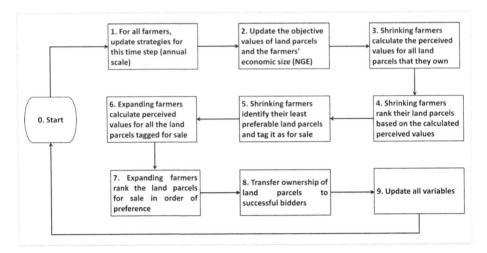

Fig. 4. An outline of the processes in the RULEX model at each time step of a simulation run.

succession can affect the model's results [18] and we aim to test these assumptions and alternative succession mechanisms in the next RULEX version.

Land Exchange. Figure 4 gives an outline of the simulation schedule at each time step (year) in the model. The model starts with loading the land use map and census data from 2009 and all assigning strategies to all farmer agents (see Table 1) based on the farmer agent's current age, land use type, total area and economic size. Shrinking farmer agents select the least preferred land parcels (the number of parcels put on sale per year is a model parameter; default=1) and put them in the market for sale. In RULEX, when a farmer agent notices that the parcel(s) it had placed in the market did not sell the previous year, i.e., it was not attractive to buyers; it puts his next least preferred parcel for sale and so on. The preferential ranking of parcels is based on a farmer's agents perceived value of a land parcel calculated using Eq. 1. This parameter can have an effect on the model outputs: If the shrinking farmer agents attempt to sell a lot of parcels then the expanding farmer agents may have a lot more parcels to choose from and thus leading to more land consolidation (as buyers prefer adjacent or nearest parcels). On the other hand, if the shrinking farmer agents sell fewer parcels at or if there are fewer sellers in the system, then the expanding farmer agent may end up buying less favorable land parcels.

Expanding farmer agents evaluate all land parcels that are available in the market by calculating their perceived values and rank them in the order of preference. An expanding farmer agent bids for only those parcels for which its perceived value is greater than 24,520 (a threshold value; calibrated from data). Here we introduce another model parameter that limits the bidding capacity of a buyer. That is, an expanding farmer agent is allowed to bid for a certain area for sale in a given time step, which is a percentage (default: 30 %) of the total area of land it currently owns. Since a farmer agent's economic size (NGE) is proportional to the area it owns, the total area owned by a farmer agent is used as a proxy for its purchasing power in the model. If there is more than one bidder for a land parcel, the one with the highest competitive power wins the bid and is transferred ownership of the land parcel. In the current model version, bidders compete based on their economic size (NGE) the bidder with the highest NGE becomes the new owner of the parcel. Notice that the RULEX model simulates land transactions without considering actual monetary values. This allows applying the model over wider spatial and temporal scales in the subsequent phase of the CARE project. Finally, following succession (described above), agents' age, area and NGE are updated.

4 Preliminary Results

In RULEX, farmer agents receive feedback on their strategies based on the performance, i.e., a change in economic size (NGE) that might be affected by a suite of climate change and socioeconomic scenarios. Since NGE is one of the factors that affect farmer agents' strategies, penalizing an expansion strategy would imply that expander agents would be less likely to expand when their economic performance is low. These scenarios will be explored in the subsequent model version following the model's validation with farmers and other stakeholders as part of the RULEX model's development process. Table 2 gives a list of the model's general and region-specific parameters and their default values. Here, we list only the intercepts of the regression equations that are used to calculate the respective probabilities for the four strategies (see Table 1) of farmer agents. One could simulate the effects of buyers' and sellers' market in the region by exploring different values of these intercepts.

We report the model's outputs based on five different parameter settings that are described in Table 3. We select three parameters: Maximum number of parcels put for sale by shrinking farmer agents in a time step (NrPrSell); maximum area to bid in a time step by an expanding farmer agent as a percentage of area it currently owns; and the intercept from the regression equation affecting the number of shrinking farmer agents in the model (ShrinkerIntercept); see Table 2. Each simulation was run for 40 time steps (years) beginning with 2009 as the starting year for which we have the census and landownership data.

Table 2. RULEX (version 1.0) Baakse Beek region-specific and general parameters

Region-specific parameters	General parameters
Regression coefficients for strategy:	Retirement age (67 years)
Expander (intercept) -2.961348	Maximum age of farmer (90 years)
Intensifier (intercept) -1.398397	Age difference between farmer and successor
Shrinker (intercept) -3.473086	(35 years)
Regression coefficients for price prepared to	Maximum number of parcels offered for sale by
pay (see Eq. 1)	shrinkers per year (1)
NGE threshold for a successor 8.2	Percentage of total area of which an expander is
Annual NGE/ha increase for intensifiers (1.7)	allowed to bid in a year (30 %)
Threshold for buying land (24520 euros/ha)	

Table 3. Five simulation settings based on different values of the model parameter: the maximum number of parcels that a shrinking farmer agent may put in the market in a year (NrPrSell); the percentage of the total area of which an expanding agent is allowed to bid in a year (PercExp) and three different values for the shrinking agent's intercept.

Setting	NrPrSell	PercExp (%)	ShrinkerIntercept
I	1	30	−1.473086
II	2	30	−1.473086
III	3	30	−1.473086
IV	3	10	−2.473086
V	1	10	−3.473086

The outputs generated by the model include the time series of the number of farmer agents with respect to their strategies and land use types and the total area covered under different land use categories. Furthermore, we look into the effect of these settings on land consolidation – i.e., assuming that farmer agents who would merge adjacent lands as one patch for more convenient land management. Whether a market-based land exchange results in further fragmentation or consolidation of land in the case study region is an important policy question for the stakeholders.

Measuring consolidated patches on land parcels in a vector-based geometry can be tricky as the delineation of land parcels in a shapefile format needs to be correct in order to determine neighboring land parcels. In contrast, for grid-based representation of land parcels, identifying consolidated patches is straightforward. Here have used a distance threshold of 20 m to determine if two land parcels are adjacent or not, and identify them as belonging to a consolidated patch if both belong to the same farmer agent. Several metrics[8] are reported in the literature for measuring land fragmentation in a study region. Here we use an adaptation of the 'patch density' measure of land consolidation, which is the total area that is owned by a farmer agent divided by the number of land parcel; we report the average patch density as a time series.

Figure 5 shows the time series for the average patch density and the total number of farmers for the five settings (see Table 3). The model parameter limiting the number of parcels that can be put on sale in a year by a shrinking farmer agent has a significant effect on the rate and extent to which farm size increases in the simulation. The more parcels that are put on sale by shrinking agents, the more choice expander agents have and thus the chances for expanders to bid for parcels that are in proximity increases with time. Notice that the expanding agents only bid for a 'for-sale' parcel if their perceived value exceeds a given threshold (Table 3). For the shrinking agents, this means that they are able to sell off their land parcels more quickly and thus the total number of agents decreases with time. The second model parameter, which limits the bidding capacity of expander agents, also affects the number of total farmer agents that survive in the system after 40 years (time steps). Unfortunately, we do not have the data to calibrate these two model parameters and this therefore requires uncertainty analysis on these parameters (currently in progress).

---

[8] See [20, 21] for more land consolidation measures.

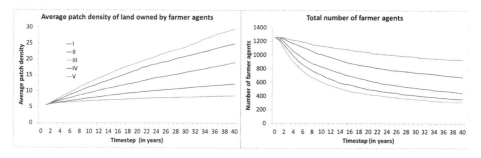

Fig. 5. Left: total area (in hectares) owned by farmer agents. Right: total number of farmer agents in the system.

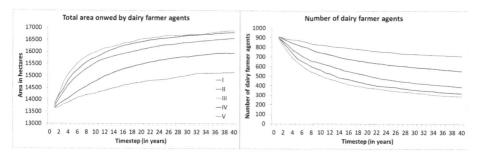

Fig. 6. Left: total area (in hectares) owned by dairy farmer agents. Right: total number of farmer agents in the system.

In the past decade, there has been a 40 % reduction in the number of farmers based on the national-level statistics. As we can see in Fig. 5, different parameter settings lead to an overall reduction ranging from approximately 20 to 70 %. Another observable trend in the case study region is the increasing dominance of dairy farmers, which is reflected from the simulation results shown in Fig. 6 and in Fig. 7, which shows two snapshots of land use spatial patterns for 2009 and 2050.

5   Outlook

The RULEX model is currently being developed to study trends in increase of farms size under different climate and socioeconomic scenarios. Land exchange in RULEX incorporates exchange and bidding processes and takes place on a spatially explicit landscape. In this paper, we have reported the first results that were run without a scenario configuration and feedbacks. Our modeling approach has been to find a neutral solution of not optimizing either from the ecological or economic perspectives, instead to mimic the observed behavior to engage the farmers in the Baakse Beek region and other stakeholders.

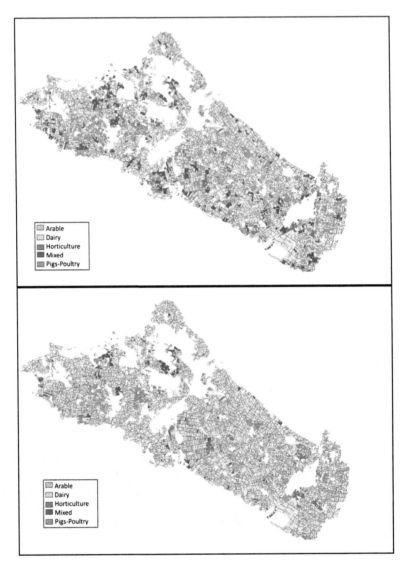

Fig. 7. Above: land use of parcels based on the respective owners in the Baakse Beek region in 2009 (time step: 0). Below: simulated land use of parcels for 2050 (time step: 40).

The model will undergo revisions following the feedback from the stakeholders and then we will introduce another type of land managers, i.e., nature manager organizations that are interested in the conservation of nature areas in the region. This will allow a cross-sectorial competition analysis for land resources between the two actor types that have different desirability for a land parcel that is on sale and different land use. Modeling nature managers' behavior (decision-making) is an unexplored subject and will be included in the next phase.

Acknowledgements. This work is supported under the Knowledge for Climate Research Programme in the Netherlands. We are thankful to our partners in the CARE Project consortium for their valuable feedback.

References

1. Schmit, C.: Analysing spatial patterns and representations of agricultural land use cata. Ph.D. thesis, Université catholique de Louvain (2006)
2. Verburg, P.H., Schulp, C.J.E., Witte, N., Veldkamp, A.: Downscaling of land use change scenarios to assess the dynamics of European landscapes. Agric. Ecosyst. Environ. **114**, 39–56 (2006)
3. Schmitzberger, I., Wrbka, T., Steurer, B., Aschenbrenner, G., Peterseil, J., Zechmeister, H.G.: How farming styles influence biodiversity maintenance in Austrian agricultural landscapes. Agric. Ecosyst. Environ. **108**, 274–290 (2005)
4. Valbuena, D., Verburg, P.H., Bregt, A.K.: A method to define a typology for agent-based analysis in regional land-use research. Agric. Ecosyst. Environ. **128**, 27–36 (2008)
5. UN Report of the Netherlands: Sustainable development in agriculture, land and rural development, drought and desertification and Africa. http://www.un.org/esa/agenda21/natlinfo/countr/nether/ (2008)
6. OECD Rural Policy Reviews: Netherlands. ISBN: 9789264041967 (2008)
7. LNV-The Netherlands Ministry of Agriculture, Nature and Food Quality. National report on Land use, land registration and land development in the Netherlands. www.icarrd.org/en/icard_doc_down/national_Netherlands.doc (2006)
8. Donald, P.F., Sanderson, F.J., Burfield, I.J., van Bommel, F.P.J.: Further evidence of continent-wide impacts of agricultural intensification on European farmland birds, 1990-2000. Agric. Ecosyst. Environ. **116**, 189–196 (2006)
9. Sattler, C., Nagel, U.J.: Factors affecting farmers' acceptance of conservation measures-a case study from north-eastern Germany. Land Use Policy **27**, 70–77 (2010)
10. Murray-Rust, D., Dendoncker, N., Dawson, T.P., Acosta-Michlik, L., Karali, E., Guillem, E., Rounsevell, M.D.: Conceptualising the analysis of socio-ecological systems through ecosystem services and agent-based modelling. J. Land Use Sci. **6**, 83–99 (2011)
11. Evans, T.P., Moran, E.F.: Spatial integration of social and biophysical factors related to landcover change. Popul. Dev. Rev. **28**, 165–186 (2002)
12. Land Tenure Studies 3: Land tenure and rural development. ftp://ftp.fao.org/docrep/fao/005/y4307E/y4307E00.pdf (2002)
13. Filatova, T., Parker, D.C., van der Veen, A.: Agent-based urban land markets: agent's pricing behavior, land prices and urban land use change. J. Artif. Soc. Soc. Simul. **12**, 3 (2009) http://jasss.soc.surrey.ac.uk/12/1/3.html
14. Filatova, T., Voinov, A., van der Veen, A.: Land market mechanisms for preservation of space for coastal ecosystems: an agent-based analysis. Environ. Modell. Softw. **26**, 179–190 (2011)
15. Parker, D.C., Brown, D.G., Filatova, T., Riolo, R., Robinson, D.T., Sun, S.: Do land markets matter? A modeling ontology and experimental design to test the effects of land markets for an agent-based model of ex-urban residential land-use change. In: Agent-Based Models of Geographical Systems, pp. 525–542. Springer, Netherlands (2012)
16. Alam, S.J., Meyer, R., Ziervogel, G., Moss, S.: The impact of HIV/AIDS in the context of socioeconomic stressors: an evidence-driven approach. J. Artif. Soc. Soc. Simul. **10**(7) (2010) http://jasss.soc.surrey.ac.uk/10/4/7.html

17. Bakker, M.M., van Doorn, A.M.: Farmer-specific relationships between land use change and landscape factors: introducing agents in empirical land use modelling. Land Use Policy **26**, 809–817 (2009)
18. Schindler, Julia: The importance of being accurate in agent-based models - an illustration with agent aging. In: Timm, Ingo J., Guttmann, Christian (eds.) MATES 2012. LNCS, vol. 7598, pp. 165–177. Springer, Heidelberg (2012)
19. Matthews, R.B., Gilbert, N.G., Roach, A., Polhill, J.G., Gotts, N.M.: Agent-based land-use models: a review of applications. Landscape Ecol. **22**, 1447–1459 (2007)
20. Irwin, E.G., Bockstael, N.E.: The evolution of urban sprawl: evidence of spatial heterogeneity and increasing land fragmentation. PNAS **104**, 20672–20677 (2007)
21. Aslan, S.T.A., Gundogdu, K.S., Arici, I.: Some metric indices for the assessment of land consolidation projects. Pak. J. Biol. Sci. **10**, 1390–1397 (2007)

Simulating Social Phenomena

Multi-Agent-Based Simulation
of *Mycobacterium Tuberculosis* Growth

Pablo Werlang, Michel Q. Fagundes, Diana F. Adamatti, Karina S. Machado, Andrea von Groll, Pedro E.A. da Silva, and Adriano V. Werhli[✉]

Grupo de Pesquisa em Biologia Computacional - Centro de Ciências Computacionais, Núcleo de Pesquisa em Microbiologia Médica - Faculdade de Medicina, Universidade Federal do Rio Grande, Rio Grande, Brazil
{pswerlang,michelqf,dianaada,karinaecomp, pedrefurg,werhli}@gmail.com,avongrol@hotmail.com

Abstract. Tuberculosis is an infectious disease that still causes many deaths around the world nowadays. It is caused by the *M. tuberculosis* bacillus. The study of the growth curve of this infectious organism is relevant as it has wide applications in tuberculosis research. In this work a Multi-Agent-Based Simulation is proposed to pursue the reproduction *in silico* of the observed *in vitro M. tuberculosis* growth curves. Simulation results are qualitatively compared with growth curves obtained *in vitro* with a recent proposed methodology. The results are promising and indicate that the chosen simulation methodology has the potential to serve as a platform for testing different bacterial growing behaviour as well as bacteria growth under different conditions.

Keywords: Multi-Agent-Based Simulation · Tuberculosis · Bacterial growth curve

1 Introduction

Determination of mycobacterial growth is relevant specially due to its implications in tuberculosis (TB) research. Recently, a new method for determination of mycobacterium growth has been proposed [8]. In the present work we are interested in modelling mycobacterial growth using a Multi-Agent Based Simulation.

There are various accepted bacterial growth models. The most employed models are Baranyi and Gompertz [13]. These methods are, by definition, deterministic and lack a proper representation of the biological components present in the system under study. This characteristic makes it difficult to include any new biological hypothesis for testing purposes directly into the model. On the contrary, stochastic models such as Multi-Agent-Based Simulations (MABS) are very flexible tools that permit the representation of each individual present in a system, thus easing the assessment of new hypothesis in the model. Usually, deterministic models present as results the averaged behaviour of its components. Contrarily, MABS models can model individual behaviour producing much more

S.J. Alam and H. Van Dyke Parunak (Eds.): MABS 2013, LNAI 8235, pp. 131–142, 2014.
DOI: 10.1007/978-3-642-54783-6_9, © Springer-Verlag Berlin Heidelberg 2014

detailed results. Moreover, MABS models have a simpler interpretation and are closely related to the real system. These peculiarities make the implementation and test of new biological hypothesis under the Multiagent framework straight-forward.

The golden goal of using biological computer simulations is to have a computational system in which a biological behaviour can be exactly reproduced. This would allow new biological hypothesis to be tested cheaper, faster and without using living organisms. After the simulations phase, only those that showed some interesting results *in silico* will be carried out *in vitro*.

This paper is organized as follows. Section 2 presents Tuberculosis and the growth curve of the *Mycobacterium tuberculosis* as well as Multi-Agent-Based Simulations. In Sect. 3 the proposed model is described. Section 4 brings the first results and a discussion. Finally, in Sect. 5, the conclusion and a proposal of future works are presented.

2   Background

2.1   Tuberculosis

TB is an infectious disease caused by the *M. tuberculosis* bacillus. The World Health Organization (WHO) in the last Global Tuberculosis Report in 2012 estimates that there were almost 9 million new cases in 2011 and 1.4 million TB deaths remaining a major global health problem and being the second leading cause of death from an infectious disease [11].

The multidrug-resistant and extensively drug-resistant TB are two forms of highly drug-resistant TB that can convert this disease untreatable and fatal, specially in poor countries with a high incidence of AIDS [2]. Due to these reasons it is necessary to investigate rapid diagnostic of drug-resistant TB and the development of new drugs to effectively treat all forms of TB.

2.2   Growth Curve of *Mycobacterium Tuberculosis*

Determination of growth curve of *M. tuberculosis* has wide applications in tuberculosis research. It has been useful in assessing the viability of the bacteria in cases of: environmental stress [18], alterations in gene regulation [17], response to different physic-chemical conditions [1], presence of gene mutations associated with drug resistance [8] and deciphering the function of unknown genes revealed by genome sequencing [14].

The fact that *M. tuberculosis* has a slow growth rate and the tendency to form clumps when grown in liquid media, makes it more difficult to study mycobacterial growth by methods commonly used for other bacteria [9]. The standard plate count method of viable cells is laborious, time consuming and requires at least 3 weeks to give results and frequently fails due to either contamination or dehydratation of the medium during the long incubation period [5]. Turbidity measurement has limited value and works best for well-dispersed cultures containing detergents [10].

Recently, von Groll et al. [8] standardized a new method to determine the growth curve based on MGIT960^{TM} system which assesses mycobacterial growth by the consumption of oxygen in the liquid medium [12]. This method allows closely monitoring the metabolic activity of the bacteria, which is measured automatically every hour by the apparatus. Unlike counting of viable cells, the main classical method to determine a growth curve, it does not require the use of detergents to disperse the bacterial cells in the medium. It is less time consuming, and the turnaround time is between 12–20 days. Besides, this system measures automatically and stores the data, which is an advantage to any current method to determine growth curve. Furthermore, it can be easily set up by any person having the Epicenter® [16] software. On the other hand, this method requires expensive equipment and they are inflexible since they depend on a single pre-packaged growth media [3,19].

The normal bacterial growth curve *in vitro* has four stages (see Fig. 1):

1. **Lag phase:** is the adaptation period of the bacteria to the culture medium. Although bacteria have metabolic activity, there is no population growth. This phase may be affected by differences in the environment prior to the bacteria was growing and also the growth phase which the bacteria was in the moment of the inoculums. Another factor that influences is the concentration of the inoculums which smaller concentration, the longer it takes to reach the minimum population that can be quantified by the method used.

2. **Log phase:** the exponential growth phase of the bacterium. Bacterial bio-mass increases linearly, with the number of bacterial cells doubling with every generation time. This growth occurs until reach a high population density, an increase of toxic metabolites and reduction of nutrients. During the growth phase, the bacterial cells can release chemical molecules (quorum sensing), which may stimulate reducing the bacterial growth rate at high population density.

3. **Stationary phase:** this occurs when there is a stable bacterial population growth. The number of cells which die is similar to the number of new cells. Furthermore, part of the bacterial cells stop to multiply, however, through the dormancy factor, they remain viable. The better the ability of the bacterium to survive in dormancy longer the stationary phase it.

4. **Decline phase (death):** eventually, death phase is reached where bacterial cells are broken down (cell lysis) due to the additional accumulation of inhibitory byproducts, depletion of cellular energy, reduction of O_2 and pH changes.

2.3   Multi-Agent-Based Simulation (MABS)

Multiagent Systems (MAS) study the behaviour of sets of independent agents with different characteristics, which evolve in a common environment. These agents interact with each other, and try to execute their tasks in a cooperative way by sharing information, preventing conflicts and coordinating the execution

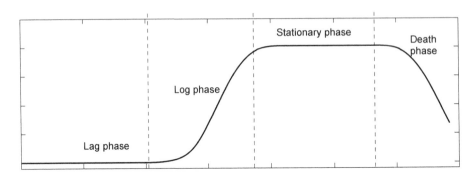

Fig. 1. Phases of a typical bacterial growth curve. See the main text for a detailed description of each phase.

of their own activities [20]. Additionally, the use of simulation as an auxiliary tool for human decision-making is very efficient, because it allows the verification of specific details with great precision.

The combination of both, multiagent systems and simulation, generates a new research area called Multi-Agent-Based Simulation (MABS), that deals with problems that involve multiple domains [7]. An example of a MABS application domain is medicine and how the diseases are disseminated. Typically, it involves researchers from various scientific areas, such as social psychology, computer science, social biology, sociology and economics. The interdisciplinary character of MABS is an important challenge faced by all researchers, while demanding a difficult interlacement of different theories, methodologies, terminologies and points of view.

MABS has provided architectures and platforms for the implementation and simulation of relatively autonomous agents and it has contributed to the establishment of the agent-based computer simulation paradigm. The agent-based approach enhances the potentialities of computer simulation as a tool for theorizing about social scientific issues. In particular, the notion of an extended computational agent, implementing cognitive capabilities, is giving encouragement to the construction and exploration of artificial societies, since it facilitates the modeling of artificial societies of autonomous intelligent agents [4]. According to Drogoul and Ferber [6], MABS goals are:

1. Testing hypotheses about the emergence of social structures from the behaviours and interactions of each individual. This is done by testing the minimal conditions given at the micro-level that are necessary to observe these structures at the macro-level;
2. Building theories that contribute to the development of a general understanding of ethological, sociological and psycho-sociological systems, by relating behaviours to structural and organizational properties; and
3. Integrating different partial theories coming from various disciplines, as sociology, ethnology or cognitive psychology, into a general framework, by providing tools that allow the integration of different studies.

In this work, our ideas are to test the goal (1), searching the global variables to help in the understanding of the mycobacterial growth.

3   Proposed Model

The model uses agents analog to the *M. tuberculosis* bacteria. Each of these agents has features that allow them to perform their role in the model, mimicking features of the real world. The agents' features are:

- **Energy**: Describes how healthy is the agent.
- **Consumption**: Determines how much nutrients the agent is consuming from the environment at each time interval. It also determines the rate at which it consumes their energy.
- **Adaptation**: Determines the time needed to the agent to make the transition between lag and log phase.
- **Sense**: Determines if the agent detected enough signalling molecules in the environment. Once this detection is positive the agent enters a reduced power state.

The model is also composed by the environment, which is the space where the agents can move. Every patch of this environment has its own characteristics. In the present model these characteristics are *nutrients* and *waste*. *Nutrients* represents the resource that agents consume to produce energy and *waste* is related to the waste that agents produce and dispose into the environment after metabolising nutrients.

Initially the agents need time to adapt to the environment where they live until they start replicating. This is the *Lag phase* in the bacterial growth.

After this period agents starts to reproduce in a process analogous to cell division in which a new agent is an exact copy of the agent that gave birth to it. However, in order for this reproduction to occur, agents need to have a certain amount of energy, due to the fact that this resource is divided between the two agents in the process. Therefore, the limiting factor for reproduction of the agents is the amount of energy that they can acquire from the environment by metabolising nutrients. This represents the *Log phase*.

At each time interval the agents consume from the environment a certain amount of nutrients. After metabolising these nutrients the agent acquires energy and produces waste. The higher the concentration of waste in the environment, less energy the agent can extract from it.

The agent also has a chance to produce a signalling molecule. This chemical signalling molecule is used by bacteria to sense their population density and communicate with each other in a process called Quorum Sensing [15]. This process is used to coordinate gene expression by several bacterial species optimizing their metabolic and behavioural activities. Thus, when the agents detect that the concentration of signalling molecules in the environment is high enough they enter in a reduced power state where they gradually consume less nutrients, generate less waste and reduce their reproduction rate. The concentration detection is an indirect measurement of how populated the environment is at the moment. It gives an indication that the population has to stop growing or it will soon face lack of nutrients which in turn may result in the death of all agents. This is the *Stationary phase*. Although there is no specific study about the Quorum Sensing in *M. tuberculosis* growth, several quorum sensing systems are intensively studied in other bacteria.

At each time interval agents also move randomly on the environment in search for patches with high concentration of nutrients, as they get more energy in this way.

The model has many variables that the user can set to adjust the different parameters of the environment to get results close to real experiments. The initial parameters that can be configured in the interface (see Fig. 2) are:

- Starting number of agents
- Nutrients from each patch
- Adaptation time of the agents
- Threshold where agents will enter the reduced power state
- Gradual rate of decay of consumption upon entering the reduced power state
- Minimum consumption
- Chance of the agent to produce a signalling molecule
- Amount of energy expended per unit time to maintain the vital functions of the agent.

3.1 Correspondence Between Real Measurements and the Simulated Model

Real growth curves are obtained with the MGIT960^{TM} system which assesses mycobacterial growth by the consumption of oxygen in the liquid medium [12]. In this method bacteria are not directly counted, instead its growth is monitored by means of measuring the fluorescence resulting from its metabolic activity. The measurement unit for bacterial growth is named *"growth units"* or [GU]. Moreover, the time in the real growth curves is measured in days.

Simulated curves are obtained from MABS in which the time is represented by "ticks" and each agent corresponds to one bacteria, therefore, bacteria is directly counted.

In order to establish a correspondence among the variables in the real curves and the ones in the MABS system, and therefore be able to compare them, we set one agent to be equivalent to four metabolic activity units and 41.88 ticks to represent one day. Note that these factors are arbitrary and determined by the choice of constants defined in the MABS system.

4 Results and Analysis

4.1 Experimental Data: The *Mycobacterium Tuberculosis* Strains and Growth Curve

To validate our MABS we need to consider experimental data about real *M. tuberculosis* growth curves. These experimental results are detailed in [8]. In this

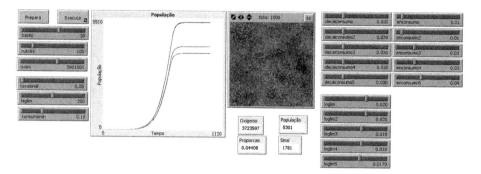

Fig. 2. Snapshot of the Environment Simulator, Netlogo.

work we are considering four *M. tuberculosis* clinical isolates from Bangladesh or Georgia countries and the reference one (H37Rv). The susceptibility profiles of the strains are in the Table 1. The strains 01-2522, 02-2761 and H37Rv were susceptible to Isoniazid (INH), Rifampicin (RIF), Ethambutol (EMB) and Streptomycin (SM). The strain 03-2922 was resistant to INH and SM and the strain 03-0850 was resistant to INH, RIF, EMB and SM, being classified as a multidrug resistant (MDR) strain.

The growth curve determined by MGIT960^{TM}: all strains were freshly subcultured on Lowenstein Jensen medium and incubated at 37 °C for exactly 3 weeks. The inoculum was prepared by suspending bacilli in 4 ml ultra-pure water containing glass beads. The suspension was vortexed for 30 s and allowed to sediment for 15 min. The supernatant was transferred to another tube, diluted to match the turbidity of a McFarland tube No. 0.5 and adjusted at 595 nm to an OD of 0.01–0.03. A dilution 1:1000 was prepared in ultra-pure water. One hundred µl of this dilution was added in triplicate to MGIT960^{TM} Mycobacteria Growth Indicator Tubes (Becton Dickinson Diagnostic Systems, Sparks, MD, USA) supplemented with 10 % MGIT960^{TM} SIRE Supplement (Becton Dickinson, USA). The tubes were entered into the MGIT960^{TM} system and incubated at 37 °C. Growth curves were obtained by monitoring the fluorescence and recording the growth units (GU) every hour using the BD EpiCente software.

Table 1. The *M. tuberculosis* strains.

Strain identification	Origin of isolates	Susceptibility			
		INH	RIF	EMB	STM
GC 02-2761	Bangladesh	S	S	S	S
GC 03-0850	Bangladesh	R	R	R	R
GC 01-2522	Georgia	S	S	S	S
GC 03-2922	Georgia	R	S	S	R
H37Rv	ATCC	S	S	S	S

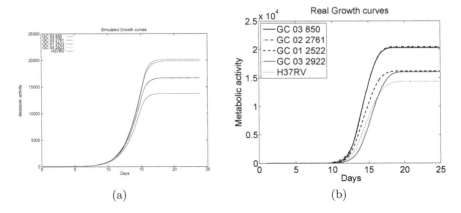

Fig. 3. Growth curves for all strains from simulated (a) and real (b) data. The simulated growth curves are obtained by averaging the results of 10 different simulations for each of the 5 strains. Real growth curves are measured by MGIT960^{TM}.

4.2   Simulation Set Up

In order to adjust the simulated growth curve with the experimental results five different populations of agents were created. These populations are analogous to the five real strains described in Table 1. For each one of the five strains we performed 10 simulations as a way to compare them with real curves. The comparison is accomplished using the average and standard deviation over the 10 simulations.

The following parameters were set for all populations as follows:

– Number of agents: 30
– Nutrients from each patch: 100
– Adaptation time: 250
– Minimum consumption: 0.1
– Chance of the agent to produce a signalling molecule: 0.05
– Gradual rate of decay of consumption upon entering the reduced power state: 0.3

The real curves do not measure the number of bacteria directly, instead they measure bacteria's fluorescence. Due to this fact we had to choose an arbitrarily low number of initial agents, 30, to imitate the initial value of fluorescence which is very low. Also, a higher number of initial agents may have had a negative impact in the computational performance of the simulations.

The following parameters were set with specific values for each population permitting each strain's behaviour to be approximately reproduced as is shown in Figs. 3 and 4.

– Threshold where agents will enter the reduced power state: 0.02, 0.02, 0.018, 0.018, 0.017.
– Amount of energy expended per unit time to maintain the vital functions of the agent: 0.01, 0.01, 0.03, 0.03, 0.04.

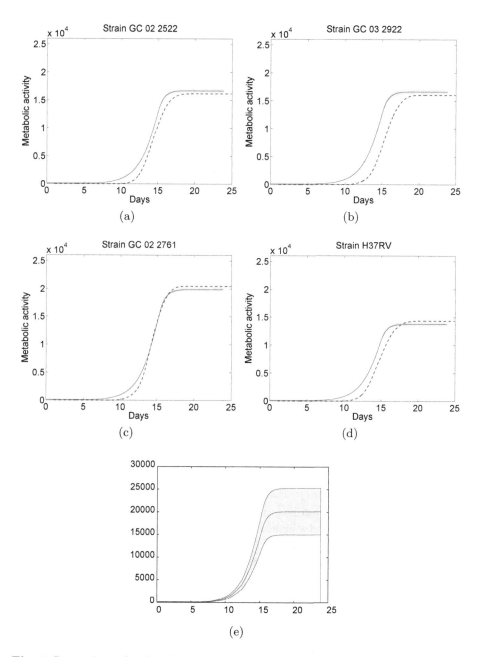

Fig. 4. Comparison of real and simulated growth curves. Each panel presents the results from simulations and real growth curves for one specific strain indicated at the top of the panel. The dashed line is the measured growth curve. The continuous line and the grey shaded area are respectively the average and the standard deviation over the 10 simulations.

The variable "Gradual rate of decay of consumption upon entering the reduced power state" causes the more or less abrupt end of the curve. It happens because once the population enter this state, they will begin to gradually reduce their consumption, which will lead them to reproduce less and therefore stabilize the curve. The intensity of this gradual reduction in consumption will dictate how quickly the curve will stabilize.

The variable "Threshold where agents will enter the reduced power state" determines the the final size of the population. This is because the variable associated with this threshold is obtained by calculating the proportion of signalling molecules in the environment compared to the total space. Therefore, for larger thresholds more signalling molecules will be allowed to populate the environment, thus more agents will be produced until the population reaches the reduced power state.

The variable "Amount of energy expended per unit time to maintain the vital functions of the agent" is associated with the inclination of the log phase of the growth curve. This is due to the fact that the more energy is required to maintain a live agent, less energy is left for him to reproduce, and therefore the reproduction speed of the population is affected.

The variables in our simulator are not directly adjusted to match the real variables and, thus, they are converted from simulated variables units to real system units. See Sect. 3.1 for a discussion about this topic.

In Fig. 3 are presented simulated (a) and real (b) growth curves. These curves show that the simulation is very near to real, mainly related to the shape of the curve, which must be similar to the typical growth curves presented in Fig. 1. For some strains the results are very similar.

If we individually analyse each strain, as is presented in Fig. 4, we can notice that growth curves (a), (b), (c) and (d) shows interesting results with low standard deviation. In the curve (e), the standard deviation at the beginning is small, but in the end of log phase and stationary phase a big difference occur between simulated and real data. Interestingly, the strain for which the higher standard deviation is observed is the GC03-0850 that is classified as multidrug resistant. This suggests that this strain has an erratic growth behaviour and needs to be further investigated from a biological point of view. It is important to underline that the simulation system depends on how the parameters were initialized. It is a very sensitive system as well as is the real system.

5   Conclusions

The determination of growth curve has important applications in the tuberculosis research. The *M. tuberculosis* has a slow growth rate turning it difficult to be studied by common methods. Due to this reason, von Groll et al. [8] standardizes a new method of determining the *M. tuberculosis* growth curve based on MGIT system. In this methodology the metabolic activity of the bacteria is automatically measured by the apparatus during 12–20 days. Despite the advantages of this methodology, it still time consuming and requires an expensive equipment.

Due to these reasons in this work we proposed a MABS to the determination of mycobacterium growth.

In this work we presented our first effort in pursuing to develop a biological hypothesis tester to the *M. tuberculosis*. The preliminary results are promising specially because with reasonable effort we can adjust our simulator to reproduce real curves obtained from different strains of *M. tuberculosis*. What is still missing is a closer relationship among the simulator and the biological system regarding their parameters and mechanisms. In fact this is not a simple task. The reason being that many parameters and mechanisms in the bacterial growth are not fully understood or accepted in the biology community and, thus, we cannot program it perfectly in a simulator.

In the future development of this simulator the main goal is to keep working together with biologists in order to unveil unknown aspects of bacterial growth. Also, as we gain knowledge about bacterial growth we intend to incorporate it into the simulator turning it closer to the main goal of reproducing the true biological behaviour. This will allow researchers to simulate and test hypothesis about the growth of other bacteria as well as bacteria growing under different experimental conditions.

References

1. Barkan, D., Liu, Z., Sacchettini, J., Glickman, M.: Mycolic acid cyclopropanation is essential for viability, drug resistance, and cell wall integrity of Mycobacterium tuberculosis. Chem. Biol. **16**, 499–509 (2009)
2. Chan, E.D., Iseman, M.D.: Multidrug-resistant and extensively drug-resistant tuberculosis: a review. Curr. Opin. Infect. Dis. **21**(6), 587–595 (2008)
3. Chien, H., Yu, M., Wu, M., Lin, T., Luh, K.: Comparison of the BACTEC MGIT 960 with Löwenstein-Jensen medium for recovery of mycobacteria from clinical specimens. Int. J. Tuberc. Lung Dis. **4**(9), 866–870 (2000)
4. Conte, R., Gilbert, N., Sichman, J.S.: MAS and social simulation: a suitable commitment. In: Sichman, J.S., Conte, R., Gilbert, N. (eds.) MABS 1998. LNCS (LNAI), vol. 1534, pp. 1–9. Springer, Heidelberg (1998)
5. Damato, J.J., Collins, M.T., Rothlauf, M.V., McClatchy, J.K.: Detection of mycobacteria by radiometric and standard plate procedures. J. Clin. Microbiol. **17**, 1066–1073 (1983)
6. Drogoul, A., Ferber, J.: Multi-agent simulation as a tool for modeling societies: application to social differentiation in ant colonies. In: Proceedings of Workshop on Modelling Autonomous Agents in a Multi-Agent World (1992)
7. Gilbert, N., Troitzsch, K.G.: Simulation for the Social Scientist. Open University Press, Buckingham and Philadelphia (2005)
8. von Groll, A., Martin, A., Stehr, M., Singh, M., Portaels, F., da Silva, P.E.A., Palomino, J.C.: Fitness of Mycobacterium tuberculosis strains of the W-Beijing and Non-W-Beijing genotype. PLoS ONE **5**(4), e10191 (2010)
9. Lambrecht, R.S., Carriere, J.F., Collins, M.T.: A model for analyzing growth kinetics of a slowly growing Mycobacterium sp. Appl. Environ. Microbiol. **54**, 910–916 (1988)

10. Meyers, P., Bourn, W., Steyn, L., van Helden, P., Beyers, A., Brown, G.: Novel method for rapid measurement of growth of mycobacteria in detergent-free media. J. Clin. Microbiol. **36**(9), 2752–2754 (1998)

11. Organization., W.H.: Global tuberculosis report. http://www.who.int/tb/ publications/global_report/ (2012)

12. Pheiffer, C., Carroll, N., Beyers, N., Donald, P., Duncan, K., Uys, P., van Helden, P.: Time to detection of Mycobacterium tuberculosis in BACTEC systems as a viable alternative to colony counting. Int. J. Tuberc. Lung Dis. **12**(7), 792–798 (2008)

13. Buchanan, R.L., Whiting, R.C.W., Damert, W.C.: When is simple good enough: a comparison of the Gompertz, Baranyi, and three-phase linear models for fitting bacterial growth curves. Food Microbiol. **14**, 313–326 (1997)

14. Sassetti, C., Boyd, D., Rubin, E.: Genes required for mycobacterial growth defined by high density mutagenesis. Mol. Microbiol. **48**(1), 77–84 (2003)

15. Sifri, C.D.: Quorum sensing: bacteria talk sense. Clin. Infect. Dis. **47**(8), 1070–1076 (2008)

16. Technologies, B.: The BD epicenter microbiology data management system. http:// www.bd.com/ds/technicalCenter/brochures/br_1_2704.pdf (January 2013)

17. Verma, A., Sampla, A., Tyagi, J.: Mycobacterium tuberculosis rrn promoters: differential usage and growth rate-dependent control. J. Bacteriol. **181**(14), 4326–4333 (1999)

18. Voskuil, M., Visconti, K., Schoolnik, G.: Mycobacterium tuberculosis gene expression during adaptation to stationary phase and low-oxygen dormancy. Tuberculosis (Edinb) **84**(3–4), 218–227 (2004)

19. Walters, S.B., Hanna, B.A.: Testing of susceptibility of Mycobacterium tuberculosis to isoniazid and rifampin by mycobacterium growth indicator tube method. J. Clin. Microbiol. **34**, 1565–1567 (1996)

20. Wooldridge, M.: An Introduction to MultiAgent Systems. John Wiley & Sons, New York (2009)

Who Creates Housing Bubbles?
An Agent-Based Study

Jiaqi Ge[(✉)]

Department of Economics, Iowa State University, Ames, IA 50011, USA
jge@iastate.edu

Abstract. This paper develops an agent-based spatial model of the housing market. A house is many families' biggest asset. It is also widely held by financial institutions, in the form of mortgage-backed securities. As a result, avoiding extreme housing price volatility is crucial for maintaining financial stability of the nation. The housing market is very unique: it is less liquid, highly regulated, highly leveraged, involves speculative behaviors, and exhibits spatial correlations. To this day, there are few housing market models that take into account all of these complications. In this paper, we propose an agent-based spatial model of the U.S. housing market. Preliminary results show that sensible aggregate outcomes that are generated from individual interaction, and a lenient lending criteria might be responsible for causing a housing bubble.

Keywords: Real estate market · Housing bubble · Agent-based model · Spatial model

1 Introduction

More than five years have passed since the sub-prime crises in the U.S. housing market and the financial crises it has triggered. Till this day, America is still seeing its consequences. About four and half million American families have lost their homes to foreclosures or were on the edge of going foreclosure. Nearly $11 trillion in household wealth has vanished, with retirement accounts and life savings swept away [11]. In fact, housing bubble is a global phenomenon. Japan experienced the property price bubble in the late 1980s. The bubble burst in the early 1990s, followed by an economy slow down in the years after. In Europe, housing bubbles occur in Norway, Spain and Ireland. Emerging economies such as South Korea, then Russia, China, India, and Brazil have also witnessed big housing bubbles. For many families, the house it owns is its biggest asset. For banks and financial institutions, real estate has become an increasingly important component in their portfolios, in the form of mortgage-backed securities.

Jiaqi Ge like to thank Dr. Leigh Tesfatsion, Dr. Steve Kautz, Dr. Catherine Kling, Dr. Joseph Herriges, and Dr. John Schroeter at Iowa State University for their advice, comments, and help. He also like to thank Tom Randall Real Estate Team, Hunziker & Associates, and an anonymous realtor for their helpful inputs.

S.J. Alam and H. Van Dyke Parunak (Eds.): MABS 2013, LNAI 8235, pp. 143–150, 2014.
DOI: 10.1007/978-3-642-54783-6_10, © Springer-Verlag Berlin Heidelberg 2014

Hence, extreme volatility in the housing market, like a housing bubble, will not only hurt homeowners, but also disturb the economy on a large scale.

The housing market is very unique: it is less liquid, highly regulated, highly leveraged, involves speculative behaviors, and exhibits spatial correlations. To this day, there are few housing market models that take into account all of these complications. This paper proposes an agent-based spatial model of the housing market. Our model set up is based on interviews with real estate personnel, in order to replicate important aspects of the business. The model will provide us with a more comprehensive understanding of the housing market and the housing bubble. Our research questions include: What are the major contributors of a housing bubble? In particular, what is the role of investors in the market? What is the role of the bank's lending criteria? Is there any spatial patterns in the housing price movements?

2   Review of Literature

There are mainly three groups of papers in the housing literature. The first group focuses on speculative behavior in the housing market. Examples are Shiller[10] and Riddel [9]. The second group of papers, mostly done after the U.S. housing crises, look at the relationship between the housing market and sub-prime lending. Examples are Goetzmann et al. [4] and [1]. The third group studies land use choice and housing supply elasticities. Examples are Goodman et al. [6] and Glaeser et al. [2].

As far as agent-based modeling goes, Goldstein [5] and Markose et al. [8] devised agent-based models for the interaction between the housing market and financial securities, such as residential mortgage backed security, collateralized debt obligations, and credit default swaps. Torrens [12] developed an three-leveled agent-based model to simulate individual housing choices. However, some important aspects such as the market price formation and price expectation are largely omitted. Moreover, the model does not have a financial sector. The agent-based housing market model proposed by Geanakoplos et al. [3] does have a sophisticated financial sector, but the model is non-spatial.

According to a recent review by Mayer [7], the current literature is not satisfying in explaining and predicting a housing bubble. Some important aspects of the housing market are still to be explored. For instance, few papers have looked at intra-city differences. Few have modeled the negotiation process and the difference between the listing and final prices. In terms of future price expectation, most studies only consider past prices, but few consider prices in neighboring areas. In short, we feel that much more can be done in this area, and our paper could fill the gap.

3   The Housing Market: Agent Class Structure

Our housing market sits on a two dimensional landscape that contains multiple regions. A region can have as many houses as its maximum capacity allows.

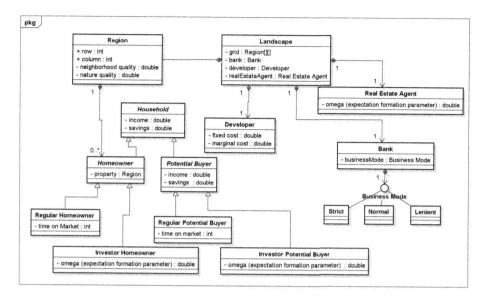

Fig. 1. Class diagram for the housing model

Two regions are neighbors if they share a common border. Each region has exogenous attributes such as nature quality, and endogenous attributes such as neighborhood quality. Neighborhood quality measures the attractiveness of a region's neighborhood environment, such as safety, public service, or school qualities. It is endogenous because it depends on who lives in the region, which is endogenously determined in the system. The nature quality, on the other hand, captures anything that is exogenously determined, such as weather, distance to the beach, or cultural heritage.

Our model has five types of market participates: the real estate agent, the developer, buyers, homeowners, and the bank. We further distinguish buyers and homeowners as investors and non-investors. Investors buyers buy a property in hope of profiting from housing price appreciation. Their purchase decisions are based on their heterogenous expectations of future housing price. Regular buyers, on the other hand, obtain utility from living in the house. Hence, their purchase decisions depends on the house's attributes: its listing price, neighborhood quality, and nature quality. We need to distinguish investor buyers/homeonwers from regular ones because the two types have very different objectives and behavioral rules. Figure 1 is a class diagram of the model. It outlines the model's class structure and demonstrates relationships between different types of agents.

At the beginning of each period, the bank will announce the mortgage rate; the developer starts to build new houses on the landscape. A bunch of new buyers enter the market in search of a house; at the same time existing homeowners may decide to put their houses on the market for sale. Both buyers and sellers submit bids or asks to a real estate agent. The real estate agent then settles the

Table 1. Bank's three business mode

case component	Normal	Lenient	Strict
mortgage rate (year 1 & 2)	0.05	0.02	0.06
mortgage rate (year 3 & more)	0.05	0.08	0.06
minimum down payment	0.05	0.00	0.20
maximum debt to income ratio	0.33	0.50	0.28

market price and completes housing transactions. Buyers become homeowners after buying a property; while homeowners leave the city after selling the property they own. Homeowners can also choose to default on the mortgage loan. When that happens, their houses go into foreclosure.

4   Treatment Factors

One of the treatment factors in the model is Bank's lending criteria. For example, a bank can adopt one of the three cases: normal, lenient, or strict lending. Each case is a package of four components: mortgage rate in the first two years, mortgage rate after the second year, minimum down payment, and maximum debt to income ratio. Here debt to income ratio is simply the ratio between monthly payment and monthly income, since we assume away any other forms of household debt. In the lenient lending scenario, homeowners enjoy a lower mortgage rate for the first two years of the loan duration. When the lower rate expires, homeowners have the opportunity to refinance. If refinance is approved, the lower rate is resumed and will be in effect for another two years. Otherwise, the higher rate is applied. Homeowners can get at most two refinance opportunities. In summary, lenient lending adopts an adjustable mortgage rate. Details of each case are listed in Table 1.

Another important treatment factor is the number of investors, as opposed to the number of non-investor buyers. Will more investors lead to a larger housing price volatility, because they tend to follow trend? Or, on the contrary, more investors will lead to less housing price volatility because they try to seize investment opportunities and buy when the market is at the bottom. Our model would provide some insight.

5   Preliminary Results

We first show the simulated housing price over 300 month or 25 years under strict, normal, and lenient lending criteria. (We eliminate 120 burn-out periods at the beginning of the simulation.) The solid line is the mean price across all regions; The blue/red line represents maximum/minimum price across all regions.

Strict Lending Scenario   Normal Lending Scenario   Lenient Lending Scenario

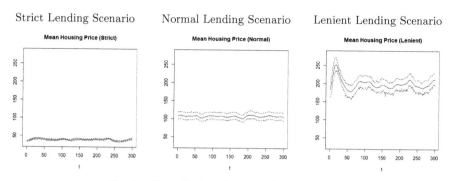

Housing Price Under Three Lending Scenarios

It is obvious that the bank's lending criteria has a large impact on the housing market. Lenient lending (see Table 1) is associated with higher housing prices, more price volatility, and a larger number of foreclosures. The reason price is higher in the lenient lending scenario is because more people are qualified for a loan. The demand is higher in the lenient lending scenario, compared with the normal and strict ones. Because the majority of buyers are qualified for a loan from the bank, including the ones whose income is only marginally higher than the minimum income required, and no down payment is required, any price perturbation will induce loan defaults and foreclosures.

Next we introduce an exogenous income shock at t = 100. At t = 100, residents' income shrunk by approximately 20 % from a mean of 2.8 (thousand) to 2.2 (thousand). The shock lasts for 24 months. After 24 months, income goes back to the original level. The housing price under strict, normal, and lenient lending criteria with an external income shock are shown below.

Strict Lending Scenario   Normal Lending Scenario   Lenient Lending Scenario

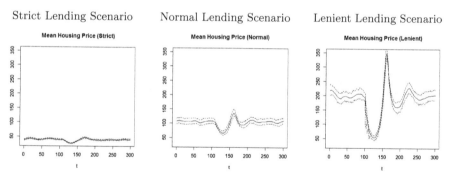

Housing Price Under Three Lending Scenarios With External Income Shock

Once again, in the lenient lending scenario, the system has the biggest price drop at the time of the income shock. Housing price plummets by nearly 70 % in 24 months. Housing price in normal or strict lending scenario also decreases at the time of shock, but to a lesser extent. Moreover, in all scenarios, price rebounds after the shock when income goes back to the original level. In the short post-shock period when income has recovered but price is still low, demand is so high that housing price rebounds to a higher level than the pre-shock average.

The rebound lasts for around 20 periods and price goes back to the pre-shock level eventually.

As for number of investors, each period we create a certain number of investors. However, the number of investors in the market is endogenously determined by the system. Investors have heterogenous expectation about future housing price. An investor will purchase a house if she thinks it profitable to do so. Similar, an investor will sell a house if she believes it's no longer a good investment. In short, we do not control the number of investors who make a purchase or sale in the market. We only control the number of investors newly created in each period to search for profitable opportunities. Figures below shows the mean prices in lenient lending when we have a smaller number of investors (200 per period) and a large number of investors (600 per period) per period. We also imposed an external income shock at t = 100.

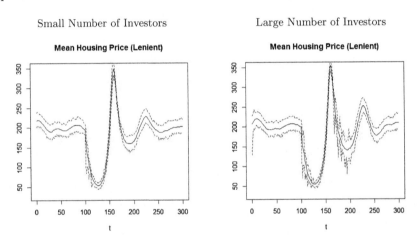

Housing Price Under Small and Large Number of Investors With External Income Shock

We see that the shapes of the two curves are really similar. The difference lies in the discrepancy between the minimum and maximum housing prices during the shock period. It seems like investors tend to invest more in high-end neighborhood than in other neighborhoods. In other words, the introduction of more investors widens the price differences between neighborhoods. As a result, high-end neighborhoods can recover from a negative shock more quickly than low-end neighborhoods.

6   Conclusions

This paper develops an agent-based spatial model of the housing market. We try to incorporate some important aspects of the housing market that are largely ignored in the existing housing literature, such as the negotiation process between buyers and sellers, household's choice of location, and the role of bank and real estate agent. Our research questions include: who creates housing bubbles? What is the role of the bank's lending criteria? And what is the role of investors?

The preliminary results are very promising. We have generated sensible aggregate results simply from individual buyer and seller interactions in the market. From the preliminary results, we can already conclude that one of our treatments, i.e., bank's lending criteria have a large impact on the housing market. Lenient lending criteria, like what we had during the recent U.S. housing bubble, have led to higher housing prices and larger price volatility.

When an exogenous income shock is imposed on the system, housing price drops in all scenarios, but it drops by the biggest amount in the lenient lending scenario. In all scenarios, prices rebounds after the shock. It rebounds by the biggest amount in the lenient lending scenario. One thing that is different in our experiment than in reality is that, in the experiment, the bank always remains lenient lending criteria during and after the shock; while in reality, banks tighten lending. We test what if the bank tightens its lending and shift to normal lending scenario when a shock occurs. We found that post-shock housing price still rebounds, but by a lesser extent.

Investors also play a role in the housing bubbles. Our model results show that investor are responsible for widening regional housing price differences, especially when housing prices move dramatically. Investors are more likely to invest in high-end neighborhoods than in low-end neighborhoods. As a consequence, prices in high-end neighborhoods recover more quickly from a shock.

To sum up, we have looked at a global phenomenon that affects household wealth, the financial market, and national economy. By talking to numerous real estate agents, we have set up a model that captures important aspects of the market. Although further exploration of the model is needed, the preliminary results we have obtained so far show that our model is able to generate from the bottom up sensible aggregated outcomes that capture important characteristics in the housing market.

References

1. Brueckner, J.K., Calem, P.S., Nakamura, L.I.: Subprime mortgages and the housing bubble. J. Urban Econ. **71**(2), 230–243 (2012)
2. Glaeser, E.L., Gyourko, J., Saiz, A.: Housing supply and housing bubbles. J. Urban Econ. **64**(2), 198–217 (2008)
3. Geanakoplos, J., Axtell, R., Farmer, J., Howitt, P., Conlee, B., Goldstein, J., Hendrey, M., Palmer, N., Yang, Ch-Y: Getting at systemic risk via an agent-based model of the housing market. Am. Econ. Rev. **102**(3), 53–58 (2012)
4. Goetzmann, W., Peng, L., Yen, J.: The subprime crisis and house price appreciation. J. Real Estate Finance Econ. **44**(1–2), 36–66 (2012). (Special Issue: SI)
5. Goldstein, J.: An Agent-Based Model of the Interaction between the Housing and RMBS Markets
6. Goodman, A., Thibodeau, T.G.: Where are the speculative bubbles in US housing markets. J. Hous. Econ. **17**(2), 117–137 (2008)
7. Mayer, C.: Housing bubbles: a survey. Annu. Rev. Econ. **3**, 559–577 (2011). (Book Series: Annual Review of Economics)

8. Markose, S., Giansante, S., Gatkowski, M., Shaghaghi, A.R.: Too interconnected to fail: financial contagion and systemic risk in network model of cds and other credit enhancement obligations of us banks. Analysis (2009)

9. Riddel, M.: Are housing bubbles contagious a case study of Las Vegas and Los Angeles home prices. Land Econ. **87**(1), 126–144 (2012)

10. Shiller, R.: Asset, low interest rates and high, prices: an interpretation in terms of changing popular economic models. Brookings Pap. Econ. Act. **2**, 11132 (2007)

11. The financial crisis inquiry commission: The financial crisis inquiry report: final report of the National Commission on the causes of the financial and economic crisis in the United States (2011)

12. Torrens, P.: New tools for simulating housing choices (2001)

Towards Simulating the Impact of National Culture on Organizations

Loïs Vanhée[1,2](✉), Frank Dignum[2], and Jacques Ferber[1]

[1] LIRMM, University of Montpellier II, Montpellier, France
lois.vanhee@gmail.com
[2] Utrecht Universiteit, Utrecht, The Netherlands

Abstract. Both culture and organizations are concepts which have been partially formalized. Only some of their aspects have been specified to build agent-based models. In this conceptual article, we identify and characterize the features that should be considered when building an agent-based model of an organization taking into account the influence of culture. In particular, we investigate the impact culture can have on the delegation, coordination, control and normative structures of organizations and on the way these structures are used. Moreover, we describe how this cultural impact would influence the three central performance criteria of organizations: efficiency, flexibility and robustness.

Keywords: Simulating organizations · Simulating social complexity · Agent models of social behavior

1 Introduction

Why do some organizations succeed to expand their operations abroad while others fail? Many reasons are given. Often, individuals from the foreign part of the organization are declared responsible of this failure. They may constantly need to be directed in order to perform any action or they may take counter-productive initiatives. They may spend their time defining how things shall be done and do nothing or even overlook specifications and produce inappropriate results. Even worse, this distrust can be reciprocal and the foreign branch might also blame the parent one. The effects of such underlying expectations are embedded in culture. Organizations, as a means to create interaction amongst several individuals, are naturally sensitive to these expectations. Hofstede et al. [9,10] studied and described the impact of culture on human behavior. They explained how copy-pasting the successful management style of one country can fail in another. Although this research is empirically grounded, it only gives a descriptive and intuitive account of the impact of cultures on organizations. In order to design, simulate and analyze models of organizations incorporating cultural influences, we must first formalize this intuitive description.

In this conceptual paper, we move one step forward the formalization of the impact of culture on an organization and on its performance. In particular, we focus on influence of culture from outside the organization, sometimes

S.J. Alam and H. Van Dyke Parunak (Eds.): MABS 2013, LNAI 8235, pp. 151–162, 2014.
DOI: 10.1007/978-3-642-54783-6_11, © Springer-Verlag Berlin Heidelberg 2014

called national culture. This culture does not emerge from within the organization, which is referred as organizational culture [10] or corporate culture. To this extent, we link each aspect of organizations with each Hofstede's cultural dimension. In order to have a perspective that integrates each organizational aspect and each cultural dimension as wholes, we describe how each organizational aspect is influenced by culture but also how each cultural dimension influences the organization. Using these orthogonal descriptions, a modeler can build a model of culture and organizations which is coherent with both theories of culture and organizations. Moreover, the effect of culture on organizations influences the organizational behavior. Thus, the cultural effect can be observed from outside of the organization. In this article, we describe how culture would affect the performance criteria (efficiency, flexibility and robustness) of an organization. This description can be used by a simulator to determine if the shift of organizational performance due to a different cultural setting is conform to *a priori* expectations.

We describe the relevant previous work about culture and organizations in Sect. 2, then we explain the impact of culture on organizations in Sect. 3. Finally, we present the consequences of this impact on the organization performance in Sect. 4.

2   Previous Work

2.1   Culture

Culture can be defined as social knowledge. For instance Hofstede *et al.* [10] defines culture as values and practices (Fig. 1). Values are a set (or an order) of dilemmas considered by individuals when interacting with the world (e.g. the "evil versus good" dilemma is more important than "rational versus irrational" one). Practices encompass rituals (e.g. saying "hello"), heroes and symbols. But, the particularity of cultural knowledge (especially of values) is that it is expected to be shared with other individuals. This expectation dramatically affects interactions, positively if they are shared and possibly negatively otherwise. (Why is the leader so bossy? Why do they lack so much subordination?)

Even if the concept of culture has not been formalized yet, Hofstede *et al.* [10] empirically classified cultures (independently of any representation) along 5 *national dimensions*: power distance (PDI), individualism (IDV), masculinity/femininity (MAS), uncertainty avoidance (UAI) and long-term orientation (LTO). *Power distance* influences the expectation and importance given to power statuses. Leaders are expected to take directions and subordinates to obey and not take initiatives. E.g.: China, Russia (high PDI) opposed to Scandinavian countries (low PDI). *Individualism* influences the definition of individual identity. The lower the IDV, the more one individual's identity is linked to his or her social context (e.g. relatives, colleagues). Thus, one's individual goals and actions (and the claim for this action) are more or less linked to him/herself or to his/her context. This context leads to a collective image that has to be preserved (helping each other, hiding errors, rejecting outsiders). Conversely, in high

IDV cultures, individuals expect a treatment independent of any social context. In this cultures, relationships between individuals are less influential on decisions than in lower IDV. E.g.: USA, Great Britain (high IDV) opposed to South American countries (low IDV). *Masculinity* indicates preferences on assertiveness, toughness, focus on performance and material success. Good performance should be recognized and rewarded, leading to competition. Conversely, low MAS cultures favor modesty, tenderness and high quality of life. Interactions focus on building cooperation and establishing consensus. E.g.: Scandinavian countries (low MAS) versus Japan, Italy (high MAS). *Uncertainty avoidance* favors the desire for clear and explicit situations with predictable outcomes. This desire leads to establishment of rules (formal or not), making everything explicit with low ambiguity. Conversely, individuals with low UAI culture dislike the presence of rules. They tend to accept more easily situations with unspecified behavior or unclear outcome. E.g.: Greece, Japan (high UAI) versus Sweden, China (low UAI). *Long-term orientation* influences the time span considered when taking decisions. In high LTO culture, rewards can be sacrificed for better ones later, relationships are built on long-lasting trust and rules are flexible. Conversely, individuals in low LTO culture focus on immediate success, avoiding failure and decisions rely on dogmatic rules (e.g. total commitment, best profit commitment). E.g.: China, India (high LTO) versus Canada, Great Britain (low LTO).

In computer science, culture has been investigated from two perspectives. The first one studies culture as a dynamic system of values (or memes) propagation. For instance, [2] studies the formation of cultural clusters or [4] the emergence of suboptimal equilibria. Nonetheless, these models consider only superficially the influence of culture on individual behavior. The second perspective focuses instead on the influence of culture on the decision making process, considering culture as a static parameter. For instance, Dignum [6] describes how cultural values can influence the plan selection process in considering the constraints imposed to the agent. In the same direction, Dechesne *et al.* [5] models the influence of culture on norm emergence. This model is used to investigate why the European smoking ban is being accepted in certain countries while not in others.

2.2 Organizations

Organizations are social structures created in order to accomplish a given goal. Morgenstern [14] describes organizations by introducing six key *organizational features*: goals, workflow, roles, structures (coordination, delegation, control and information), failures and norms.

An organization aims at achieving a *goal*, which is a set of *tasks*. Tasks are solved in executing unitary *operations* which may require some specific *competence*. The *workflow* [15] defines how these operations are linked to each other. Each operation is associated to a *role* possessing the right competencies. These roles are connected with each other via the *coordination structure*, which should match the order of operations defined by the workflow. Individuals are allocated to roles and they are *responsible* for successfully performing the operations attached to their roles. Finally, a role can delegate an operation to another role if they are linked in the *delegation structure*. Delegation can be used to balance the workload and divide the work. The *control structure* determines roles in charge of monitoring operations of other roles. This information can be used to verify the success of an operation, the state of a task or to change the organization but also to prevent costly *failures*. Failures can be caused by operations incorrectly performed or tasks not handled by the workflow. In this case, *exception handling* rules can be used to find a solution to resolve these failures. *Norms* can be developed in order to avoid failures or to standardize processes of the organization. Finally, the *information structure* determines which information shall be transferred to whom and when. This structure encompasses other structures but can also be necessary for other purposes (e.g. storing information about the past failures). This information can then be used for longer-term *learning*. Organizational learning is a background process gathering past experiences of an organization in order to improve future performance.

Mintzberg [13] synthesized 5 frequent organizational patterns, each one fitting a particular purpose: simple structures, machine bureaucracies, professional bureaucracies, divisionalized forms and adhocracies. *Simple structures* are flat hierarchies composed of few leaders tightly supervising large groups of subordinates. This pattern is fit for simple tasks in dynamic environments (e.g. a grocery). *Machine (or full [10]) bureaucracies* are pyramidal hierarchies of specialists. Each branch is specialized in a domain, leaders encompass the specializations of their subordinates. This hierarchy centralizes all structures: leaders delegate, control and handle exceptions of their subordinates. Norms standardize the work processes, coordinating operators at the lowest level. This pattern fits repetitive tasks in simple and stable environments (e.g. mass production). *Professional bureaucracies* are composed of teams of autonomous experts. Training leads to a standardization of skills allowing complex sequences of operations to be performed while requiring minimal coordination. This pattern fits stable and complex environments (e.g. hospitals). *Adhocracies* are unstructured networks. Their structures are flat, thus anyone can coordinate, delegate or control anyone else. Individuals tend to cluster in working teams depending on the task to be solved. This structure is fit for complex and dynamic environments (e.g. software development). Finally, *divisionalized forms* are macro-organizations containing multiple sub-organizations. Each sub-organization (which tends to become a machine bureaucracy) aims at different markets. The key part of these organizations is the link between the top direction and each sub-organization. This pattern is more balanced and fit various environments.

Organizations have also been studied in the field of computer science. These studies have two main purposes: model organizations to build software [1] and study human organizations. This article focuses on the latter approach. Reference [8] uses Morgenstern's description to model organizations. They are represented with a 3 layer directed multigraph. Vertexes represent the roles and the edges determine the delegation, coordination and control structures. The authors use this representation to build organizational performance measures and describe properties of the organizational behavior. Reference [12] investigates organizational performance evaluation through simulations. Simulations are used in particular to evaluate the costs involved by congestion and evolving

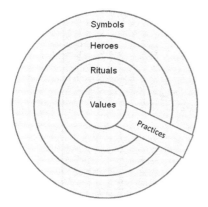

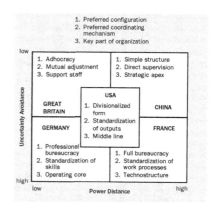

Fig. 1. Hofstede's model of cultures (onion diagram) [10]

Fig. 2. Mintzberg's five preferred configurations of organizations, from [10]

tasks. This evaluation of performance can be used to propose new organizational shapes. For instance, [11] uses genetic algorithms to optimize organizational design. Similarly, [3] presents an expert system proposing organizational change and supporting its propositions. The long-term goal of this article is to introduce the influence of culture in a model evaluating the performance and proposing adaptations for multi-cultural organizations.

3   Culture and Organizations

Hofstede [10] links culture and organizations in two ways: the emergence of an organizational culture and the influence of national cultures on organizations. The first approach considers that organizations, as relatively closed interaction system, grow a culture. This culture is highly domain dependent: bank cultures are relatively similar but different from factory cultures. In this article, we focus instead on the second approach, which investigates why and how two organizations with similar purposes differ due to the influence of national cultures. Hofstede [10, chap. 9] illustrates the Mintzberg type of organization that would emerge if organizations were only influenced by culture (Fig. 2). In practice, this influence is not so extreme: even in a low UAI culture, hospitals require experts and a minimal amount of regulations. Nonetheless, culture can still influence some aspects of the organization (e.g. emphasize care vs efficiency). Similarly, a local sport club is more easily culturally driven than a hospital. Describing in detail the influence of each cultural dimension on each organizational feature would require a large amount of space. A summary of these links is presented in Table 1. Nonetheless, in order to build coherent models of culture and organizations, in the following sections we describe how each cultural dimension can influence organizations and how culture can influence each organizational feature. Note that cultural influence drives organizational behavior, but actual implementation also depends on other parameters like the environment.

Table 1. Hofstede's cultural dimensions applied on organizations. The description of the impact on an organizational feature of a low cultural dimension value is described in the first row of each cell and the high value is described in the second row.

	Power distance	Individualism	Masculinity	Uncertainty avoidance	Long-term orientation
Organization goal	set by members / set by leaders	group interest / joint interest	security, member care / high risks and rewards	undefined, opportunism / well defined, specialism	immediate / sum reward over time
Individual goal	unconstrained / advancement	group goal / personal	quality of life / earning, advancement	exploration / stability	immediate reward / advancement, savings
Workflow definition	democratic / by the leader	linked to groups / task oriented	modest, balancing / by well-performer, assertive	informally defined / by expert	on the fly / evolving with time
Role allocation	democratic / by leaders	roles created for individuals / individual selected for a role	by affinity / by performance	generalism / roles linked to expertise	unstable / consider experience
Coordination structure	dedicated roles / encompass hierarchy	links individuals / links tasks	consensual / efficient	informal, global / explicit, restrictive	unstable / evolve with workflow
Delegation structure	dedicated roles / matches hierarchy	moral relationship / optimize human resource	balance workload / assertive delegation	informal, global / explicit, restrictive	based on reward / based on trust
Control structure	dedicated roles / encompasses the hierarchy	evaluation under context / egalitarian evaluation	part of the cooperation / performance measure	subjective, casual / objective, explicit	intrusive / provides feedback
Information structure	unconstrained, no locus / encompass hierarchy	in-group propagation / unrestricted circulation	interpersonal care / task oriented	informal networks / standard process	abstract / pragmatic
Failure responsibility	responsible / downwards	hidden in-group / aim at the responsible	forgiveness / blame, discredit	change practice / change the rule	rejection, shame / accepted, learning
Exception handling	unrestricted / hierarchically upwards	hidden in-group / defined by organization	solve together / challenge	find solution / exception protocol	avoid aggravation / get feedback
Learning	self-driven / leader-driven	match group needs / match personal needs	improve cooperation / improve performance	generalism / specialism, formal	side effect / calculated effect
Norms	democratic / top-down	in-group favoritism / equity expected	consensual / by the most efficient	informal, influential / formal	abstract, dogmatic / concrete, pragmatic
Efficiency	redundant communication / tight coordination	driven by group needs / driven by personal success	cooperation / competition	redundant structure / efficient protocols	(over) fitting / sparing resource
Robustness	decentralization / central hierarchy	groups hide failures / interchangeability	cooperative solving / failure as a challenge	redundancy / restricted by rules	unexpected failure / prevention
Flexibility	possibly inefficient / restricted by hierarchy	change group identity / interchangeability	cooperative changes / challenging	dynamic network / restricted by rules	invest on the present / prepare the future

3.1   The Impact of Each Cultural Dimension on Organizations

Power Distance: PDI influences the perception of power associated with individuals. Power, in general, is the capability of an individual to influence or restrict the behavior of another individual (e.g. affecting his/her welfare). In high PDI cultures, individuals expect to be lead by one unique individual while in low PDI cultures, power is expected to be spread. The organizational context is particularly favorable to the creation of formal and informal power. Formal power arises mainly through organizational structures and the possibility to establish and apply norms. Informal power results from the praise given to an individual (high MAS), informal networks (low IDV), and/or expertise (high UAI). In high PDI cultures, individuals want the power to be concentrated in few hands, leading to a fusion of structures. Leader uniqueness stresses the structural shapes towards trees. In low PDI, individuals prefer decentralized power. So, structural merging is avoided, leading to more balanced networks. PDI also influences the importance given to individual status. Thus, in high PDI cultures, a leader's opinion and welfare are more valuable than those of the subordinates, which impacts decision making processes (e.g. autocratic delegation).

Individualism: IDV influences the importance given to one individual's context. This context can introduce important side-effects on organizations. Since the identity of an individual is linked to his/her context, individuals sharing a context tend to protect each other and reject outsiders. Thus, the notion of fairness depends on IDV: in low IDV cultures, in-group favoritism is expected while in high IDV ones equality is expected. IDV influences individual goals, towards personal or context interest. The responsibility for a failure charged on an individual or on his/her context depends on IDV. To this extent, in low IDV cultures, a failure notification from an out-grouper is more troublesome than from an in-grouper.

Masculinity: MAS influences the preference towards performance and success over care and stability. Thus, organizations in high MAS cultures prefer assertive goals (even if potentially risky or unachievable) and members, stressing on individual performance. Conversely, low MAS organizations favor modest and achievable goals keeping their members satisfied. MAS also influences the workflow and the role allocation. The stress on performance impacts in turn the tendency towards competition (high MAS) or cooperation (low MAS). Moreover, MAS influences the importance given to performance measure (carried by the control structure), success recognition and failures. In high MAS cultures, failures display discredit the individual (potentially leading in turn to retrogradation or removal) while in low MAS settings, failures can be forgiven in order to pursue cooperation.

Uncertainty Avoidance: UAI influences the need of well defined and predictable situations. In organizations, this need impacts the accuracy of the process definition. Thus, workflow, roles (through expertise), processes (operations to be performed, how the task flows in the organizational structure), operation outcomes and norms are more explicit. In high UAI cultures, processes strictly follow the predefined structures and a regular control validates the completion of a task. Conversely, in low UAI cultures, structures are less formally defined, paths taken by tasks are less predictable and control is more rare. This lack of formalism can be represented with an organic informal structure.

Long Term Orientation: LTO influences the importance of immediate rewards and lack of failures versus investments leading to greater expected benefits in the future (e.g. training individuals, updating machines). Thus, low LTO organizations tend to dramatically change their activity to any more profitable one while high LTO organizations update their strategy more smoothly. LTO influences the revision of rules for decision: from dogmatic commitment to rules versus pragmatic rules evolving with time and experience. This choice influences the dynamism of structures and norms. LTO also influences the importance of trust in interactions. In low LTO cultures, these interactions are more efficient but also more risk-prone (e.g. members can more easily quit).

3.2   The Impact of Culture on Organizational Aspects

Structures: Organizational structures (coordination, delegation, control, information) link individuals with each other. Structures can be merged and centralized in a single hierarchy of power (high PDI). This hierarchy determines leader/subordinate relationships where leaders instruct, help and verify subordinates' operations. Conversely, power can also be spread in organization with low fusion and no hierarchical distribution of structures (low PDI). Thus, an individual can have several leaders (e.g. in a matrix structure) or two different roles can manage the delegation and the control of a third one. In extreme cases, organizations can be represented by a complete graph (e.g. adhocracies). Thus, for instance individuals may delegate tasks to anyone else. In addition, the importance given to expertise (influenced by UAI) also influences the shape of the organization. Expertise can be important for role creation and to link individuals (high UAI). Then, the organization tends to be structured in teams (low PDI) or hierarchies of experts (high PDI, where leaders encompass their subordinates' expertise). Otherwise, links are less restricted by formal structures, leading to unrestricted teams (low PDI) or hierarchies of power (high PDI). Figure 2 links this description with Mintzberg's synthetic organizations. Finally, note that organizations can be attached to their formal structures and experts (high UAI) making individuals rely explicitly on these structure to handle tasks, or they can rely on informal structure emergence (low UAI).

Organizational structures can evolve with time. Goals can change, leading to changes in workflow and thus in structure. But, roles in charge of managing organizational change differ depending on the organization and culture. Adding or removing new members can be done by a leader (high PDI), influenced by experts (high UAI) or the opinion of best performers (high MAS). Otherwise, this process can be more democratic and consensual. The reasons for hiring or firing employees are also culturally driven: by expertise (UAI), by apparent efficiency (MAS), by familial background (IDV) and the way to manage the organizational agenda (LTO).

Moreover, culture also influences how interactions are carried out through these structures. Taking the decision to interact with someone else is dependent on culture. This decision can be made explicit and objective through procedures (UAI, e.g. a procedure describes to control one item for every 1000). Status differences can influence the decision to initiate it (PDI e.g. an individual may prefer to avoid using delegation links towards individuals with higher status). Individuals can care or not about the state of mind of the other one (MAS, e.g. an individual may prefer to avoid delegating a task to an individual with personal problems in low MAS. Contrarily, demands can be voluntarily set above the capability of the receiver in order to force him/her to outperform in high MAS). Individuals may expect a degree of fairness (e.g. balance the ungratifying work) or accept different treatment due to context (IDV). Finally, trust and longer-term goals can be taken into consideration when initiating an interaction (LTO, e.g. always delegate tasks to the most profitable individual or delegate simple tasks to newcomers who need experience).

The protocols underlying interactions are also culturally driven. In some cultures, the subordinates expect to receive instructions before acting while in others they expect a degree of autonomy (PDI). Similarly, communications can be more assertiveness or consensual and explanatory (MAS). Thus, the balance between proposing and imposing is dependent on PDI and MAS. PDI influences the acceptance of decision from higher power individuals, while MAS influences the care given to other's desires in decision. Thus, for instance, in a high PDI, low MAS organization, a leader can delegate a task if he/she considers that the subordinate is willing to do it. In addition, the UAI influences the amount of standardization of the interactions (e.g. standardized delegation messages). Finally, the amount of context in the message is influenced by the IDV.

Failures: Defining a failure and deciding how to handle it are also culturally dependent. Some organizations can recognize as a failure a document wrongly filled in while others are not worried unless a factory is destroyed overnight. The occurrence of a failure is linked to the detail given to the processes and its expected outcome (UAI). Moreover, an organization which performs intensive control is more sensitive to failures (UAI, PDI). The consequence is that more failures are reported but their gravity is generally lower.

When a failure is observed, it may be fixed with a failure handling mechanism. Organizations centralized in a hierarchy tend to transfer the failure upwards and delegate it to the correct service (high PDI). A standard failure handling mechanism can be designed (high UAI) or it is solved by hand with the informal network (low UAI) to handle it. The group where this failure occurred can try to solve it locally (IDV). Some individuals may look forward to failures to gain recognition by solving them or lose this recognition and solve them through cooperation (MAS). Finally, the behavior when faced to error handling can vary, like trying to resolve it and forget about it or trying to get more feedback about its origin but possibly without any additional reward (LTO).

When a failure occurs, for various reasons organizations may want to determine a responsible. The failing individual can be classified as inefficient (high

MAS), unfit for his/her position (high PDI) and endangering the group (low IDV). Some tolerance can be accepted to avoid hurting the faulty individual (low MAS) or because failure is part of a learning process (high LTO). The blame can be determined by explicit and objective rules (UAI), or by a special role, like a leader (PDI) or a special control institution (UAI). Individuals can expect more or less fairness from the system with regard to their context (IDV). The context itself may be in charge of blaming the faulty individual. Leaders can try to reject the responsibility in order to avoid being discredited (PDI).

Norms: Norms are rules restricting the individual's behavior, but they can nonetheless be violated in exceptional cases. In an organization, norms can serve to improve performance or avoid failures (e.g. a vaccine should be kept below 15 °C). The category of individuals determining the norm is influenced by culture. As for decision making, this individual can be a leader (PDI), an expert (UAI) or the best performer (MAS). These norms can be more or less democratic and consensual (PDI, UAI, MAS). The definition and the content of the norm are also influenced by culture. Rules can be more or less explicit and objective (UAI) and they can be connected to various features of the organization, like expertise (UAI) and position (PDI, MAS). Finally, the individuals in charge of applying the norm can vary. This individual can be a leader (PDI), a special role (UAI), the best performer (MAS) or any colleague (low PDI, low UAI). Some organizations can more easily forgive violations than others (LTO, MAS). The importance of blame can also vary (MAS, PDI). Individuals can also expect a relative fairness or group favoritism when being judged (IDV).

4   Consequences of Culture on Organizational Performance

Efficiency measures the costs to achieve a task. In multi-agent and multi-task goals, the cost can be defined in various ways (e.g. individuals can cost over time or by operation). The number of messages exchanged in order to achieve a task is a generally reliable indicator for efficiency. Efficiency is dependent on the task complexity and the variability of the task space (see Fig. 2).

Simple tasks have low coordination costs and predictable operations. A strong leader (high PDI), as a central node, can optimize coordination while keeping inter-individual communication low. Conversely, complex tasks require better competence and communication costs are higher. In this case, efficiency is gained by giving more autonomy to individuals (low PDI). Static tasks are efficiently handled via standardization (being a formal work process or a formal training), leading to specialization (high UAI). Contrarily, dynamic tasks require that individuals are not bound to rules (low UAI). IDV has a positive effect on efficiency: high IDV cultures make individuals responsible for their operations. In low IDV cultures individuals' accomplishment is blurred by the group, reducing incentives to perform well. The impact of MAS on efficiency is mitigated: the desire of success is a motive which may also create inefficient competition.

Reference [7] proposes a twofold approach to *robustness:* congestion and connectivity. *Congestion robustness* measures the organizational capability to cope with concurrent tasks, highlighting bottlenecks. *Connectivity robustness* measures the organizational capability to cope with the disappearance of some members (e.g. sick leave). For both approaches, robustness increases when a task can be performed through multiple paths and actors which implies the creation of redundant roles and links.

PDI has a negative impact on this redundancy: the higher the PDI, the more individuals prefer to obey a single leader, driving the organization to a tree-like structure without redundancy. Similarly, UAI influences the use of explicit links: in case of failure, alternate routes must have been conceived beforehand. MAS has a mitigated influence on robustness. In high MAS cultures, individuals expect recognition when doing extra work when the organization has a problem while in low MAS ones, individuals want to cooperate and protect the organization even at the cost of extra work. LTO has a positive effect: organizations with high LTO culture tend to pragmatically consider failures and establish appropriate prevention and learn from past failures.

Flexibility measures the range of tasks that can be coped with by the organization. Thus, organizations with individuals that are generalist and not bound to formal structures (low UAI) are naturally more flexible. Similarly, PDI prevents the task to flow without validation of the leader which may lead to excessive costs. The assertiveness and competition driven by high MAS cultures have a positive influence on flexibility. Low MAS cultures are more conservative and less risk-taking. LTO has mitigated influence on flexibility: high LTO organizations are prone to early and smoothly shift their activity to increase their long-term profit while low LTO organizations can sharply change their activity as soon as the new goal is more profitable.

5   Conclusion and Future Work

In this conceptual article we highlight how cultural backgrounds influence structures and interactions occurring in an organization. We describe how cultural dimensions influence organizations and how organizational features are influenced by culture, emphasizing the individual level. Moreover, we present the consequences of cultures on organizational performance (efficiency, robustness, flexibility). This way, a modeler can use our work as a guideline to integrate culture and organizations in a single agent-based model. This model can be used to simulate organizational operations in various or multiple cultural settings, which can provide data about the cultural influence on organizational performance.

In the future, we plan to use this conceptual work as a reference point to build agent-based models of culture and organizations. In particular, we are interested in reproducing phenomena occurring in multi-cultural organizations or cross-cultural replication of organizational structures. For instance, we expect to observe an increase of inter-individual clashes due to cultural mismatch or inefficiency due to a misuse of an organizational structure. This work, in a longer term, aims at helping decisions makers in providing them deeper insight into how culture can influence the way their decisions will be interpreted and applied.

Acknowledgments. The first author wishes to thank Gert Jan Hofstede for his fruitful interaction and Melania Borit for her feedback while writing this paper.

References

1. Argente, E., Julian, V., Botti, V.: Multi-agent system development based on organizations. Electron. Notes Theoret. Comput. Sci. **150**, 55–71 (2006)
2. Axelrod, R.: The dissemination of culture: a model with local convergence and global polarization. J. Confl. Resolut. **41**(2), 203–226 (1997)
3. Baligh, Burton, Obel.: Validating an expert system that designs organizations. In: Computational Organization Theory, pp. 179–193 (1994)
4. Bura, S.: Minimeme: of life and death in the noosphere. In: From Animals to Animats 3 Proceedings of the Third International Conference on Simulation of Adaptive Behavior, pp. 479–486. MIT Press, London (1994)
5. Dechesne, F., Tosto, G.D., Dignum, V., Dignum, F.: No smoking here: values, norms and culture in multi-agent systems. Artif. Intell. Law **21**(1), 79–107 (2012)
6. Dignum, F., Dignum, V.: Emergence and enforcement of social behavior. In: 18th World IMACS Congress and MODSIM09 International Congress on Modelling and Simulation (2009)
7. Dodds, P.S., Watts, D.J., Sabel, C.F.: Information exchange and the robustness of organizational networks. Proc. Natl. Acad. Sci. U S A **100**(21), 12516–12521 (2003)
8. Grossi, D., Dignum, F.: Structural aspects of organizations. In: Dignum, V. (ed.) Handbook of Research on Multi-Agent Systems: Semantics and Dynamics of Organizational Models, pp. 190–219. IGI Global, Hershey (2009)
9. Hofstede, G.: Motivation, leadership, and organization: do American theories apply Abroad? Organ. Dyn. **9**(1), 42–63 (1980)
10. Hofstede, G., Hofstede, G.J., Minkov, M.: Cultures and Organizations: Software of the Mind, 3rd edn. McGraw-Hill, New York (2010)
11. Crowston, K.: Evolving novel organizational forms. In: Computational Organization Theory, pp. 19–38 (1996)
12. Levitt, R.E., Cohen, G.P., Kunz, J.C., Nass, C.I., Christiansen, T., Jin, Y.: The "Virtual Design Team": simulating how organization structure and information processing tools affect team performance. In: Computational Organization Theory (1994)
13. Mintzberg, H.: Structure in 5's: a synthesis of the research on organization design. Manage. Sci. **26**(3), 322–341 (1980)
14. Morgenstern, O.: Prolegomena to a theory of organization. Technical report (1951)
15. Van Der Aalst, W.M.P., Ter Hofstede, A.H.M., Kiepuszewski, B., Barros, A.P.: Workflow Patterns. Distrib. Parallel Databases **14**(1), 5–51 (2003)

Author Index